BEYOND **CAPITALISM** & **SOCIALISM**
a new statement of an old ideal

THE SMALL LANDHOLDERS ARE
THE MOST PRECIOUS PART OF A STATE.

—Thomas Jefferson

THE ESSENTIAL POINT IS THAT AGRICULTURE OUGHT
TO BE SAVED AND REVIVED BECAUSE AGRICULTURE IS THE
FOUNDATION FOR THE GOOD LIFE IN SOCIETY;
IT IS, IN FACT, THE NORMAL LIFE.

—T. S. Eliot

*Dedicated to the social Catholics of all times
and their fellow apostles of sanity, along with those
who today would follow in their footsteps.*

BEYOND
capitalism
&*socialism*

A New Statement
of an
Old Ideal

A TWENTY-FIRST CENTURY APOLOGIA
FOR SOCIAL AND ECONOMIC SANITY
BY TWELVE CATHOLICS

Tobias J. Lanz, Ph.D. | EDITOR
Kirkpatrick Sale | FOREWORD • *John Sharpe* | INTRODUCTION

featuring contributions by

AIDAN MACKEY • ANTHONY COONEY • GARY POTTER
DALE AHLQUIST • CHRISTOPHER BLUM, PH.D.
PETER CHOJNOWSKI, PH.D. • THOMAS STORCK • RUPERT EDERER, PH.D.
EDWARD MCPHAIL, PH.D. • FR. LAWRENCE SMITH
WILLIAM FAHEY, PH.D. • TOBIAS LANZ, PH.D.

Light IN THE Darkness
PUBLICATIONS
An Imprint of IHS Press

Norfolk, Virginia • 2008

Footnotes to the contributions are their authors' except where indicated. Information from periodicals available through the Internet is referenced as "online" (or identified by the web-based source title) in lieu of page numbers or URLs. References to scholarly works have been standardized by the editors across contributions.

Sources for decorative quotations throughout the book are as follows: title page: Jefferson, letter to James Madison, *op. cit.* at p. xxv n3 of the present volume, and Eliot, *Criterion* XI, 1942, p. 42, quoted in Michael R. Stevens, "T. S. Eliot's Neo-Medieval Economics," *Journal of Markets & Morality* 2 (2), Fall 1999, p. 237; p. x: Nolan, *Orate Fratres*, quoted in Dorothy Day, "Articles on Distributism – 2," *The Catholic Worker*, July-August 1948, 1, 2, 6, from the Dorothy Day Library on the Web (http://www.catholicworker.org/dorothy-day/, accessed December 12, 2007); p. 1: Lytle, *op. cit.* at p. xxviii n2, p. 32; p. 2: Distributist League of New England, *op. cit.* at p. xlvi n4, p. 43; p. 8: Heseltine, *The Change* (London: Sheed and Ward, 1927), p. 111; p. 29: Weaver, *op. cit.* at p. xv n1, p. 147; p. 30: Murphy, *op. cit.* at p. xvi n2, p. 30; p. 40: Troy J. Cauley, *Agrarianism* (Chapel Hill: University of North Carolina Press, 1935), p. 210; p. 66: Davidson, *op. cit.* at p. xxiv n4, p. 45; p. 82: David B. Danborn, "Romantic Agrarianism," *Agricultural History* 65 (4), Autumn 1991, p. 11; p. 117: Davidson, "Agrarianism and Politics," *The Review of Politics* 1 (2), Mar. 1939, 125; p. 118: Belloc, "The Modern Man," *op. cit.* at p. xxvi n2, p. 342; p. 152: Conkin, *op. cit.* at p. xx n2, p. 171.

Frontispiece: *Spring in Town* by Grant Wood, Oil on panel, 26 x 24½ in., inscribed lower center: "Grant Wood 1941"; at the Swope Art Museum, Terre Haute, Indiana. When the painting appeared on the cover of the *Saturday Evening Post* in 1942, Grand Wood's comments were included, as follows: "In making these paintings, as you may have guessed, I had in mind something which I hope to convey to a fairly wide audi-ence in America – the picture of a country rich in the arts of peace; a homely, lovable nation, infinitely worth any sacrifice necessary to its preservation."

ISBN-10: 1-932528-10-5
ISBN-13: 978-1-932528-10-7

Library of Congress Cataloging-in-Publication Data

Beyond capitalism & socialism : a new statement of an old ideal : a twenty-first century apologia for social and economic sanity / by twelve Catholics ; Tobias J. Lanz, editor ; Kirkpatrick Sale, foreword ; John Sharpe, introduction.
       p. cm.
    Includes bibliographical references and index.
    ISBN 978-1-932528-10-7 (alk. paper)
    1. Capitalism--Religious aspects--Catholic Church. 2. Socialism and Christianity--Catholic Church. I. Lanz, Tobias J.
    BX1795.C35B49 2007
    330.12--dc22

2007040933

Printed in the United States of America.

Light in the Darkness Publications is an imprint of IHS Press. IHS Press is the only publisher dedicated exclusively to the Social Teachings of the Catholic Church.

For information on current or future titles, contact IHS Press at:

toll-free phone/fax: 877.447.7737 (877-IHS-PRES)
e-mail: info@ihspress.com
e-mail: info@lidpubs.com

Contents

Editor's Preface

Tobias J. Lanz, Ph.D.

THIS BOOK HAS SEVERAL INFLUENCES AND POINTS OF origin. First there are my own personal experiences. I grew up in a Catholic home. My father ran a small business and my mother raised children and the home was the center for both. I worked for my father and also had many household duties. Working with parents and siblings created a close-knit family and a healthy appreciation of physical work. Most importantly, I learned that work was a broader part of the art of living. Thus, I experienced subsidiarity and solidarity, which is the very essence of Catholic economics, first hand – long before I knew what they meant.

These ideas were further enriched during my education at a monastery school run by the Benedictines. Here work and intellectual life were integrated for the good of the community. I observed how brothers and priests followed St. Jerome's dictum of the monk tied to a place, like Christ to the cross. Their goal was to make that particular place a center of love, beauty, and holiness. Although I couldn't fully appreciate their message and way of life at the time, it stayed with me and emerged in later years.

The first reawakening was in graduate school in the early 1990s where I studied economic and political development and did field research in Africa and India. When I encountered vibrant subsistence economies rather than abject poverty, I felt like E. F. Schumacher who was supposed to find the same thing on his first trip to Burma in the 1950s. Like Schumacher I saw a difficult life, where nature established harsh limits and often exacted a high price. But I also noticed how different work was there than in industrial societies. People had livelihoods, rather than jobs, and work was connected to every other facet of life. Each person lived out his drama through his daily labors. Life was struggle, but when mastered the rewards were great.

This experience was my first conscious realization that wealth and poverty had many meanings. Wealth was not just money – something abstract and mutable. Wealth was something concrete. It was land and a home, the fruits of nature and human relationships. Most importantly this wealth was rooted in life itself. As such it had a profoundly spiritual character – ultimately pointing to Creator and Creation. How utterly different than "advanced industrial economies" where everything revolves around money and products that are derivative of nature. A whirlwind of dead things!

Similarly poverty was not simply the lack of material goods. Poverty could also be defined in spiritual and emotional terms. A society awash in material goods could still be emotionally and spiritually poor. This is the poverty of advanced socialist and capitalist economies in which the industrial cycle has replaced the life cycle. Ironically, the constant pursuit of material goods to fill this spiritual and emotional vacuum intensifies the cycle and only worsens the poverty.

It was this realization that sparked my interest in alternatives to the dominant political economy. I sought out individuals who shared these views and lived according to alternative economic values. They existed, but were scattered about and were socially and politically unorganized and usually marginalized. Sadly, most were not Catholics, or even Christians. That latter fact disappointed me most, since so many critics of the dominant political economy were Catholic. Papal Encyclicals, the English Distributists, E. F. Schumacher and many others outlined and defended what seemed like viable alternatives to both capitalism and socialism.

Yet when I spoke to Catholics and read contemporary pundits and writers about the subject, I encountered widespread ignorance, even hostility. "Conservative" Catholics were the most hypocritical. I had always agreed with their positions on certain specific moral issues. Yet when it came to the morality of the modern economic system, there was only selective criticism, or none at all. I remember one RCIA class (which I helped to teach) where I was almost crucified on the spot for suggesting that capitalism and socialism are both incompatible with Church teaching!

This frustration led me to ask why a greater number of Catholics and other Christians aren't more critical and skeptical of a materialist system that can only be described as the rule of Mammon. One reason is simply apathy and laziness. The system works; why change it? And even if one wants to change it, it is simply too large, too complex, and too entrenched. So to even try to do so is futile. Another reason is denial. Many Catholics simply deny that the modern economic system is problematic. To them, Catholics simply have to adjust to the new economic realties and reap the benefits like everyone else. An even bigger problem is ignorance. Most Catholics do not even know what the Church teaches in general, let alone on the specifics of economics.

But the biggest problem, and one that touches on all of the above, is a lack of imagination. G. K. Chesterton saw this lack as a fundamental condition of the modern world. In the past, nature and tradition formed the basis of life and provided rich images to inspire and guide society. Today the images that guide society are manufactured by the system itself. It is a closed loop. For the majority of people caught in the system it becomes almost impossible to imagine any alternative. It is really a form of intellectual, moral, and aesthetic slavery.

The goal of this book is to inspire Catholics, their fellow travelers, and anyone else who is willing to look at with open eyes, and consider with an open mind, the vision that the Church proposes, in order to break free of this system by providing images and ideas that challenge its totalitarian vision. There are also practical paths to follow. Most are very simple and straightforward because they are based on timeless principles, but while these have always been easy to understand, they are often difficult to follow given the human tendency towards both sloth and disobedience.

The teaching of the Catholic Church, as well as that of common sense and the collected wisdom of many thoughtful people from the beginning of civilization, is that economies must be built around the human being and the natural community. It is also that the goal of economics is to harmonize the material with the spiritual, namely to create the conditions that allow for greater spiritual development. Ultimately economics must be tied to salvation itself. If it is not, economics will, of necessity, lead us in the opposite direction, for social no less than physical nature abhors a vacuum. The stakes are high. Change must happen soon.

"Too long has idle talk made out of Distributism something medieval and myopic, as if four modern popes were somehow talking nonsense when they said: the law should favor widespread ownership (Leo XIII); land is the most natural form of property (Leo XIII and Pius XII); wages should enable a man to purchase land (Leo XIII and Pius XI); the family is most perfect when rooted in its own holding (Pius XII); agriculture is the first and most important of all the arts (Pius VII); and the tiller of the soil still represents the natural order of things willed by God (Pius XII)."

—Joseph T. Nolan

Foreword

Kirkpatrick Sale

FRITZ SCHUMACHER USED TO TELL THE STORY OF THE three professionals sitting around arguing about whose was the oldest profession. The doctor said that his was the oldest because God operated on Adam to remove his rib to make Eve. The architect, however, declared that even before that God built the world out of chaos. And who, said the economist, do you think made that?

Yes, indeed, economists have made chaos, and they have done it on a worldwide if not universal scale, and for some reason are richly rewarded for it. They have created a system, in both capitalist and socialist guises, that favors the using up of the world's resources at ever-faster rates, that encourages their processing in ways that produce pollution and waste, that puts wealth into ever-fewer hands in the countries of the favored few, that allows for great sickness, poverty, ignorance, and starvation across the world, and that celebrates all of the Seven Deadly Sins including sloth.

There must be a better way. And, of course, there is, and has been for a very long time. It is a society based on small self-sufficient regions, empowered communities, vibrant neighborhoods, gainfully employed families, individual self-satisfactions, decentralized politics, local economies, sustainable organic agriculture, cooperative work, environmental humility, and careful nurturing of the earth. It is the way many people have lived, probably in most places and for most of the time, for the greatest part of the last eight thousand years, punctuated by some periods of empire and kingship, until the rise of capitalism five hundred years ago.

It was nearly a hundred years after the ravages of industrial capitalism had spread across the United Kingdom that a group of people in England began to talk about this sort of society, and they gave it the name of Distributism. It was a largely literary movement, with giants like Hilaire Belloc and G. K. Chesterton, and it set out in careful and inspiring terms what the good society would look like, giving a framework and a name to what had long been seen as an ideal, or at least more reasonable, way of life. It did not have a great deal of success, on the ground as it were, because of all the 20th-century forces stacked against it, but it suggested the ways people might organize their lives insofar as those forces permitted it and the kind of world to be working for.

That philosophy is still alive today, as this book attests, though it is not always named Distributism, and so, surprisingly enough, are some of the actual elements of it, taking shape at the edges of the dominant society. To suggest but a few, there is the bioregional movement, deep ecology, farmers markets, community-supported agriculture, organic farming, homegrown gardens, local- and slow-food movements, alternative currencies, alternative medicine, alternative energy, intermediate technology, Buy-Nothing Day, simple living, home schooling, neo-Luddism, worker ownership, anti-globalization, anti-free trade, environmental interest groups, ecological restoration, land trusts, and land preservation. All of these would be welcomed by Distributists as living out their legacy.

What's more, if the predictions for the future prove to be accurate—peak oil and the end of long-haul transportation, global warming and the end of agribusiness—the world and its destructive capitalist/socialist economy will be forced to change radically and in the direction of Distributist principles.

As James Kunstler puts it in *The Long Emergency*, when these crises hit, national and supranational economies will disintegrate and

> the focus of society will have to return to the town or small city and its supporting agricultural hinterland . . . .
> It will require us to downscale and re-scale virtually everything we do and how we do it, from the kind of communities we physically inhabit to the way we grow our food to the way we work and trade the products of our work . . . .
> Anything organized on the large scale, whether it is government or a corporate business enterprise such as Wal-Mart, will wither as the cheap energy props that support bigness fall away.

And then, of necessity, the world will reconstruct itself on the lines of a more human-scale, community-based, local-resource-dependent societies, something that the Distributists would recognize as what they'd been talking about all along.

ℰ

Introduction

John Sharpe

> The price of Liberty is eternal vigilance, and we have slept. The price
> of Justice is responsible government, and our rulers are irresponsible.
> The price of Security is self-support, and we have yielded up our
> independence.
>
> —*Manifesto of the Distributist League*

> In politics we are losing our freedom. In economics we are losing our
> independence. In life we are losing our proper sense of values.
>
> —*Statement of Principles*, Committee for the
> Alliance of Agrarian and Distributist Groups

I N 1937, AMERICAN ARCHITECT AND SOCIAL CRITIC RALPH
Adams Cram made the rather audacious claim that "today here in the
United States of America, and in all industrialized countries . . . there
is a class of men and women, perhaps the majority, that, within the
comprehension of the State, and in their relation to the State, is unfree." Had
his words been uttered a century earlier, the meaning would have been clear-
er, but in a wholly different sense, given that he was speaking in Richmond,
Virginia. But what could he have meant by this just seventy years ago?

"I mean," he continued,

> all those who subsist on a wage, the price paid for the commodity they have
> and who have no other means of maintenance for themselves and their fami-
> lies. I mean the "hands" (significant name) in mills, workshops, and factories,
> the diggers in the earth for metals and coal, the share-cropper and the farm
> laborer, shop assistants, domestic servants, clerks, teachers in grade schools,
> in fact, as I have said, all those who subsist on a wage that is paid to them by
> those who are, in actuality, their masters; a wage that may be withdrawn at
> any time and for any reason, leaving them to go on the dole, or to starve, if

they can find no new job in a market that has reached the point of saturation. These are not free men in any rational and exact sense of the word.[1]

As hard as it may be to believe, and as contrary as it may be to our Whiggish and "progressive" idea that things constantly get better and better, the situation is worse today. Even our conception of "freedom" has atrophied to the point where the constraints – sometimes in a real sense life-threatening – that most of us would face upon the loss of a job with its steady paycheck are no longer imagined to constitute an infringement of our "freedom." It would "cramp our style," indeed, but affect our *freedom*?

This is precisely what this architect-*cum*-critic was driving at. But though it is a simple concept, understanding it depends upon a frame of reference that today is largely a thing of the past. We get to vote periodically and can drive to the supermarket whenever we want. We are "free" in this sense. But measured against another more enduring standard – one that is increasingly difficult for us to comprehend, if not merely to envision, from lack of experience – this is an *empty* freedom, if it is one at all. That which Cram had in mind is of a wholly different kind, and for its defense he appealed to what the American founding fathers Thomas Jefferson and John Adams would have taken for granted:

> [I] venture to unite myself with these greatest of American statesmen in holding that he only is a free man who owns and administers his own land, craft, trade, art or profession and is able, at necessity, to maintain himself and his family therefrom. One hundred years ago, excluding slaves, eighty percent of the male population of the United States came within this category. We were then a nation of free men. Today less than forty percent can be so counted.[2]

---

1. Ralph Adams Cram, "What Is a Free Man?," *Catholic Rural Life Objectives* (St. Paul, Minn.: National Catholic Rural Life Conference, 1937), pp. 36–7. Cram was a High Episcopalian architect and medievalist social critic from New Hampshire who went to Boston to learn and practice architecture. According to one sketch, he "dabbled in royalism and Christian socialism" but then converted at least in spirit and emotion to Catholicism (though he was unwilling to embrace "the Church of the immigrant"). His 1893 essay, "On the Restoration of Idealism," set forth the program which he would defend for the rest of his life, arguing for an alternative to "modern fragmentation" and the rupture between art, religion, and community by a return to the application of medieval principles to modern society. His vision was one of a medieval Europe "as an aesthetic, religious, and social paradise lost where all men were artists, all women revered, and all social classes bound in an organic, deferential social order. In his work he quoted from Arthur Penty and William Morris, contributed to Seward Collins's *American Review*, and claimed kinship with Lewis Mumford and the Southern Agrarians. See T. J. Jackson Lears, *No Place of Grace: Antimodernism and the Transformation of American Culture 1880–1920* (New York: Pantheon Books, 1981), pp. 203–9.

2. *Ibid*, p. 37. See also the comment from the old *Catholic Encyclopedia* of Fr. Victor Cathrein, S.J., where he writes, "Man is not really free unless he can, at least to a certain degree, dispose of external goods at will, not only of goods of consumption but also of productive goods" (*The Catholic Encyclopedia* (CE) (New York: Robert Appleton Company, 1907–12), s.v. "Property").

One shudders to think what the statistic would be today! But it is in fact to this ideal that the following essays are dedicated, along with the broader social concepts that underpin the vision that Cram and others of his school and generation were defending. It is the position articulated by Richard Weaver when he praised the arrangement where "the individual [gets] his sustenance from property which bears his imprint and assimilation . . . ." Indeed, it was not *security* he was after with such a scheme, which would only mean

> being taken care of, or freedom from want and fear – which would reduce man to an invertebrate – [but rather] stability, *which gives nothing for nothing but which maintains a constant between effort and reward* [emphasis added].[1]

It is this stability and direct proportion of effort to result that led Cram, Weaver, and others to defend this vision of personal and private property ownership because of the central position such a vision occupied in their conception of the kind of social life befitting rational, civilized men. Anything less, they thought, was worthy of mere animals (if them, in some cases!). The lynchpin of their vision was this ownership by men and families of the means of getting a livelihood, such that they could depend, more or less, upon themselves alone, and not be beholden to the state or "the boss," either of whom might quite easily interfere in an illegitimate way with that freedom that becomes responsible and independent citizens.

In such a context, the crucial issue is *control* of real property, not the mere possession of tokens or slips of paper that are as free from the dominion of their owner as is the machine upon which the wage slave labors. In a later essay, Frank L. Owsley, an original Southern Agrarian and contributor to the manifesto of 1930, highlighted the point:

> [W]hat was the Jeffersonian conception of private property: not great corporations, trusts, monopolies, banks, or princely estates – in brief, not great wealth concentrated in the hands of the few, but land and other property held or obtainable by all self-respecting men. Such property thus widely held must, of course, in the very nature of things be personally controlled, or it would cease to have much value as the basic instrumentation of the right to life, liberty, the pursuit of happiness, and self-government. The ownership and control of productive property sufficient for a livelihood gave a man and his family a sense of economic security; it made him independent; he was a real citizen, for he could cast his franchise without fear and could protect the basic principles of his government. Jefferson regarded stocks and bonds as an insecure economic basis for a free state, for even in the eighteenth

---

1. Richard Weaver, *Ideas Have Consequences* (*IHC*) (Chicago and London: University of Chicago Press, 1984 [1948]), p. 141.

century directors and presidents of corporations understood, perfectly, the art of avoiding the payment of dividends to small stockholders who had no voice in directing the management of the business. The insecurity of citizens who depended upon such property over which they no longer had control was doubtless a strong factor in the Jeffersonian advocacy of the agrarian state. Perhaps the Jeffersonians believed that city life was not a good life, but the loss of economic independence and security which accompanied this life was what made the great Virginian and his colleagues fear urbanization and look upon land as the best form of private property and the only safe basis of a free state.[1]

The philosophical context in which this vision was set regarded a freedom of this kind, based upon private ownership and independent means, as a prerequisite for a properly religious and virtuous life – and for those who had no interest in revealed religion but were able to hold onto some sense of what "the good life" of the ancients was all about, this freedom was just as central; as one contemporary historian has nicely put it, for the Agrarians "traditional culture depended on a premodern economy and its particular material establishment."[2] However remote this line of discussion sounds today (and it is our task to remedy that), in the 1930s it was a living, breathing concern among a host of different circles of thought and study and action.

Indeed, something serious *was* happening, intellectually, before 1945, as a casual review of the journals and books from the period will attest. But thereafter something seems to have gone wrong with the ability of a large number to think and reason dispassionately, from first principles, about societal problems and issues. That "something" was addressed with precision by what is said to be a classic of "conservative" thought: *Ideas Have Consequences* – though for my part I can find nothing "conservative" about it except the author's obvious desire to conserve what little in 1948 may have been left of the values of the Schoolmen of the Middle Ages.

For the same reason that the reference point taken by Richard Weaver (who was not himself a Catholic) in his monumental indictment of modernity was the work and thought of the medieval Scholastics, who were the intellectual custodians of all that was, and still is, good about "the West," the essays that follow are by Catholics working with a traditional, Catholic approach to social and economic issues. But although the book is *by* Catholics, it is not just *for* Catholics. Because this traditional and yet radical[3]

---

1. Frank L. Owsley, "The Foundations of Democracy," in Emily S. Bingham and Thomas A. Underwood, eds., *The Southern Agrarians and the New Deal* (Charlottesville: published for the Southern Texts Society by the University Press of Virginia, 2001), pp. 223–4. Owsley's article originally appeared in the 1936 *Who Owns America?*, of which we will hear more.

2. Paul Murphy, *The Rebuke of History* (Chapel Hill: University of North Carolina Press, 2001), p. 234.

3. In the genuine sense of going back to "roots" of political and social thought.

Catholic approach to thinking about society and economic affairs partakes of a tradition that came to us from the best of the pre-Christian Greek and Roman thinkers, and – though it was adopted by and conserved within the Church, from her medieval philosophers to her 19th- and 20th-century socio-economic scholars – it remains offered to and at the disposal of all of humanity, Catholic or otherwise. As opposed to purely religious dogma that requires a gift of Faith to accept, the moral wisdom of Catholicism expressed in the following essays deals primarily with the natural law and the issues we confront in temporal and civil affairs. Strictly speaking, the solutions our Catholic authors offer to these problems require not Faith for their acceptance (though it doesn't hurt!), but merely good will and a substantial dose of common sense.

The title of the volume should indicate the uniqueness of this Catholic approach to social and economic affairs. The idea that there is some "third alternative," some other "thing" that offers a vision of sanity, of humanity, of justice, of independence and responsibility to men and their families in their daily lives and the earning of their daily bread, still lives, and it lives within the Catholic social tradition along with those more secular movements, such as that of the Southern Agrarians of Nashville and Vanderbilt fame, largely inspired by it.[1] (Note that we're not here talking about the "soft socialism" or "compassionate conservatism" of modern parlance, which succeed, in reality, in doing nothing other than amalgamating the worst features of both sides of the spectrum.) The authentic and organic "third way" beyond capitalism and socialism lives underground, marginalized and disfranchised by the monopoly over political life, thought, and discourse possessed by the modern, two-headed political monster, and kept from the playing field by the economic incarnation of the same set scheme. Party politics and loyalties, along with the old desire for power and profit, have for *at least* centuries succeeded in divorcing common sense and the sincere discussion (and solution) of real problems from the business of statecraft and the formulation and implementation of public and economic policy.

That such a vision does still live may come as a surprise to those who are professedly "on the right" and who have looked to the Church for (alleged,

---

1. Indeed, in one of his many defenses of the agrarian position, Donald Davidson, a contributor to the original manifesto, wrote (to Virginius Dabney of the Richmond *Times-Dispatch*) that the "agrarian economy . . . offers a third choice to a country staggering between the alternatives of a decaying and bewildered Capitalism and a Socialism, or Communism, that gains adherents every day" ("From the Richmond *Times-Dispatch*," University of Virginia special collections, p. 2). Fifty years later, Lyle Lanier, another original contributor, noted that the manifesto emerged from conversations among the participants and resulted in an "effort to find a third way, another way. Perhaps it's a fourth way . . . " ("Discussion: The Agrarian-Industrial Metaphor: Culture, Economics, and Society in a Technological Age," in William C. Havard, and Walter Sullivan, eds., *A Band of Prophets: the Vanderbilt Agrarians After Fifty Years* [Baton Rouge: Louisiana State University Press, 1982], pp. 161–2).

rather than real) sanction of neoconservative conceptions of private owner-ship and the rights of capital, business, and finance. Indeed the Church's doctrine is not simply a "morale builder," as Fulton Sheen noted (also in 1948), or a "rubber-stamp [for] the policies of a party in power,"[1] even if the that party is composed of leading figures in government or its auxiliaries like the American Enterprise Institute or the Ethics and Public Policy Cen-ter. Many of these old "cold warriors" – along with the post-Cold War world they inhabit – no doubt make the mistake (we are being charitable) of read-ing into the mutual opposition to Soviet expansionism and atheism of both the Church and the modern, materialist West the unconditional support by the former of the social and philosophical system of the latter. From such a viewpoint, any "third way" beyond capitalism and communism would seem a futile, if not dangerous, compromise between the forces of evil and the forces of evident good.

But what a mistaken assumption! Condemned by a whole host of think-ers, Catholic and otherwise, the notion was eminently refuted by (then Mon-signor but eventually Archbishop) Fulton Sheen, whose solid explanation of the authentic, traditional position bears quoting in full.[2] "If by capitalism is meant, not diffused ownership of property, but monopolistic capitalism in which capital bids for labor on a market, and concentrates wealth in the hands of the few," Sheen says,

> then from an *economic point of view alone*, the Church is just as much op-posed to capitalism as it is to communism. Communism emphasizes social use to the exclusion of personal rights, and capitalism emphasizes personal rights to the exclusion of social use. The Church says both are wrong, for

---

1. Fulton J. Sheen, *Communism and the Conscience of the West* (Indianapolis and New York: The Bobbs-Merrill Company, 1948), p. 79.

2. Many others could be added who approach the problem from similar or different, albeit equally in-teresting and persuasive, angles. Indeed a constant refrain one hears from orthodox Catholic thinkers from both before and after the World Wars is that rather than being opposites, among whom one must choose (and the implication is usually that one must side with the "freedom" of the "market," not-withstanding its inaccessibility to a whole range of people for ownership of any substantial productive property), capitalism and communism are based upon the same materialist errors and are related more as parent and offspring, or warring siblings, rather than diametrically opposed systems. In this light it is easy to understand why a number of the Agrarians (e.g., Allen Tate, Robert Penn Warren, Andrew Lytle, and Lyle Lanier) lobbied for the title of their manifesto being *Tracts Against Communism* rather than *I'll Take My Stand*, insofar as they saw communism as the inevitable outcome of the a system that concentrated wealth and industry, unless the agrarian alternative be pursued. Support for capitalist industrialism equated therefore into at least tolerance, if not advocacy, of communism. As Tate put it, entitling the symposium *Tracts Against Communism* would startle "the ordinary reader who might be inclined to call us [Agrarians] 'radical' by charging him with ultimate 'radicalism' if he continues to support the industrial system" (letter to E. F. Saxton of *Harper's*, September 3, 1930, quoted in Virginia Jean Rock, *The Making and Meaning of* I'll Take My Stand: *A Study in Utopian Conservatism, 1925–1939* (University of Minnesota: Ph.D. dissertation, 1961, p. 258). Andrew Lytle summed up: "[T]he defense of agrarianism was, itself, an attack on Communism" (letter to Tate, Spring 1930, quoted in *ibid.*, p. 260).

though the right to property is personal, the use is social. It therefore refuses to maintain capitalism as an alternative to the economic side of communism. Monopolistic capitalism concentrates wealth in the hands of a few capitalists, and communism in the hands of a few bureaucrats, and both end in the proletarianization of the masses. The true Christian must rid himself of the delusion that in opposing communism the Church thereby puts itself in opposition to all those who would seek thus to change the present economic system. The Christian concept denies there is an absolutely owned private property exclusive of limits set by the common good of the community and responsibility to the community. The more anonymous and impersonalistic property becomes, the less is the right to it. The Church agrees with communism in its protest against the injustice of the economic order, but it parts with it in the collectivity being made the sole employer, for this reduces the individual to the status of a serf or a slave of the state. Concentration of wealth is wrong whether it is done on the Hudson or the Volga.

The Church is not opposed to communism because the Church is a defender of the status quo. In every movement one must distinguish between *protests* and *reforms*. One can protest against a headache without advocating decapitation. The protests of communism are often right; but the reforms are wrong. The Church agrees with some of the protests of communism. In fact, there is a far better critique of the existing economic order based on the primacy of profit in two Encyclicals of Leo XIII and Pius XI than there is in all the writings of Marx. But the reforms of communism are wrong, because they are inspired by the very errors they combat. Communism begins with the liberal and capitalistic error that man is economic, and, instead of correcting it, merely intensifies it until man becomes a robot in a vast economic machine. There is a closer relation between communism and monopolistic capitalism than most minds suspect. They are agreed on the materialistic basis of civilization; they disagree only on who shall control that basis, capitalists or bureaucrats. Marx himself admitted he got many of his economic ideas from liberal economists such as Ricardo and the author of an anonymous work on interest. Capitalistic economy is godless; communism makes economics God. It is Divinity itself. Capitalism denies that economics is subject to a higher moral order. Communism says that economics is morality. Communism is not a radical solution of our economic problem; however violent be its approach, it does not touch the roots of the evil . . . .

Those who look to the Church in this hour of peril to pluck out of the fire the chestnuts of liberalism, secularism, materialism, and monopolistic capitalism are doomed to disappointment . . . . It is so easy for those who have made their money under a given system to think that that system must be right and good. Conservatism is for that reason often nothing else than a pseudo philosophy for the prosperous. The Church, however, knows that the disorganization of the world is largely due to the fact that it is not organized by any conscious acceptance of purpose other than the immediate interest of a capitalistic class on one hand, or a Communist class on the other hand.

That is why the economic policy of the Church is consistently in opposition to both capitalism and communism.[1]

Distributists and Agrarians both appreciated this fact; only to partisans of one camp or another was it (and does it remain) unapparent. Allen Tate complained of the reality – that these two "alternatives" are really twin variants of the same inhuman and ultimately unpalatable system – in a rather well-known letter to Malcolm Cowley: "[Y]ou and the other Marxians are not revolutionary enough: you want to keep capitalism with the capitalism left out."[2] While Eric Gill confirmed Sheen's judgment in advance, calling the so-called "revolutionaries" of the left

simply "progressives." They want, [he wrote,] instead of the present world, the world which the present one implies. They want the same thing only more so – the same things only more of them . . . . Merely to transfer ownership from private persons to the state is no revolution; it is only a natural development. Government by the proletariat is no revolution; it is only the natural sequel to the enfranchisement of lodgers. But to abolish the proletariat and make all men owners – and to abolish mass-production and return to a state of affairs wherein "the artist is not a special kind of man but every man is a special kind of artist" – that would be a revolution in the proper sense of the word. And merely to proclaim an atheist government is no revolution – for that would be to make explicit what is already implicit in capitalist commercialism; but to return to Christianity would be truly revolutionary.[3]

The work of Weaver, we have noted, has long been considered foundational in the canon of American conservatism.[4] It should therefore be of comfort to those "conservatives" of good will that the denunciation of "capitalist commercialism" and "monopolistic capitalism" by Sheen and Gill (to cite just the two above) is no more strident than the warning that Weaver

---

1. Sheen, *op. cit.*, pp. 79–81.

2. From Daniel Aaron, *Writers on the Left* (Oxford and New York: Oxford University Press, 1977), quoted by Edward S. Shapiro, "Decentralist intellectuals and the New Deal," *Journal of American History* 58 (4), March 1972, p. 939. Confirming our judgment on the Agrarian understanding is historian Paul Keith Conkin, who wrote that "[t]he equating of finance capitalism with communism distinguished the Agrarians from most American intellectuals" (*The Southern Agrarians* [Knoxville: University of Tennessee Press, 1988], p. 174).

3. From *Work and Property* (London: Dent, 1937), pp. 53–54, quoted by Donald Attwater, "Eric Gill," in Donald Attwater, ed., *Modern Christian Revolutionaries* (New York: The Devin-Adair Company, 1947), p. 228.

4. Robert Nisbet's comment on the jacket of the Chicago paperback says that that *IHC* "launched the renascence of philosophical conservatism in this country." Elsewhere, Weaver and his work have been called the "source and origin of the contemporary American conservative movement" (Forrest McDonald, "Conservatism," in Jack P. Greene, ed., *Encyclopedia of American Political History* [New York: Scribner, 1984], p. 366). Most of the secondary literature dealing with the Southern Agrarians and their so-called "neo-Agrarian" disciples places Weaver and his critique, rightly or wrongly, in a "conservative" paradigm.

offered in his magnum opus against this right-wing pole of our two dead-end "ism's," to which, unfortunately, so many more novel "conservatives" continue to cling as an ostensible refuge from statist collectivism.

[The] kind of property brought into being by finance capitalism . . . is . . . a violation of the very notion of *proprietas*. This amendment of the institution to suit the uses of commerce and technology has done more to threaten property than anything else yet conceived. For the abstract property of stocks and bonds, the legal ownership of enterprises never seen, actually destroy the connection between man and his substance without which metaphysical right becomes meaningless. Property in this sense becomes a fiction useful for exploitation and makes impossible the sanctification of work. The property which we defend as an anchorage keeps its identity with the individual.

Not only is this true, but the aggregation of vast properties under anonymous ownership is a constant invitation to further state direction of our lives and fortunes. For, when properties are vast and integrated, on a scale now frequently seen, it requires but a slight step to transfer them to state control. Indeed, it is a commonplace that the trend toward monopoly is a trend toward state ownership; and, if we continued the analysis further, we should discover that business develops a bureaucracy which can be quite easily merged with that of government. Large business organizations, moreover, have seldom been backward about petitioning government for assistance, since their claim to independence rests upon desire for profit rather than upon principle or the sense of honor. Big business and the rationalization of industry thus abet the evils we seek to overcome.

The moral solution is the distributive ownership of small properties. These take the form of independent farms, of local businesses, of homes owned by the occupants, where individual responsibility gives significance to prerogative over property. Such ownership provides a range of volition through which one can be a complete person, and it is the abridgment of this volition for which monopoly capitalism must be condemned along with communism.[1]

*****

A S WILL BE clear enough early on, if it is not already, the particular approach taken by many – though not all – of the authors of the essays that follows can be broadly characterized as an advocacy of Distributism, a school of thought of English Catholics supported also (explicitly or otherwise) by Americans such as Allen Tate, Herbert Agar, Ross Hoffman, Richard Weaver and others, who looked at the sane and sound social principles running through this tradition, conserved largely but not exclusively by the Church, and applied them to the situation of modern social and economic life.[2] And they looked at one problem in particular, which was the modern

1. Weaver, *op. cit.*, pp. 133–4.

2. See the essays of Aidan Mackey and Anthony Cooney for the historical and philosophical sketch; both

xxii ~ BEYOND CAPITALISM & SOCIALISM

separation of property from work, owing to the historical accident of the industrial revolution coupled with bad policy regarding the employment of money and machinery, inspired by a rationalist and erroneous philosophy stemming from the "liberation" of science and philosophy from the salutary influence of Catholic morals. To this problem they proposed the solution of the re-integration of property and work via the widespread distribution of property, especially land (and hence one aspect of the emphasis on ruralism and agriculture, especially among the Southern Agrarians and the English ruralists), but also shops, trades, and businesses, to those who already possessed their labor power.

For Catholics the ideal of the yeoman farmer or independent small businessman – not just as an individual, but in a community of correspondingly independent men and families – is obvious enough, owing to the social philosophy underlying it. As one Georgetown professor contemporary with the Distributists and Agrarians, and a disciple of the German Jesuit thinker Heinrich Pesch, S.J.,[1] put it,

> to live the life of a saint under the urban conditions which the rank and file of Christians face, presupposes a saintliness which we apparently cannot expect from the average man; therefore our social and economic institutions must be built in such a way that not only the hero and the saint but also the average Christian can find his way to his ultimate salvation without struggling heroically and with the grace of a selected saint against the daily things tempting him toward unnatural and graceless life.[2]

In the face of this task, Dr. Briefs, with others who supported the National Catholic Rural Life Conference during the inter-war years, called the "rural problem" the "predominant" one. "Our fundamental task," he wrote, in defense of the agrarian vision of small property holders drawing at least a portion of family needs from a piece of productive property both owned and worked by the family,

> is to restore the *natura* which presupposes the *gratis*. By doing it, we restore conditions of life which permit man to escape collectivism, impersonalism, secularism, the three great menaces of our age, the deep rooted sicknesses which poison State, Church, and society, and form the trinitarian heresy of our time. I am deeply convinced that the greatest contribution the Catholic Church has to offer to the present generation, to the American people and to the salvation of the occidental world lies here, in restoring *natura hominis* and

---

of these men were young when – and in touch with – the generation of Distributists that followed the death or retirement of the original Distributist Englishmen such as Hilaire Belloc and G. K. Chesterton.

1. About whom see Rupert Ederer's essay, Chapter 8.

2. Goetz Briefs, Ph.D., "The Back-to-the-Land Idea," *Catholic Rural Life Objectives* (St. Paul, Minn.: National Catholic Rural Life Conference [NCRLC], 1937), p. 98.

societatis in order that the grace of God, this great historical causality, can work its way to the salvation of man and to the welfare of our modern world.[1]

There is no argument against this approach as the traditional, typical, and commonly held and accepted opinion of Catholic moral thinkers and social critics from the first days in which such a problem came to be treated by Catholic commentators. The question of family ownership of property was not, and cannot ultimately, be separated from the question of rural life and ownership of land, insofar as that ownership is the chief way in which productive property is made available to individuals, with its obvious benefits that contrast with the owning of mere shares in a factory where drudgery is the order of the day. B. A. Santamaria, the chief figure of Catholic action, the Catholic rural movement, and Catholic politics in Australia – then and into the late 1990s – perhaps put it best:

> There is a unique Catholic tradition of the land . . . . For the land is linked peculiarly with the ideas and institutions which are inseparable from the Christian way of life and in defence of which the blood of Christians has been shed in every age. The Family, as an institution, flourishes best when it is linked to the land, for on the land children are an economic asset, whereas in the city they are a liability. *The moral freedom of the individual person has no counterpart in the regimentation and servility which are the handmaids of industrial civilization. It lives only if a man is his own master and is free from the threat of economic pressure and insecurity. In the modern world this can be only on the land, if the land is free from the incubus of debt. That liberty which comes only from the control of property can be realized only on the land. The Christian doctrine of property can be applied only imperfectly to the conditions of the factory and the industrial system.* There is no faith which is stronger than the Faith of the tillers of the soil. There is much to be said for the view of those who hold that there can be no Christian society which is not based on the solidity and permanency of the rural life [emphasis added].[2]

The three Popes who spoke most definitively upon the question of land ownership by families as the anchor upon which to build a social structure

---

1. *Ibid.*

2. B. A. Santamaria, *The Fight for the Land: The Program and Objectives of the National Catholic Rural Movement* (Carnegie, Vic.: Renown Press, n.d.), p. 6. American Catholics forcefully advanced the same argument; "[T]he Catholic religious ideal can best be fulfilled in the rural parish. Both family and communal life find there their most stable expression. The rural parish offers unparalleled advantages for the popular cultivation of the liturgy of the Church, while its young are shielded from many, though not all, of the dangers that beset them in non-rural surroundings" (Rev. John La Farge, S.J., "The Church and Rural Welfare," *Catholic Rural Life Objectives* [St. Paul, Minn.: NCRLC, 1935], p. 38); and, "The burning concern of the Catholic Church with agriculture arise from the altogether unique relations which exists universally between the agricultural occupation and the central institution of Christian, nay, of all, civilization; namely, the family" (Most Rev. Edwin V. O'Hara, D.D., "A Spiritual and Material Mission to Rural America," *ibid.*, p. 3).

that would benefit the family and provide an atmosphere conducive to the practice of religion and virtue were Leo XIII, Pius XI, and Pius XII. In his fiftieth anniversary commemoration of the great *Rerum Novarum* – Leo's encyclical on the condition of the working class, which was the first "official" Catholic crown placed upon the head of the already longstanding Catholic social movement – Pius XII refers explicitly to "the insistent call of the two Pontiffs of the social Encyclicals."[1] The call is for ownership of a homestead or smallholding as that which nearest approximates to the ideal form of productive property that can be possessed by the family, necessary for safeguarding its liberty to pursue and fulfill its economic, social, moral, and spiritual duties:

> Of all the goods that can be the object of private property, none is more conformable to nature, according to the teaching of *Rerum Novarum*, than the land, the holding on which the family lives, and from the products of which it draws all or part of its subsistence.[2]

He then goes so far as to state, "in the spirit of *Rerum Novarum*," that "*as a rule*, only that stability which is rooted in one's own holding makes of the family the vital and most perfect and fecund cell of society . . . . "[3]

In terms that parallel the Catholic argument, the Agrarians that trace their roots not explicitly to the Church, but to the traditions of Greece, Rome, and medieval Europe as transmitted to the early American republic, envisioned a small-is-beautiful, human-scale, person-above-profits social and economic vision that saw the independent family of independent means, united with other families in rural farming villages or modest towns of trades, crafts, and exchange, as the socio-economic foundation of "the good life," in the best and most virtuous sense of the term.[4] In many ways

---

1. *La Solennità della Pentecoste*, from *Principles for Peace* (Washington, D.C.: National Catholic Welfare Conference, 1943), p. 728. That this understanding was not merely that of Catholic social thinkers can easily be seen by the comment of a contemporary political scientist, who noted – echoing both Pius XII and Santamaria – that "[m]any of the [historical and philosophical] arguments for private property have no validity except in reference to a situation in which the ordinary individual owns the property upon which he labors for his livelihood" (Francis W. Coker, "American Traditions Concerning Property and Liberty," *The American Political Science Review* 30 (1), Feb. 1936, p. 15).

2. *Ibid*, p. 727.

3. *Ibid*, p. 727, emphasis added. He continues by stating (pp. 727–8, emphasis added): "If today the creation of vital spaces is at the center of social and political aims, should not one, before all else, think of the vital space of the family and free it of the fetters of conditions which do not permit one even to formulate the idea of a homestead of one's own?"

4. Most commentators agree with William Havard's description of the Southern Agrarian position as consistent "with the political doctrines of Plato and Aristotle" (Robert B. Heilman, "Spokesman and Seer: The Agrarian Movement and European Culture," in William C. Havard et al, *op. cit.*, p. 100). Furthermore, Davidson was at one with Allan Tate's call, in this vein, for opposition to "the low-grade but often pretentious life reflected in the succulent pages of *Life* and *Time*, in the TV show, in the blaring radio with its singing commercials, and in the stream of 'remorseless motors' on street and highway"

the Southern section of the United States became sole heir to this position as early as the middle 1800s, though it took until 1930 for that tradition to find its most able spokesmen.[1]

As might be expected, this tradition, while not necessarily the *Catholic* one argued by the Church on principally religious terms, is to be found within Catholic circles as well as without. While the Agrarians and others make more narrow claims that exclude aspects of the Catholic position, the Catholics tend to incorporate the natural, philosophical, and social arguments made by their allies outside the Church.

Charles Devas, a Catholic economist of early last century, declared "flourishing populations of small farmers or peasants" to be "the ideal of all great statesmen from Solon to Leo XIII."[2] He could justifiably have added Thomas Jefferson, whose apologia for a republic of independent yeomen farmers was well known among Agrarians and others advocating widely distributed productive-property ownership. "I am conscious," he wrote to James Madison,

> that an equal division of property is impracticable, but the consequences of this enormous inequality producing so much misery to the bulk of mankind, legislators cannot invent too many devices for subdividing property, only taking care to let their subdivisions go hand in hand with the natural affections of the human mind . . . . It is too soon yet in our country to say that every man who cannot find employment, but who can find uncultivated land, shall be at liberty to cultivate it, paying a moderate rent. But it is not too soon to provide by every possible means that as few as possible shall be without a little portion of land.[3]

---

by a recovery of the "classical-Christian world, based upon the regional consciousness, which held that honor, truth, imagination, human dignity, and limited acquisitiveness could alone justify a social order however rich and efficient it may be . . . " (Donald Davidson, "Counterattack, 1930–1940: the South Against Leviathan," *Southern Writers in the Modern World* [Athens: University of Georgia Press, 1958], p. 59).

1. See Christopher Hollis, *The American Heresy* (New York: Minton, Balch & Company, 1930), and Richard Weaver, "The Tennessee Agrarians," in George M. Curtis III and James J. Thompson Jr., eds., *The Southern Essays of Richard M. Weaver* (Indianapolis: Liberty Press, 1987).

2. *CE*, s.v. "Agrarianism."

3. Letter to James Madison, Fontainebleau, October 28, 1785, in Jean M. Yarbrough, ed., *The Essential Jefferson* (Indianapolis and Cambridge: Hackett Publishing Co., Inc., 2006), p. 154. Earlier (QUERY XIX: "The present state of manufactures, commerce, interior and exterior trade?," in *ibid.*, pp. 132–3), Jefferson had made the same point, with slightly different emphasis: "Those who labor in the earth are the chosen people of God, if ever he had a chosen people, whose breasts he has made his peculiar deposit for substantial and genuine virtue. It is the focus in which he keeps alive that sacred fire, which otherwise might escape from the face of the earth. Corruption of morals in the mass of cultivators is a phenomenon of which no age nor nation has furnished an example. It is the mark set on those, who not looking up to heaven, to their own soil and industry, as does the husbandman, for their subsistence, depend for it on the casualties and caprice of customers. Dependence begets subserviency and venality, suffocates the germ of virtue, and prepares fit tools for the designs of ambition. This, the natural progress and consequence of the arts, has sometimes perhaps been retarded by accidental circumstances: but, generally speaking, the proportion which the aggregate of the other classes of citizens bears in

The reception afforded by *Commonweal* to the Agrarian-Distributist volume *Who Owns America?* that in 1936 followed the celebrated Agrarian manifesto, *I'll Take My Stand* (*ITMS*), of 1930, offered a confirmation, from a Catholic source, of the centrality of the vision here advocated to "the standard of traditional American liberty." The widespread ownership of property was said to offer

> that real liberty which cannot exist materially speaking, in any nation, unless the determining mass of the nation is constituted by individuals and families and free groups possessed of true property in land and in houses and in tangible things – not merely jobs, and some paperholdings of shares in enterprises in the direction of which they have no part. For that mode of life tends toward servility, and regimentation, and degradation of human values as surely, if more slowly, and less directly, and less openly, than Communism or Fascism.[1]

Herbert Agar, who with Allen Tate was largely responsible for coordinating the 1936 volume, put it this way:

> Our common ground is a belief that monopoly capitalism is evil and self-destructive, and that it is possible, while preserving private ownership, to build a true democracy in which men would be better off both morally and physically, more likely to attain that inner peace which is the mark of a good life.[2]

That "inner peace" characteristic of the "good life": here we find the essence of the moral and natural, as distinguished from the more overtly religious, argument of the Agrarians, and the Distributists too, for private ownership of real, tangible productive property. The case was made most eloquently, as is not surprising, by Weaver a decade later, referring to the exercise of choice and self-direction afforded by private property as man's "birthright of responsibility." Private property, he wrote,

> provides indispensable opportunity for training in virtue. Because virtue is a state of character concerned with choice, it flourishes only in the area of volition. Not until lately has this fundamental connection between private property and liberty been stressed; here in the domain of private property, rational freedom may prove the man; here he makes his virtue an active principle, breathing and exercising it, as Milton recommended. Without freedom, how is anyone to pass his probation? Consider Thoreau, or any hard-bitten New England farmer of Thoreau's day, beside the pitiful puling

any state to that of its husbandmen, is the proportion of its unsound to its healthy parts, and is a good-enough barometer whereby to measure its degree of corruption . . . . "

1. "To Make America Free," *Commonweal*, May 8, 1936, quoted in Edward S. Shapiro, "*Who Owns America?*: A Forgotten American Classic," *Intercollegiate Review* 35 (1), Fall 1999, p. 44.

2. Herbert Agar, "Introduction," *Who Owns America?* (Freeport, New York: Books for Libraries Press, 1970 [1936]), p. ix.

creature which statism promises to create. The comparison points to this: a great virtue is realizable here, but we must be willing to meet its price . . . . [1]

And again:

That I reap now the reward of my past industry or sloth, that what I do today will be felt in that future now potential – these require a play of mind. The notion that the state somehow bears responsibility for the indigence of the aged is not far removed from that demoralizing supposition that the state is somehow responsible for the criminality of the criminal. I will not deny that the dislocations of capitalism afford some ground for the former. But that is another argument; the point here is that no society is health-ful which tells its members to take no thought of the morrow because the state underwrites their future. The ability to cultivate providence, which I would interpret literally as foresight, is an opportunity to develop personal worth. A conviction that those who perform the prayer of labor may store up a compensation which cannot be appropriated by the improvident is the soundest incentive to virtuous industry. Where the opposite conviction pre-vails, where popular majorities may, on a plea of present need, override these rights earned by past effort, the tendency is for all persons to become politi-cians. In other words, they come to feel that manipulation is a greater source of reward than is production. This is the essence of corruption. [2]

As we noted, the Catholics accepted all of these arguments, along with those of their own. Devas noted that

the instinct of private property is truly human; and the proper unfolding of human liberty and personality is historically bound up with it, and can-not develop where each person is only a sharer in a compulsory partnership, or, on the other hand, where property is confined to a privileged few. Suit-ably, therefore, the same Pope [Leo XIII] who had defended the true dignity and true liberty of man urged *the diffusion of property as the mean between Socialism and Individualism,* and that where possible each citizen should dwell secure in a homestead which, however humble, was his own [emphasis added]. [3]

The Agrarians of the South also saw the connection of this defense of widespread ownership with the advocacy of rural life and agriculture for a large percentage of the population. "[T]he answer," Lytle wrote in his contri-bution to the manifesto of 1930,

lies in a return to a society where agriculture is practiced by most of the people. It is in fact impossible for any culture to be sound and healthy with-out a proper respect and proper regard for the soil, no matter how many

---

1. Weaver, *IHC*, p. 137.

2. *Ibid.*, pp. 138–9.

3. Devas, *op. cit.*, s.v. "Agrarianism."

urban dwellers think their victuals come from groceries and delicatessens and their milk from tin cans.[1]

Twenty years later, Donald Davidson defended this vision with a similar insistence upon the connection between agriculture, rural life in general, and the full development of human personality. "The farm, whether large or small," he wrote in a 1952 *ITMS* retrospective published in the journal *Shenandoah*,

> together with all allied establishments partaking of its organic and natural character, obviously would furnish the basis for such a [traditional] society, rather than the non-organic, artificial "organizations" that industrialism is always busily erecting and always, just as busily, throwing on the junk-heap. I have not heard of any other kind of society in which human beings can hope to come as near as they can in this kind of traditional society to realizing their capacities as "whole persons" or "real persons" – a thing all but impossible under an industrial regime, which wants only specialists, or pieces of men.[2]

A survey of the individuals, movements, and arguments of the ruralist and agrarian stripe would be incomplete without mention of the English "rural reconstruction" school that included Harold J. Massingham, Adrian Bell, Gerald Wallop, the Viscount Lymington, Rolf Gardiner, Jorian Jenks, and others in the "Kinship in Husbandry" group, the Economic Reform Club and Institute (ERCI), and the Rural Reconstruction Association, which English architect and Distributist Arthur J. Penty helped to found alongside Montague Fordham.[3] Collectively and apart, these individuals and associations looked to a restoration of the values and practices of English rural life, as intimately connected to – and essential for – the defense of private property, the proper relationship between man and nature, and the cultivation of that style of life that resisted the plastic and "disposable" trend in modern, industrial culture. Massingham was perhaps the most prolific and representative voice among these dozens of rural-restoration activists; he captured, better than many others, the spirit and vision of rural England,

---

1. Andrew Nelson Lytle, "The Hind Tit," *ITMS* (New York: Harper Torchbooks, 1962), p. 203. Further citations are from this edition of *ITMS* unless otherwise indicated.

2. "A Symposium: The Agrarians Today," *Shenandoah* 3 (2), Summer 1952, p. 19.

3. See Richard Moore-Colyer, "Rolf Gardiner, English Patriot and the Council for the Church and Countryside," *Agricultural History Review* 49 (2), pp. 187 209; "Back To Basics: Rolf Gardiner, H. J. Massingham and 'A Kinship in Husbandry,'" *Rural History* 12 (1), 2001, pp. 85–108; "Sir George Stapledon (1882–1960) and the Landscape of Britain," *Environment and History* 5, 1999, pp. 221–236; Philip Conford, "A Forum for Organic Husbandry: *The New English Weekly* and Agricultural Policy, 1939–1949" *Agricultural History Review* 46 (2), pp. 197–210; "Finance versus Farming: Rural Reconstruction and Economic Reform, 1894–1955," *Rural History* (2002) 13 (2), pp. 225–241; Conford and Moore-Colyer, "A 'Secret Society'? The Internal and External Relations of the Kinship in Husbandry, 1941–52," *Rural History* 15 (2), 2004, pp. 189–206; and Frank Trentmann, "Civilization and Its Discontents: English Neo-Romanticism and the Transformation of Anti-Modernism in Twentieth-Century Western Culture," *Journal of Contemporary History* 29 (4), Oct. 1994, pp. 583–625.

and its importance in the cultural struggle that raged then (and which rages still) between modernity and social tradition. He advocated the vocation of the gardener as a means of keeping "soil and person intact against the corruption of the modern world," arguing that the gardener would be

> the base of the society of tomorrow. For he and his like obey the primary laws of nature and within himself. His private ownership has the sanction of millennia and the voice of the wise men. His responsibility is the first condition of man's moral and his usefulness of man's physical being, while the beauty he creates is part of the whole visible universe.[1]

Working within the same ambit as these groups were the Catholic land associations and movements that existed across the English-speaking world, and from some of whose spokesmen we have already heard. In England the land movement formally began in 1929 with the Scottish Catholic Land Association (CLA), based in Glasgow; in 1931 the English CLA was founded in London (and patronized by Cardinal Bourne of Westminster), later becoming the South of England CLA with the inauguration of the Midlands CLA in Birmingham that same year. The following year saw the foundation of the North of England CLA in Liverpool. The key figures of the land movement in England included Mgr. James Dey, Fr. Vincent McNabb, O.P., Rev. John McQuillan, and Distributists Harold Robbins, K. L. Kenrick, and Reginald Jebb. Supporters included other prominent Distributists such as Hilaire Belloc, G. K. Chesterton, and Herbert Shove, and Ditchling village craftsmen such as George Maxwell, Eric Gill, and Hilary Pepler.[2]

In the U.S. the National Catholic Rural Life Conference (NCRLC) began in 1923 in St. Louis, under the patronage of the Archbishop there, and was effectively founded by then Fr. Edwin V. O'Hara (later Bishop of Great Falls, K.C., and given personal title of archbishop by Pope Pius XII). American supporters of the movement included a number of the clergy, such as Bishops Aloysius J. Muench of Fargo and George Speltz of St. Cloud, Minn. (author of a significant Catholic University dissertation entitled *The Importance of Rural Life According to the Philosophy of St. Thomas Aquinas*, written with the hope that he could "add to the work of the [agrarian-decentralist movement]"[3]), Frs. Howard Bishop, Luigi Ligutti, and John Rawe, who were affiliated with the NCRLC through its routine conferences and activities; American academics such as Drs. Goetz Briefs, Walter Marx, and Willis Nutting;

1. *This Plot of Earth* (London: Collins, 1944), p. 280.

2. See Harold Robbins, *The Last of the Realists: G. K. Chesterton, His Work and His Influence* (Norfolk, Va.: IHS Press, 2008 [1946], forthcoming), originally serialized in *The Cross & the Plough*; *Flee to the Fields* (Norfolk, Va.: IHS Press, 2003 [1934]); and Fr. Vincent McNabb, O.P., and Cdr. Herbert Shove, *The Catholic Land Movement* (London: Catholic Truth Society, 1932).

3. Washington, D.C.: The Catholic University of America Press, 1945 (pp. xiv–v).

and journalists and Distributists such as Carol Robinson and Ed Willock of *Integrity Magazine* in New York.[1]

Elsewhere – such as Australia, for instance – there was the National Catholic Rural Movement (NCRM), founded in 1939 by Bishop F. A. Henschke, who was appointed Episcopal chairman by the Australian hierarchy; in 1947 he declared that the "success of the Rural Movement is the condition of the success of all Catholic Action." The mainstay of support for the NCRM came from those associated with the Australian Catholic Social Movement of Archbishop Daniel Mannix and B. A. Santamaria.[2] These three bodies constituted the specific organizations in the U.S., England, and Australia – alongside the other sympathetic and variously related groups and movements – dedicated to promoting the Catholic vision of rural life and acting consciously to foster it.

The period in which the CLAs and similar groups were most active saw not just an intellectual renaissance of classical and Christian ruralism and economic thought, but also a resurgence of very practical interest in "back-to-the-land" schemes of all kinds. Operating to some extend under the influence of Belloc, with his elaboration of the Servile State in the early twentieth century, Fr. Luigi Ligutti and his Granger homesteads were just one of numerous land settlement projects attempted in various venues during the New Deal era, when such initiatives as solutions to unemployment – in the spirit of the English Distributists' Birmingham Scheme – were most in vogue. Not surprisingly, Ligutti's efforts are reckoned by historians of the period as among the most successful, owing to the solid religious and philosophical foundation of his efforts, along with his own insistence that land-movement cooperation among Catholics was important enough to become almost a matter of "moral compulsion."[3] Additionally, there were other community house-raising initiatives, such as that of Ed Willock of *Integrity Magazine*, who helped to pioneer "Marycrest," two dozen miles outside of New York City, along with others who were interested in "decentralism, back to the land, and Christian-humanism."[4]

---

1. See Dan Dorsey, *Reverend William Howard Bishop: Toward an Understanding of His Charism as Founder of the Glenmary Home Missioners*, unpublished thesis, www.glenmary.org; Fr. George H. Speltz, *The Importance of Rural Life According to the Philosophy of St. Thomas Aquinas* (Washington, D.C.. Catholic University of America Press, 1945); Raymond Philip Witte, *Twenty-Five Years of Crusading: A History of the National Catholic Rural Life Conference* (Des Moines: The National Catholic Rural Life Conference, 1948); and Frs. Luigi G. Ligutti and John C. Rawe, *Rural Roads to Security: America's Third Struggle for Freedom* (Milwaukee: Bruce Publishing Co., 1940).

2. See *Fruits of the Vine*, Handbook of the National Catholic Rural Movement (Fitzroy, Vic.: Australian Catholic Publications, 1958) and Santamaria, *op. cit.*

3. Paul Keith Conkin, *Tomorrow a New World: the New Deal Community Program* (New York: Da Capo Press, 1976), pp. 25, 28–9, 300–1.

4. Editorial, *Integrity Magazine* 6 (10), July 1952, p. 7. See also James Terence Fisher, *The Catholic Coun-*

In Canada, to take one example, Fr. Francis McGoey was a priest at a To-ronto parish who in 1934 founded a rural community of five families on 10 acres, supplemented initially with 50 chickens per family, and two common cows: "If," McGoey said,

> giving men, women,, and children an opportunity to use their brains in the development of art, music, work, entertainment, and play, as against the ar-tificial city life, is part of progress, then we have it. Land ownership and agrarianism gives the poor something better than a choice between finance-capitalism and communism.[1]

More well-known in Canada were the efforts of Frs. Coady and Tompkins, pioneers of a rural cooperative movement which worked "to break down the barrier that the profit system erected between produced and consumer."[2] The Vatican Secretary of State under Pope Pius XI offered the movement high praise on behalf of the Holy Father: "May the work undertaken grow and flourish and, with unswerving purpose of mind and will, be carried on to complete fulfillment."[3]

In England, the CLAs established six training farms, which succeeded for at least a brief time in demonstrating the viability of the "back-to-the-land" vision and its credibility as a solution to the pervasive problem of un-employment. Also well known is the effort at Ditchling to unite men on the land in an effort of husbandry and handicraft. "The communities of crafts-manship with a foothold on the land were very valuable to the [Distributist] movement," Robbins wrote in 1946, "and exist and flourish still, at Ditchling Common and High Wycombe." The guild at Ditchling survived until 1989.[4]

These land movements, principally of the U.S. and England, were pos-sessed of a wide range of propaganda vehicles – in the best and Catholic sense of the term. *Flee to the Fields*, originally subtitled "The Faith and Works of the Catholic Land Movement," was effectively the manifesto of the move-

---

terculture in America, 1933–1962 (Chapel Hill and London: University of North Carolina Press, 1989). Chapter 4, "The Limits of Personalism: *Integrity* and the Marycrest Community, 1946–1956," is full of useful facts and information on Willock and *Integrity*, but overall the work is characterized by an almost violent bigotry towards integral Catholicism, and engages in more than a fair share of super-ficial and judgmental generalization towards any number of things, including, e.g., G. K. Chesterton, whom – as one indication of the book's seriousness – the author calls "ridiculous."

1. Ligutti et al, *op. cit.*, p. 147.

2. National Catholic Rural Life Conference, *Manifesto on Rural Life* (Milwaukee: Bruce Publishing Co., 1939), p. 164, quoting from *The Land Helps Those*, by Bertram B. Fowler.

3. Ligutti et al, *op. cit.*, p. 342.

4. See Robbins, *Last of the Realists, op. cit.* (especially the "Birmingham Scheme," included as an ap-pendix); W. P. Witcutt, *The Dying Lands: A Fifty Years' Plan for the Distressed Areas* (London: The Dis-tributist League, 1937); and "The Collection," on the Guild of Ss. Joseph and Dominic, at the Ditchling Museum website (http://www.ditchling-museum.com/collection_guild.html, accessed on December 30, 2007).

ment in England; the Catholic Truth Society pamphlet on the land movement by Fr. McNabb and Cdr. Shove – which featured an Introduction by G. K. Chesterton – identified in clear and simple terms the motives and the aims and methods of the movement. The pamphlet also featured a revealing advertisement for the South of England Catholic Land Association which read, in part, "The aim of the Catholic Land associations is to encourage and assist Catholic families to live and work on the land"; the headline above stated, "Plant the Faith by Planting the Faithful."[1]

Periodicals in the U.K. that covered the movement were the *Catholic Times*, *G. K.'s Weekly*, the *Cross & the Plough* (organ of the Catholic Land Associations of England and Wales), and *Land for the People* (the organ in Scotland). In the U.S. a number of journals either supported a return to rural life or formed an official part of the NCRLC's information activities; these included, e.g., *Free America, Integrity, St. Isidore's Plow, Catholic Rural Life, Landward, Rural Bureau Notes, Catholic Rural Life Bulletin*, and *Land and Home*.[2] The Conference, in addition, published some thirteen pamphlets, including *For This We Stand*, an address by Fr. Luigi Ligutti for Farmers' Day of the National Convention of the NCRLC in Green Bay, Wis., October 14, 1946; its *Rural Life in a Peaceful World* offered "principles and policies underlying [the Conference's] postwar program for rural life." Related periodicals in the U.K. supporting a recovery of rural culture, the restoration of agriculture, and a new "organic husbandry" included A. R. Orage's *New English Weekly*, the Soil Association's journal *Mother Earth*, and the ERCI journal *Rural Economy*.[3] Interestingly, the masthead of *Rural Economy*, originally "A Monthly Commentary for all interested in the full development of a Healthy Agriculture," was later and illustratively changed to "A Non-Party Commentary devoted to the development of a Sound National Economy rooted in the Soil."[4]

*****

BEYOND ITS MERE usefulness as a historical introduction and context, this broad consideration of the range and diversity of the early-twentieth-century Agrarian, Distributist, and land movements affords us an opportunity to understand the importance of the Catholic foundation for the social and political philosophy we have been looking at – an importance which, perhaps, non-Catholics might begin to appreciate in view of

---

1. See McNabb and Shove, *op. cit.*

2. See Witte, *op. cit.*

3. Conford, "Finance," *op. cit.*, pp. 225, 231.

4. *Ibid.*, p. 234.

the Southern Agrarians' (none of whom were Catholic) evolved understanding of their own agenda.

Notwithstanding the sincere welcome that Catholics extended to the Agrarians' anthology, a number of them also frankly criticized their rather "hazy" notion of religion, maintaining that it provided an ultimately unsatisfactory foundation for the defense and restoration of civilization.[1] The differences, as well as the similarities, between Southern Agrarian and Catholic ruralist and Distributists positions was plain, and, though it didn't prove a bar to collaboration, it did represent a serious point of philosophical divergence.

None of this would have been news to the Agrarians themselves, as Allen Tate frankly admitted the inadequacy of the Southern religious idea in his contribution to *ITMS*.[2] As Paul Murphy relates, it was not more than a month after the publication of the manifesto that Tate was lamenting – or at least worrying – that the Agrarians were "Trying to make a political creed do the work of a religion."[3] Which isn't to say that the Agrarians were not concerned with religion, or didn't see it as fundamental. Quite the contrary. John Crowe Ransom made no secret of his belief that "[r]eligion is the only effective defense against Progress, and our vicious economic system; against empire and against socialism, or any other political foolishness."[4] Davidson wished, years later, that more emphasis had been placed upon religion in the discussions of the 1930s,[5] while Tate, for his part, wished that he could demonstrate, as a starting-point for the Agrarian argument, that

> the remote source of the old Southern mind was undoubtedly Catholicism or at least High Church-ism . . . and perhaps something could be done towards

---

1. See, for instance, Rev. Joseph H. Fichter, S.J., "A Comparative View of Agrarianism," *Catholic Rural Life Objectives* (St. Paul, Minn.: NCRLC, 1936), pp. 111–16.

2. "[The South] had a religious life, but it was not enough organized with a right mythology. In fact, their rational life was not powerfully united to the religious experience, as it was in mediaeval society, and they are a fine specimen of the tragic pitfall upon which the Western mind has always hovered. Not having a rational system for the defense of their religious attitude and its base in a feudal society, they elaborated no rational system whatever, no full-grown philosophy; so that, when the post-bellum temptations of the devil, who is the exploiter of nature, confronted them, they had no defense" (Allen Tate, "Remarks on the Southern Religion," *ITMS, op. cit.,* p. 173).

3. Letter, Tate to John Gould Fletcher, Dec. 3, 1930, quoted in Murphy, *op. cit.,* p. 75.

4. Letter, Ransom to Tate, Jul. 4, 1929, in Thomas Daniel Young and George Core, eds., *Selected Letters of John Crowe Ransom* (Baton Rouge: Louisiana State University Press, 1985), quoted in Murphy, *op. cit.,* p. 56.

5. Donald Davidson, *Shenandoah* symposium, p. 19. In the same article he even noted the predictable flow of Protestant youth into the Catholic Church, owing to the secularism of the Southern Protestant clergy at the time (*ibid.,* p. 21). Cleanth Brooks seconded this notion during the 1982 Agrarian reunion, pointing out how the Agrarians admitted during their 1952 symposium that they "should have dropped back to a deeper line of defense; [and] ought to have talked more about religion" (William C. Havard et al, *op. cit.,* pp. 159–60).

showing that the old Southerners were historically Catholics all the time. If that could be done, we have a starting point. For, as [Gorham] Munson says, we need a "master-idea."[1]

The problem for Tate and for the other Southern thinkers was that such a master idea was not convincingly connected to their conception of politics and society. It was not in dispute that the civilization of the South was worth preserving, in its agrarian and traditional aspects. The arguments for such a defense needed, however, to be anchored in transcendent and ultimate terms – and these terms were difficult for the Agrarians who had eschewed any authoritarian or hierarchical approach to Christianity.

In 1956 Tate tried to enunciate what he and his colleagues were defending by referring to it as a "religious humanism."[2] But the notion was vague enough that even sympathetic commentators removed many of the teeth from the Agrarians' original critique, turning it into simply a defense of "civilized values" or Southernism against a kind of cultural philistinism.[3] And ultimately this was not a wholly unfair interpretation, owing to the contradictions in Tate's position; he "was an admirer and advocate of Christian feudal society," but he could not, in 1930, submit to religious authority, nor did he believe – correctly – that the South, considered politically, "had inherited . . . a Christian tradition of 'unity of being.'"[4] In later years the ambivalence in the Agrarian political philosophy, and even more in the way it was interpreted by some of the neo-Agrarian commentators, would make it susceptible (as we shall see below) to co-option by the "Buckleyite" forces of *National Review* fame, so that a radical and uncompromising critique of industrialism, rooted in an intransigent religious and philosophical position, could be watered down into a generic "conservatism" that would offer no obstacle to the "free marketeers" of the "right."[5]

---

1. Letter, Tate to Ransom, Jul. 27, 1929, quoted in Murphy, *op. cit.*, p. 56.

2. *Fugitives' Reunion; Conversations at Vanderbilt, May 3–5, 1956* (Nashville: Vanderbilt University Press, 1959), p. 183.

3. As Paul Murphy relates (*op. cit.*, p. 221), summarizing Louis D. Rubin Jr., *The Wary Fugitives* (Baton Rouge: Louisiana State University Press, 1978), "the choice of the term 'agrarianism,' [Rubin] argued, was a 'strategic error of considerable magnitude.' They resorted to it because 'religious humanism' was an insufficient symbol and, moreover, the Agrarians themselves had forsaken religious orthodoxy. Their religion was in fact, the South, Rubin claimed. 'They thought and felt about the South in terms appropriate to religious belief.' Rubin's perspective, greatly indebted to Tate's later interpretation of Agrarianism, discounted the Agrarians' socio-economic argument; in his view, they should have simply championed the idea of the South."

4. Murphy, *op. cit.*, p. 89.

5. As Paul Murphy narrates (*op. cit.*, p. 254), "a cultural criticism originally insistent on the interconnection between culture and the economy came to be replaced by a traditionalist conservatism oriented around the image of the South as a synecdoche for Christian orthodoxy and a patriarchal social order. Contemporary traditionalist conservatives, if heeding much of the neo-Agrarian commentary on Agrarianism, stand to lose sight of the radical conservatism of *I'll Take My Stand*."

With a merely "hazy notion of religion"[1] upon which to build a political philosophy, the Agrarians could not have elaborated a vision as con-
vincing and coherent as the Scholastic tradition founded upon the Faith
of our fathers and the realism of Aristotle – the tradition with which the
Distributists and other Catholic agrarian thinkers were working. This was
something that Weaver himself attempted, however, in referring repeatedly
to the Schoolmen in *Ideas Have Consequences*.[2] And it would be unfair not
to point out that within the limits of their metaphysic, the Agrarians themselves were seeking – and effectively, if incompletely, articulated – a vision of
Christendom, of radical opposition to industrialism, and, at least implicitly,
of Catholic social doctrine and the Social Reign of Christ.

For it's not true what some critics have maintained – that the Agrarians
were simply romantic seekers after some mythical, Arcadian antebellum
South. One of Davidson's early letters outlining the aims of the then-pro-
spective *ITMS* explicitly rejected such a notion.[3] Contributors to the manifesto (e.g., Andrew Lytle and Robert Penn Warren, respectively) made it
clear, in retrospect, that "in defending what was left of Southern life, we were
defending our common European inheritance," and that the relationship
between the book and the geographical South was a completely "peripheral
and accidental question . . . ."[4] Tate wrote that those of his colleagues who
"imagine[d] they [were] writing pleasant essays on the old South" were "de-
ceiving themselves," and counseled that they had better "leave us quickly."[5]

Indeed the Agrarians wanted a full opposition to industrialism – not some
vague myth of a pastoral life that would be later watered down into what Louis Rubin would simply call "an extended metaphor." In the face of such an
assertion, Donald Davidson rightly countered that "[i]f you say that, it's very
easy, because you don't have to believe it at all."[6] Happily, some very cred-

1. Fichter, *op. cit.*, p. 115.

2. In this vein Paul Murphy (*op. cit.*, p. 223, citing M. E Bradford, *Remembering Who We Are: Observations of a Southern Conservative* [Athens: University of Georgia Press, 1985], pp. 15, 24, 74, 76) para-
phrased Bradford's contention "Weaver completed the Agrarian tradition by providing philosophical
system and depth. Weaver, Bradford suggested, sought to root Agrarianism in a larger Western intellectual tradition."

3. "We don't advocate a restoration of the 'Old South' scheme, and we are not going to give ourselves
up to a purely sentimental and romantic recession to the past" (letter, Davidson to Herman Clarence
Nixon, January 5, 1930, incorrectly labeled 1929, cited from the Nixon papers at Vanderbilt University's Special Collections, in Sarah N. Shouse, *Hillbilly Realist: Herman Clarence Nixon of Possum Trot*
[University, Ala.: University of Alabama Press, 1986], p. 52).

4. William C. Havard et al, *op. cit.*, pp. 164–5, and Andrew Lytle, "Afterword: A Semi-Centennial,"
Why the South Will Survive (Athens: The University of Georgia Press, 1981), p. 225.

5. Letter, Tate to Fletcher, Dec. 3, 1930, quoted in Murphy, *op. cit.*, p 287 n31.

6. *ITMS* (Baton Rouge and London: Louisiana State University Press, 1977), pp. xvii and xxviii, quoted
in M. Thomas Inge, "The Continuing Relevance of I'll Take My Stand," *Mississippi Quarterly* 33, 1980,
p. 449.

ible historians of the Agrarians have rejected the "metaphorical or symbolic" approach to the Agrarian position as a deplorable tactic, "as unfair as it is ahistorical," used rather for "evading the content of their criticism."[1] As Paul Murphy notes, "[t]he leading Agrarians took the socioeconomic elements of *ITMS* . . . very seriously." And for the most committed of the original group, Agrarianism remained, even fifty years on, "more than a metaphor . . . . It was a program of action, and the enemy was still industrial capitalism."[2]

More than this, the Agrarians seemed to be seeking – even if at times unwittingly – what Catholics recognize as the social doctrine of the Church, and the Social Reign of Christ over politics and society that its implementation is intended to bring about. How else, ultimately, to make sense of the Agrarian interpretations, years later, of the focus of *I'll Take My Stand*? As William Elliott put it during the 1956 reunion of Fugitive poets and original Agrarians, "a poet's affirmation of the values that should be used to govern, [is one of] the things that I thought the *I'll Take My Stand* boys were concerned with" – and this notion of transcendent values establishing the foundation for politics and economics is nothing if not (at the very least) parallel to the Catholic notion of the dependence of political rectitude upon right morals.[3] Andrew Lytle must have had the same idea in mind when, in explaining the ethos of the 1930 symposium, he remarked that "Christian kings . . . are the secular agents of God."[4] With twenty or so years of hindsight, Allen Tate stated that what he had in mind with the manifesto was "the order of a unified Christendom," as presupposed by "the possibility of the humane life."[5] With characteristic precision, Davidson summed up the whole enterprise: "There can hardly be such a thing as a 'society,' in any true sense, without religion as the all-pervasive arbiter of value."[6] It is not likely a coincidence, then, that the only European head of state to recognize Dixie's President as the leader of an independent nation – a nation whose inherited ways of life the Agrarians felt called to defend, in a stubborn resistance to a destructive "progress" – also himself condemned the suggestion that "the Roman Pontiff can, and ought to, reconcile himself, and come to terms with, progress, liberalism, and modern civilization."[7]

---

1. Conkin, *Southern Agrarians*, *op. cit.*, pp. 167–8.

2. Paul Murphy, *op. cit.*, pp. 4 and 49. In the second reference Murphy is referring to the Agrarians' remarks during their 1980 reunion (William C. Havard et al, *op. cit.*, especially pp. 162–3 and 180).

3. *Fugitives' Reunion*, *op. cit.*, p. 186.

4. Lytle, "Afterword," *op. cit.*, p. 225.

5. *Shenandoah* symposium, *op. cit.*, p. 29.

6. *Ibid.*, p. 20.

7. See Murphy, *op. cit.*, p. 274; Pius IX, *Syllabus of Errors*, December 8, 1864, condemned proposition 80; and Gary Potter, "Catholicism and the Old South," *www.catholicism.org*, accessed January 4, 2008.

As should be expected, where the Agrarians had to rely upon a vague notion – and one perhaps learned late, after much reflection – of the religious foundation of all healthy political and social arrangements, the Distributists, along with the other Catholic and Anglo-Catholic ruralists in both England and the U.S., could tap directly into the religion whose Founder articulated the Beatitudes, and the vicar of Whom in 1891 issued the workers' "Magna Carta." Even our contemporary historians recognize this difference,[1] and it is to the Agrarians' credit, of course, that in the decades following *ITMS* they came more and more to understand what Weaver would refer to as the dependency of all valid political conceptions upon a transcendent "metaphysical dream" – a dream possessed, he reminds us, by the Schoolmen of the Middle Ages.

Perhaps a consciousness of the relative inadequacy of a merely "Southern" and historical stand for agrarianism and widely distributed property, and the need for a deeper, more substantial religious and political philosophy, were among the motives that inspired Seward Collins to bring together the various traditional and anti-modern schools in his promising, if all too typically short-lived, intellectual and propaganda effort that appeared from 1933 to 1937 as the *American Review*. Distributists, Southern Agrarians, and land-movement leaders made up the bulk of the contributors. Along with the New Humanists led by Irving Babbitt and the European Neo-Scholastics, among whom Christopher Dawson was numbered, they offered a "traditionalist" critique of modernity, in the vein of what follows in the present volume, but with perhaps a greater dose of refinement and finesse.[2] Summa-

---

1. Paul Murphy noted "[t]he greater depth of Distributism in both moral philosophy and political economy," and highlighted the fact that Distributist thinkers "tapped into a deep stream of anti-modern social thought and literature; their appeal to the Catholic tradition presented them, at least in theory, with a rather large, international audience" (*op. cit.*, p. 75). There is a parallel case in Flannery O'Connor and Walker Percy, two Southern writers much indebted to the Agrarians but whose thought was Catholic rather than just "Southern." As one literary critic has noted, Flannery O'Connor "won the admiration of the Fugitive-Agrarian circle with her portraits of a fading rural South, but her intense theological interests – largely shaped by the revival in European Catholicism at the mid-century – finally marked her ultimate concerns as quite distinct from theirs. [Furthermore, O'Connor and Percy's] critique of modernity … finally owed more to an internationalist Roman Catholicism than to Southern heritage. Indeed, in their fictions, traditional regional mores and reverence for the past ultimately present only flawed and futile counterpoints to the encroaching consumer society of the larger United States (Farrell O'Gorman, "The Fugitive-Agrarians and the Twentieth-Century Southern Canon," Charles L. Crow, ed., *A Companion to the Regional Literatures of America* [Oxford and Malden, Mass.: Blackwell Publishing, 2003], pp. 299–300).

2. As Collins explained in his first editorial, the critique was to be made "from the basis of a firm grasp on the immense body of experience accumulated by men in the past, and the insight which this knowledge affords" (*American Review* 1, p. 122, quoted in Albert E. Stone Jr., "Seward Collins and the American Review: Experiment in Pro Fascism, 1933–37," *American Quarterly* 12 (1), Spring 1960, p. 5). Collins, though not a Catholic, had the good sense to call for "the end of Communism and capitalism and a return to the life of the Middle Ages" (quoted in Edward S. Shapiro, "American Conservative Intellectuals, the 1930s, and the Crisis of Ideology," *Modern Age* 23 (4), Fall 1979, p. 370).

rizing the vision offered during these exciting few years of feverish thinking and writing during the inter-war period, Albert Stone writes that

> [t]he "Property state" of Belloc and Douglas Jerrold was an anti-capitalist scheme for the sort of nation believed to have existed in Western Europe in the latter Middle Ages, based upon small landowners, a strong King and a social order cemented by family, guild and Church. Here in America, Donald Davidson, Frank Owsley, Andrew Lytle and other Southern Agrarians were also urging a sharp break with industrialism; their Utopia consisted of a politically autonomous South of subsistence farmers whose social pattern would approximate that of the early nineteenth century. Less political than either of these, the Humanists nevertheless were striving, in the spirit of Irving Babbitt, toward balance, detachment, aristocracy and discipline in personal life. These virtues, especially when combined with the New Scholastics' reverence for revealed religion and tradition, could fit neatly into a philosophy which regarded "society as a spiritual organism" and government as properly authoritarian and elitist.[1]

In the genuine spirit of the Distributists, Agrarians, and others who defended the vision of widespread property ownership as an alternative to both forms of big, impersonal, and ultimately tyrannical social and economic organization, the *American Review* conducted a campaign in defense, and for the recovery, of the humane and noble values of the "old world," while insisting that they be brought to bear on current problems. It was the vision of its editor, and its contributors, that no other solution would do. As Hilaire Belloc had it, the collective sentiment was that "the choice [lies] between property on the one hand and slavery, public or private, on the other."[2] This is our vision and our sentiment as well.

*****

A T THIS POINT it may further profit a reader coming into the Distributist, social Catholic, and agrarian tradition "from out in the (industrial) cold," to have a brief introduction to the basic theoretical principles that will be encountered. They are not demonstrated with mathematical precision, but they form the basis of much of the writing contained in this volume, and especially in the second section, where sketches of G. K. C.'s vision parallel the outline of Fr. Heinrich's Pesch's Solidarism, the Corporatism of French social Catholic René de La Tour du Pin, and the "first-things-first" simplicity of Fr. Vincent McNabb.

Distributist, agrarian, and "third way" thought in the "traditionalist" mode will draw upon a number of principal ideas, of which a few are as

---

1. Stone, *op. cit.*, p. 5.

2. Hilaire Belloc, *An Essay on the Restoration of Property* (Norfolk, Va.: IHS Press, 2002), p. 22.

follows. Economic "science" must subordinate itself to morals; or, in other words, the study and application of "what is" (and which we are asked or expected just to "live with"), must give way to an understanding and striving after of *what ought to be*. Economists saying that "it's not their place" to take into account what people *should* want (rather than merely cataloging what they do want and how they go about getting it) just won't do, here, where the needs, rights, and duties of real people and families are concerned.[1]

Next, the needs of profit and production must be subordinated to the needs of people. Where these interests conflict, readers will find that the authors of essays in this book – and the thinkers whose views they advocate – put the people first. This is common sense, and is often a well-received idea, until it involves people potentially not being able to amass as much wealth as they want, especially in the face of indigence. But there it is.

Flowing from these premises are a number of additional principles. There is an emphasis on consumption rather than production, insofar as the purpose of production is ultimate consumption.[2] There is also an emphasis on production insofar as it is superior to the needs of money and finance. In other words, while consumption is the ultimate destiny of manufactured goods, production is valued as well insofar as goods need to be produced in order to be consumed. The natural consequence is that profit and money take a back seat to the production of useful goods and their consumption by those who genuinely need what is being produced. One profoundly intelligent thinker of the Neo-Scholastic school should be quoted at some length here, for the point is an important one.

> In theory and in the abstract, a system of association between money and productive labour may easily be conceived in which the money invested in an undertaking represented an owner's share in the means of production and was used to feed the undertaking, enabling it to procure the needful material, equipment and resources in such a way that, the undertaking being productive and producing profits, a share in such profits should be returned to the capital. No fault can be found in such a scheme. In reality and in the concrete, this same faultless scheme works in an absolutely different fashion and does harm. In the human judgments which mould the economic system values have in fact been reversed, while the fundamental mechanism has retained

---

1. As Donald Davidson pointed out, none of this is to decry legitimate improvement of material and technological conditions, but it is to insist upon the subordination of that drive for improvement for other concerns that should predominate. "An agrarian is not an ascetic," he wrote. "He would be glad to see economic conditions improve. He enjoys comfortable material circumstances as much as anybody. But he is obliged to argue that economics is too narrow a foundation for a political theory. Or, still worse, a politics founded on economics is not a politics at all, but the negation of politics; and a government which devotes itself exclusively to economic concerns is not a government but a function of the economic system" ("Agrarianism and Politics," *The Review of Politics* 1 (2), Mar. 1939, p. 119).

2. This is the principle of Fr. McNabb, whose thought is detailed by Dr. Chojnowski in Chapter 6.

the same configuration. Instead of being considered as a mere feeder enabling a living organism, which the productive undertaking is, to procure the necessary material, equipment, and replenishing, money has come to be considered the living organism, and the undertaking with its human activities as the feeder and instrument of money; so that the profits cease to be the normal fruit of the undertaking fed with money, and become the normal fruit of the money fed by the undertaking. That is what I call the fecundity of money. Values have been revised, and the immediate consequence is to give the rights of dividend precedence over those of salary, and to establish the whole economy under the supreme regulation of the laws and the fluidity of the sign money, predominating over the thing, commodities useful to mankind.[1]

Another principle hinted at or implied by what follows is the necessary subordination of money and machinery to the purposes they serve. The great thinker in this regard from those occupying important places in the tradition we seek to recover is Arthur J. Penty, whose views are not expounded upon here.[2] But his principles for the right use of machinery, though unpalatable to the modern temperament pampered by convenience and unaccustomed to salutary exertion, are required reading for those who have the desire and the fortitude to question the assumptions upon which modern society rests. That his principles were endorsed by Dr. Walter John Marx of the Catholic University of America, in his *Mechanization and Culture*, is significant. His position, furthermore, on machinery and mass production dovetailed with the observations of other persuasive critiques of industrialism and its culture, along the lines of which T. S. Eliot's observation is representative:

> The tendency of unlimited industrialism is to create bodies of men and women – of all classes – detached from tradition, alienated from religion, and susceptible to mass suggestion: in other words, a mob. And a mob will be no less a mob if it is well fed, well clothed, well housed, and well disciplined.[3]

The remainder of the ideas are those we have explored at length above. They deal with the re-integration of those things that were split apart by the twin phenomena of "rationalist" economic science and the industrial revolution. Work and ownership are seen to be in need of re-uniting, such that disputes between capital and labor are reduced to friendly discussions between a man and his land or a man and his tools. A re-integration of work

---

1. Jacques Maritain, "Religion and Culture," in Christopher Dawson and T. F. Burns, eds., *Essays in Order* (New York: The Macmillan Co., 1931), pp. 56–7. Tragically, Maritain's thought became increasingly contradictory from this point on, as he attempted to force the round peg of liberal democracy into the square hole of sanity and human nature. Those interested in an alternative perspective to Maritain's on such issues should consult the works of Charles de Koninck and Fr. Julio Meinvielle.

2. God willing they will be covered at length in the book, forthcoming from IHS Press, *The Medieval Future of Arthur Joseph Penty: The Life and Work of an Architect, Guildsman, and Distributist*, by Dr. Peter Grosvenor.

3. T. S. Eliot, "The Idea of a Christian Society," *Christianity and Culture* (New York: HBJ, 1977), p. 17.

and personality is also desired, in the form of a restored, non-industrial and not-very-mechanical husbandry of the land along the lines of small farms and family gardens, coupled to personal and hand crafts (that would also help to re-integrate products for sale with a long-forgotten attribute called "quality"). Work and family are to be reunited by the ending of the drastic and now pervasive dislocation of labor from the home, where it took place for literally millennia, excepting our last 150 years.[1] And work and community are to be re-united in an updated form of the ancient worker's guild, that did such good in making friends of employers and employees before the institution was forcibly suppressed by revolutionary governments bent on forcing modernity down unwilling throats at gunpoint.[2]

It is of more than passing historical interest for us to know how the chief advocates of the Distributist and Agrarian movements put their programs forward, built upon the principles noted above. Several quick snapshots, from their own literature and in their own words, follow, as a backdrop for the re-presentation of these and other related branches of our common tradition that the present volume hopes to make.

Chesterton introduced the Distributist League in its first pamphlet in the following terms:

> The League for the Restoration of Liberty by the Distribution of Property is the only society of its kind. Yet it presents the social idea which nine men out of ten would probably in normal circumstances regard as normal. It offers a criticism and correction of our abnormal capitalist and proletarian society which differs from all those current in politics and press, not in degree but in direction. It is not merely a moderate sort of Socialism. It is not merely a humane sort of Capitalism. Its two primary principles may be stated thus:—
>
> 1. That the only way to preserve liberty is to preserve property; that the individual and the family may be in some degree independent of oppressive systems, official or unofficial.
>
> 2. That the only way to preserve property is to distribute it much more equally among the citizens: that all, or approximately all, may understand and defend it. This can only be done by breaking up the great plutocratic concentration of our time.[3]

The pamphlet included K. L. Kenrick's short but useful definition of Distributism against the alternatives that were, and are still, its competitors:

---

1. This is born out in works such as Allan Carlson, *From Cottage to Workstation* (San Francisco: Ignatius Press, 1993), Karl Polanyi, *The Great Transformation* (New York and Toronto: Farrar & Rinehart, Inc., 1944), and Herbert Shove, *The Fairy Ring of Commerce* (Birmingham: The Distributist League, 1930).

2. See Chapter 5 by Dr. Blum, on Count La Tour du Pin's advocacy of a corporate order of society, for just one example.

3. G. K. Chesterton, *The Purpose of the League* (London: The Distributist League, 1926), p. 5.

There are three economic theories struggling for supremacy in the modern world. They are Capitalism – the doctrine that property is best concentrated in large masses in the hands of a few people; Socialism – the doctrine that property is best owned and controlled by the State; and Distributism – the doctrine that property is best divided up among the largest possible number of people. Broadly speaking, we may say that Distributism means every man his own master (as far as possible); Socialism means nobody his own master, but the State master of all ; Capitalism means a select few their own masters and the rest of us their servants.[1]

The *Distributist League Manifesto*, issued a number of years later, ran to fourteen short pages, and had this to say about the essence of the property it hoped to put back into the hands of the average man:

In material things there can be no individual security without individual property. The independent farmer is secure. He cannot be sacked. He cannot be evicted. He cannot be bullied by landlord or employer. What he produces is his own: the means of production are his own. Similarly the independent craftsman is secure, and the independent shopkeeper. No agreements, no laws, no mechanism of commerce, trade, or State, can give the security which ownership affords. A nation of peasants and craftsmen whose wealth is in their tools and skill and materials can laugh at employers, money merchants, and politicians. It is a nation free and fearless. The wage-earner, however sound and skilful his work, is at the mercy of the usurers who own that by which he lives. Moreover, by his very subjection he is shut out from that training and experience which alone can fit him to be a responsible citizen. His servile condition calls for little discretion, caution, judgement, or knowledge of mankind. The so-called "failure of democracy" is but the recognition of the fact that a nation of employees cannot govern itself. Therefore we assert that the only way to remove the evils of insecurity and servility is to make, so far as possible, every man the owner of the tools and materials on which his life depends. Further, it is the only way to secure liberty, because the propertied citizen, no longer dependent upon the State to defend him against the rich, who cannot harm him, nor against famine which his own foresight can avert, will no longer accept the orders of officials whose assistance he can do without. Free to work out his own prosperity, and to discharge his natural duties by the exercise of his natural rights, the Englishman will restore to its proper dignity that natural and ancient unit of society which has been the stem of all civilization : the home and the life of the family. The Englishman's home will be his castle, and the family will be the centre of his allegiance. As in the State he will be a responsible worker and citizen, so in the home he will be a responsible husband and father; and as his normal desire and duty will be to labour and think rightly in the places where men toil and plan, so it will be his desire and duty to love and guide wisely in the place where men rest and rejoice – in the home.[2]

---

1. K. L. Kenrick, *What is Distributism?* (London: The Distributist League, 1926). p. 3.

2. *The Distributist League Manifesto* (London: The Distributist League, 1930), pp. 11–2.

Finally, in 1934 the League produced a "Distributist Programme" that was printed by St. Dominic's Press of Ditchling in Sussex, England, and ran to 33 pages. The challenge that it presented to the Englishmen of its day was set forth in the following terms:

> Distributism as a social system combines the *principle* that every human being has a right to liberty with the *application* of that principle that liberty can only be maintained through the ownership of property. The right to liberty is not limited to one particular liberty; to liberty of religion, conscience, action, or so on; it is the right of choice in all things in which the exercise of the choice does not injure the right of choice of others. The mere existence of such a state of liberty is, however, insufficient in itself to secure two other material elements essential to the full development of the human soul; and they are security and material sufficiency. We regard any political system which does not intend to provide the opportunity for each man to ensure for himself the existence of all these three conditions as a menace to civilisation, and as based upon an incomplete understanding of, or a deliberate attempt to thwart, the nature of man. We use the term justice as describing what every system ought to attempt to bring about, and a just society is our aim.
>
> Distributism is therefore equally opposed to modern monopolistic capitalism and to socialism. The one, preserving the name of liberty as a cloak for the power of the rich to exploit the poor, does not even pretend to provide either security or sufficiency; the other, undertaking to provide the two latter, only professes to do it at the expense of every vestige of political freedom.
>
> The opposition is even more fundamental than this. Distributism implicitly rejects that conception of inevitability in the development of political systems which has always been a foundation of the Socialist cure, and is now also seen in the trend of modern capitalist thought. It absolutely repudiates that servile counsel of despair which attempts to graft on to human institutions those characteristics which a mechanistic philosophy of biological evolution – itself repudiated by modern science – would attribute to animal life. It begins with the conviction that it is the human will which alone can and does change human institutions, and it disputes the right of the State or other external force to dictate to the citizen the conduct of his everyday life.
>
> Thus Distributism is a challenge; to the present order of chaos, poverty and suffering; and to the present so-called revolutionary schools of thought, which deny that the system can be changed except through the operation of irresistible and inevitable forces, and at the cost of most of the things which have made life worth living. Distributism is the only revolutionary creed; it calls for instant and individual action on the part of all. Each man can disprove for himself the lie that things must drift or evolve to a state which, so far as he can foresee it, he does not desire. Each man can, to some extent even under the present system, work out his own salvation. Our purpose is to show what each can do for himself, and what a determined few can do in co-operation.[1]

---

1. *Distributist Programme* (London: The Distributist League, 1934), pp. 1–2. Following this, the next

The Agrarians, for their part, outlined their program in a number of places. The most comprehensive was the "Statement of Principles," included with the 1930 Agrarian manifesto, to which each of the twelve Southerners that contributed to it subscribed. Smaller sketches of the Southern Agrarian agenda were made on and off by contributors to the original symposium. Frank Owsley's summation was printed as "Pillars of Agrarianism" for the *American Review* 4 (5) of March 1935, to which the preamble went as follows:

> We are on the side of those who know that the common enemy of the people, of their government, their liberty, and their property, must be abated. This enemy is a system which allows a relatively few men to control most of the nation's wealth and to regiment virtually the whole population under their anonymous holding companies and corporations, and to control government by bribery or intimidation. Just how these giant organizations should be brought under the control of law and ethics we are not agreed. We are, however, agreed with the English Distributists that the most desirable objective is to break them down into small units owned and controlled by real people. We want to see property restored and the proletariat thus abolished and communism made impossible. The more widespread is the ownership of property, the more happy and secure will be the people and the nation. But is such a decentralization in physical property as well as in ownership possible? We are confident that it is, however much we may differ among ourselves as to the degree of decentralization that will prove desirable in any given industry. We are all convinced, though we hold no doctrinaire principles as to method, that these robber barons of the twentieth century will have to be reduced and civilized in some form or other before any program can be realized by our state and Federal governments.[1]

Building upon the foundation Owsley established, Donald Davidson sketched an interesting history of the original 1930 anthology, and offered his own take on the bedrock Agrarian views:

> We consider the rehabilitation of the farmer as of first importance to the South, the basis of all good remedial procedure; and we therefore favour a definite policy of land conservation, land distribution, land ownership. At the risk of appearing socialistic to the ignorant, we favour legislation that will deprive the giant corporation of its privilege of irresponsibility, and that will control or prevent the socially harmful use of labour-saving (or labour-evicting) machinery. We advocate the encouragement of handicrafts, or of modified handicrafts with machine tools. In this connection, we believe that the only kind of new industry the South can now afford to encourage is the small industry which produces fine goods involving craftsmanship and art. We oppose the introduction of "mass-producing" industries that turn out coarse goods and

---

official statement of Distributism was A. J. Penty's 1937 *Distributism: A Manifesto*, included in *Distributist Perspectives* (Norfolk, Va.: IHS Press, 2003), pp. 86–110.

1. Frank Owsley, "The Pillars of Agrarianism," in Bingham et al, *op. cit.*, p. 202.

cheap gadgets. We favour the diversion of public and private moneys from productive to non-productive uses – as for example to the arts that over-accumulation of invested capital may be forestalled. We hold very strongly for a revision of our political framework that will permit regional governments to function adequately; and that will enable the national government to deal sensibly with issues in which the interests of regions are irreconcilable, or prevent the kind of regional exploitation, disguised as paternalism, now being practised on the South. That is to say, we favour a true Federalism and oppose Leviathanism, as ruinous to the South and eventually fatal to the nation.[1]

Finally, a Catholic approach to agrarianism is illustrated by the short program presented by Rev. W. Howard Bishop at the 13th annual conference of the 1935 National Catholic Rural Life Conference, held in Rochester, N.Y.

(1) The new order should be based upon man and his human needs and values of body, mind, and soul, not on mammon and the pursuit of money for money's sake.

(2) Civilization's heart should be the home and its soul the Church, instead of the factory and the money market which take their place at present.

(3) Production of home necessities should be returned to the home so far as possible, by restoration of the home crafts on the farms and even to a limited extent in towns and cities. Small business enterprises centered about the home should be given every protection and encouragement.

(4) Civilization's stronghold should be the farms, rather than the cities, farms on a family basis, cultivated for a living, first and primarily, rather than solely for profit, with high self-sufficiency and low dependence on cash income, with the family home as the throbbing heart of each little enterprise, and the Church its inspiration.

(5) The State should facilitate the widest possible distribution of farm, home, and business ownership and proprietorship.

(6) Every department of agriculture should be organized cooperatively to function harmoniously with similar organizations of industry, business, and the professions as vocational groups, with the Government standing by as monitor or referee to prevent abuses and conflicts, but leaving the actual work of managing the various occupations for their own best interests to the autonomous action of the organized groups themselves.[2]

Back on the other side of the Atlantic, the English land movement spokesmen, still "taking their stand" as of 1944, made not dissimilar demands:

[T]hat the English be spared the horrors of mass-unemployment or a planned slavery (probably both) by being placed again in organic independent communities on the soil of their fathers. That the production of goods be the work of craftsmen sanctifying themselves in their work, not of Combines

1. Donald Davidson, "*I'll Take My Stand*: A History," *American Review* 5 (3), Summer 1935, pp. 318–9.

2. W. Howard Bishop, "Agrarianism: the Basis of the New Order," *Catholic Rural Life Objectives* (St. Paul: National Catholic Rural Life Conference, n.d.), pp 51–2.

degrading men into robots. That the aim of English husbandry be not the greatest production of food per man, but the greatest production of food per acre; for only so can the tractor be banished and our island feed its children in peace and permanence.[1]

Across these various groups and movements there was a fair amount of mutual interest and awareness, if not outright collaboration. *I'll Take My Stand* was reviewed in the Catholic press and discussed by the National Catholic Rural Life conference. Fr. McNabb, the Distributist, followed the activities of the English land associations and corresponded with the Rural Life Conference in America.[2] The Southern Agrarians knew the Distributists through Herbert Agar, who was involved with *G. K.'s Weekly* while in London, and was instrumental in bringing together the contributors – including Hilaire Belloc – to *Who Owns America?* There was even, at the initiative of Tate and Agar, a joint Distributist and Agrarian committee that met in Nashville, June 4–5, 1936, and produced a report demanding "a wide distribution, and responsible ownership, of property" against the enemies of liberty that included finance capitalism, communism, and fascism. It also recognized "the primacy of agriculture," and looked for the decentralization of populations and "the public ownership of or control over natural monopolies."[3] Owsley, for his part, echoed Belloc by referring to the "tone" given to society by the widespread distribution of productive property; Andrew Lytle referred, fifty years after *ITMS*, to the danger of the "servile state"; and the *Cross & the Plough*, edited by Harold Robbins of one of the English Catholic Land Associations, boldly declared "We Take Our Stand," and praised the efforts of Santamaria's land movement in Australia. Meanwhile, the Distributist League of New England adopted and synthesized the vision of all of these, highlighting the potential, in those days, of a vibrant and effective Distributist "international."[4]

1. "We Take Our Stand," *The Cross & the Plough* 10 (4), Ss. Peter and Paul 1944, p. 6.

2. In one letter of support to the NCRLC, McNabb wrote: "Land workers who, as St. Thomas says, belong to the necessary organization of mankind cannot be expected to look upon their divinely appointed craft as subservient to town luxuries. Indeed the land-worker, so fitly called HUSBANDMAN, whose craft demands and provides the home and the homestead, is alone efficient to safeguard family life which the modern town has proved itself unable to preserve" (Witte, *op. cit.*, pp. 81–2, quoting Cincinnati Convention publicity materials, Des Moines files, 1926).

3. Paul Conkin, *The Southern Agrarians, op. cit.*, p. 125. As Paul Murphy explains (*op. cit.*, p. 74), "The high point of the Agrarian-Distributist coalition occurred in June 1936, when a convention for the Committee for the Alliance of Agrarian and Distributist Groups met in Nashville. By this time the movement consisted of the Agrarians (with a large contingent of the Nashville circle in attendance, including eight of the original Agrarians as well as Broods), Distributists, the Catholic Land movement, the Cooperative movement, the national Committee on Small Farm Ownership, and eccentric planners such as Ralph Borsodi, a writer from New York who organized modern homesteading operations in order to rejuvenate the moral character of Americans."

4. As Owsley noted, "We had in mind a society in which, indeed, agriculture was the leading vocation; but the implication was more than this. We meant that the agrarian population and the people of the

*****

WITH THIS FOUNDATION, a reader will be, hopefully, more prepared profitably to engage the newly (and, with any luck, adequately)
articulated but long-ripened wisdom of the best that Catholic, traditional,
and agrarian social wisdom has to offer to our frenetic and superficial age.

It is may tempting, though, to ask just what happened between the 1930s,
when the vision articulated in these pages was being argued with unique
force and persuasive power, and today, when it is largely unknown and almost forgotten. A hazarded guess would pin the blame on the Second World
War, which appointed, by default, American globalism and liberal capitalist
democracy as the "savior" of the world from the Soviet menace that would
emerge relatively soon after the war. As we noted above, perceptive thinkers like Sheen didn't fall for it; but for the "average" observer it worked out
as a "P.R." stunt of colossal proportions. Any sense that something *besides*
modern capitalism was out there, was worth trying, and was even better for
health, sanity, virtue, and civilization was eclipsed by air-raid sirens and
occasional missile crises. Even leading traditionalist "conservatives," who
until that point had treated industrial capitalism with appropriate skepti-
cism, fell into the trap.[1] Notwithstanding the sincerity of those who at the
time felt obligated to throw in their lot with the capitalist machine in the
face of threatening Russian hordes, many of the leading lights of the American "right" peddled a free-market "conservatism" that intentionally sought
to co-opt the term and the movement, marginalizing the radical critique of
capitalist (and communist) industrialism offered by the original Agrarians.
William F. Buckley Jr., with his *National Review*, was one of the front men
for this transformation, aiming to join a certain "social" conservatism with
an apologia for corporate capitalism and an interventionist foreign policy.[2]
While successful on a superficial level, more perceptive commentators still
point to the "chasm" between "southern conservatism and the free-market
liberalism that today calls itself conservatism."[3] It is this comprmise be-

---

agricultural market towns must dominate the social, cultural, economic, and political life of the state
and give tone to it" ("The Pillars of Agrarianism," *op. cit.*, p. 201). See also *The Cross & the Plough, loc.
cit.*, pp. 4–6, and Distributist League of New England, *A Declaration of the Independents* (Scotch Plains,
N.J.: Published for the Distributist League of New England by the Sower Press, ca. 1945).

1. See, for instance, Richard Weaver, "Rhetorical Strategies of the Conservative Cause," in Gerald
Thomas Goodnight, *Rhetoric and Culture: a Critical Edition of Richard M. Weaver's Unpublished
Works*, Ph.D. dissertation (University of Kansas, 1978), p. 585. See also Weaver's "Conservatism and
Libertarianism: The Common Ground" (Eliseo Vivas, ed., *Life Without Prejudice and Other Essays*
[Chicago: Henry Regnery Co., 1965], pp. 157–67), in which there is no longer a trace of Weaver's earlier
appreciation for the essential antagonism between a traditionally constrained social order and one
shaped by the unfettered free market.

2. See, for instance, Paul Murphy, *op. cit.*, pp. 120, 133, 271–2.

3. Eugene D. Genovese, *The Southern Tradition: the Achievement and Limitations of an American Con-*

tween Christ and Belial that the genuine Agrarians (and others with them) reject, for, as Mark Malvasi correctly pointed out, Tate, M. E. Bradford, and others saw that "in the spiritual, intellectual, and political milieu of the late twentieth century, merely to *conserve* sometimes meant to perpetuate the outrageous and the horrible [emphasis added]."[1]

Meanwhile, along came what one "traditionalist" cleric termed "World War Three": the Second Vatican Council. Without getting into theological hair splitting, it is a historical fact that it "knocked the guts out of" perhaps the greatest English writer of the mid- to later-twentieth century, and it seemed to do the same, in a manner of speaking, to the Catholic social doctrine that until that time had paralleled the "traditionalist" wisdom that Collins tried to put into the pages of his *American Review*. Happily, the Church has continued to articulate the basic moral truths upon which her authentic social message is built, but the emphasis upon the genuine ownership of private property and its widespread distribution among families has suffered in the face of the "mass and technology" that in many quarters are now taken for granted as the only options given an allegedly inexorable and inevitable technological and industrial expansion.

So here we are, still in desperate need of what Ross J. S. Hoffman, one of Collins's most frequent contributors, called a "constructive revolution." One contemporary commentator happily admits that the "urgency of the question posed by *Who Owns America?* has not changed since 1936," and "nor has the answer."[2] That said, we do well to remain on our guard against partisans of the "right" who would refute the position of Sheen, Weaver, and the Distributist-Agrarian "traditionalists" by arguing – along the same old deceptive lines – that the "conservative revolution" of Tate and his colleagues has already come to pass, and that the "third way" contemplated by Belloc, Chesterton, and others is indeed upon us. "None of the contributors [to *Who*

---

servatism (Cambridge, Mass.: Harvard University Press, 1994), pp. 81–2. Elsewhere, Genovese perceptively notes that "But southern conservatives understand the contradiction that neither Ronald Reagan nor George Bush nor even William Buckley has faced squarely. Capitalism has historically been the greatest solvent of traditional social relations. Thus, Marx and Engels praised capitalism and the bourgeoisie precisely for their destructive impact on traditional society and culture. Ronald Reagan has had every right to celebrate capitalism as the greatest revolutionary force in world history, against which, in at least a few important respects, the late and lamented socialist countries looked like the last bastion of cultural conservatism." Tate made this point some years earlier in his contribution to *ITMS*, where he asked, rhetorically, "[W]here can an American take hold of tradition? His country is supposed to have preserved none from Europe, and if we take the prototype of the European tradition to be mediaeval society, we must confess that America has performed wonders, considering her youth, in breaking it down" (Tate, "Remarks," *op. cit.*, p. 166).

1. Mark Malvasi, *The Unregenerate South* (Baton Rouge: Louisiana State University Press, 1997), p. 222.

2. Shapiro, "*Who Owns America?*," *op. cit.*, p. 45.

Owns America?]," commented a review (from a likely source!) of the new edition of the 1936 anthology, envisioned

the astonishing expansion of asset ownership over the last half of the twentieth century. Millions of Americans became home owners. The dramatic expansion of pension accounts, IRAs, 401 (k)s, profit sharing, and Employee Stock Ownership Plans has given millions an ownership stake in – if not control of – large economic enterprises. Tax-favored medical and education savings accounts and individual Social Security accounts have arrived or are about to do so.

Advances in technology and communications have spawned a population dispersal that would have gladdened the hearts of the agrarians, even though the globalized, fiber-optic-connected new arcadians bear little resemblance to the Jeffersonian yeomen of felicitous memory.[1]

Caveat lector! For there is *little resemblance indeed* of the real ownership of real property advocated in these pages and in the writings of those inspiring them to the "rent-from-the-bank" home "ownership" (sic) of most American families. Nor is there any correspondence between the amassing of the paper assets noted (increasingly valueless, as it happens) and the possession of that kind of property that offers stability, an outlet for salutary labor, and a forum for the exercise of choice and responsibility advocated by those arguing from the main rampart of the Western tradition. For an *American Enterprise* hack to argue that the "profound insight" of the Distributist-Agrarian project has "emerge[d] triumphant decades later"[2] requires that the tradition be distorted out of all recognition or the actual writings of its chief advocates be effectively ignored![3]

---

1. John McClaughry, "Lost cause found," *The American Enterprise* 11 (7), Oct./Nov. 2000, p. 59.

2. *Ibid.*

3. America's original "conservative" categorically refuted such a conflation of the widespread owning of paper assets with the conception of a society of owners of real property: "Ownership through stock makes the property an autonomous unit, devoted to abstract ends and the stockholder's area of responsibility is narrowed in the same way as is that of the specialized worker . . . . As property becomes increasingly an abstraction and the sense of affinity fades, there sets in a strong temptation to adulterate behind a screen of anonymity. A Spanish proverb tells us with unhappy truthfulness that money and honor are seldom found in the same pocket. Under present conditions money becomes the anonymous cloak for wealth; telling us how much a man has no longer tells us what he has. In former times, when the honor of work had some hold upon us, it was the practice of a maker to give his name to the product, and pride of family was linked up with maintenance of quality. Whether it was New England ships or Pennsylvania iron or Virginia tobacco, the name of an individual usually stood behind what was offered publicly as a tacit assumption of responsibility. But, as finance capitalism grew and men and property separated, a significant change occurred in names: the new designations shed all connection with the individual and became 'General,' 'Standard,' 'International,' 'American,' which are, of course, masks. Behind these every sort of adulteration can be practiced, and no one is shamed, because no one is identified; and, in fact, no single person may be responsible. (The most striking illustration is the Spanish phrase for corporation, *sociedad anónima*.) Having a real name might require having a character, and character stands in the way of profit" (Weaver, *IHC*, p. 141).

We can take heart, however, that in more intellectually honest circles there is an appreciation for the wisdom and the sanity that this strong current of Western thought and tradition offers, no matter how under-appreciated. "Can you imagine Will or Krauthammer contemplating these thoughts?" one pair of "progressive" writers asked approvingly of the 1936 anthology, illustrating the increasing dismay of both sides of the spectrum with "business as usual."[1]

Meanwhile, the antidote for any doubt that this humane and simple vision is worth recapturing and putting into practice is a short reflection upon day-to-day life. Remember the ideas captured in this volume the next time you are stuck in an automated voice-mail labyrinth just to get "help" (from overseas!) with your new clothes iron; the next time your "quality" piece of furniture warps under the weight of a few paperbacks or simply disintegrates into sawdust; or the next time that the price has gone up, yet again, on a product that seems to be more poorly made than ever. Ask yourself, with these and dozens of other daily frustrations in mind, whether the solution is as easy as a faster Internet connection or the new highway that promises to "unclog" the old road – or whether there isn't something to this "small is beautiful" after all, and whether we oughtn't try it before we are forced to do so whether we want to or not.[2]

*****

ACCORDING TO Allan Carlson, it was not that long ago that the "home-centered economy" began to be demolished, with its "consequent decay of the foundations of liberty."[3] Actions taken a mere century and a half ago by the operation of human will can be reversed through its exercise today. Unhappiness, stress, and uncertainty need not be our lot, if only we come to understand and follow the way up and back towards sane and normal living.

What follows is not a party platform or a program of policy. Nor is it "economics," with all the dependence of these upon figures, statistics, and abstract models. It is rather a sketch of a vision that must be recovered and re-introduced to the mass of men if we are to get a solid platform, good policy, and an economic science that puts men before money and machines. A detailed program of implementation of the views of the Distributists, Agrarians, and social and economic "traditionalists," whose authentic "third way"

---

1. Russell Mokhiber and Robert Weissman, "Who Owns America?," *Commondreams.org*, February 28, 2000, online.

2. This is the frightening but intriguing vision of James Howard Kunstler's *The Long Emergency* (New York: Atlantic Monthly Press, 2005).

3. Allan C. Carlson, *From Cottage to Workstation* (San Francisco: Ignatius Press, 1993). p. 17.

beyond capitalism and socialism is both the subject of this volume and the unique hope for the future, would fill a number of volumes, far larger than the present one. It would constitute nothing less than a wholesale re-thinking of our social and economic system, its priorities, and, most importantly, its ends.

Though much of this book looks back to the thought, life, and times of the giants upon whose shoulders we must needs stand to see our way forward, what appears most clearly is the relevance for today of their solid and still timely vision, as a basis for the radical re-evaluation so sorely needed and so plainly lacking in the largely sham alternatives presented by mainstream politics. Meanwhile, we can begin in our own lives, and that of our local communities, to put "first things first," as Fr. McNabb would have it.[1] His vision of the "primary things" does not need – no matter how much we would welcome it! – a macro-economic restructuring prior to our incorporation of his perspectives, and those of his contemporaries, bit by bit, into the details of our daily grind.

To my knowledge, no original work quite like this one has appeared since *ITMS* was published by twelve Southerners in 1930 (with its later quasi-successor, *Who Owns America?*), or since *Flee to the Fields* appeared in 1934 on the other side of the Atlantic with contributions from the English Distributists and land-movement pioneers, notwithstanding the few *ITMS* "retrospectives" that have appeared here and there in the decades since its publication.[2] Certainly I make no claim – nor, I believe, would the authors herein do so – that the essays that follow necessarily live up to the standards of thought and style possessed by our fathers in this tradition. But if what is lacking in literary grace can be made up for by sincerity of conviction, soundness of argument, and the utility to our troubled world of the principles herein articulated, then we will not have disserved our shared convictions or the memory of those, greater than ourselves, who fought for them before us.

They too were faced with what was alleged to be the so-called "inevitability" of the continuous depersonalization, mechanization, industrialization, and concentration of wealth and work. In the face of such a claim, their response was clear, and it is instructive for us. Looking back on *ITMS* some twenty years later, Donald Davidson responded to the notion in terms that echoed the position of the *Distributist Programme*, saying that one of "the most vicious of modern errors" was the idea that mechanical forces operate upon human subjects with equally mechanical necessity. On the contrary, Davidson said; the Agrarians

---

1. See Dr. Chojnowski's contribution, Chapter 6, "Fr. Vincent McNabb's 'Call to Contemplatives.'"

2. The most notable of which was the Fifteen Southerners' *Why the South Will Survive*.

did not surrender then, and I do not surrender now, to the servile notion that the existence of a powerful "trend" is a mark of its "inevitability." All the works of men result from human choices, human decisions. There is nothing inevitable about them. We are subject to God's will alone . . . . [1]

In which case, we have not the loss of the past to lament, but a new future to construct. But as Brainard Cheny put it a half century ago, we must not be deceived as to what we are up against, nor delude ourselves that it is simply a "memory lane" to which we hope to return for a lazy, noncommittal stroll. Victory over materialism and the power of unleashed and unlimited mass production and technology – a power that, he wrote, "threatens to enrich and enslave the world" – will take an uncompromising return to our "Christian heritage." More than that, it requires "Christians with the blood of martyrs in their veins, and ready to spill it."[2] It is, therefore, up to us to make sufficient and right use of the Truth, of God's grace, and of the encouragement offered by the example of those who carried the torch of sanity and wisdom through the first troubled period of industrialism's maturity. It is up to us – upon whom the outcome of this unprecedented cultural, political, and spiritual struggle ultimately depends.

Carrollton, Virgina
January 2, 2008
The Holy Name of Our Lord Jesus Christ

---

1. *Shenandoah* symposium, 1952, p 16–7.

2. "What Endures in the South," *Modern Age* 2 (4), Fall 1958, p. 410.

~ I ~

PASSING ON THE TRADITION

GREGORY THE GREAT HAD THE VISION TO USE ST. BENEDICT'S ORDER TO
RECOVER THE FIELDS AND WOODS AND STREAMS WHICH WAR HAD MADE OVER TO
THE BEASTS AND, BY WITHDRAWING FROM THE CHAOS OF THE FAILING EMPIRE,
SAVE THE WEST. WE HAVE NOT YET REACHED THAT EXTREMITY, BUT WE CAN.
WE ARE AT THE TAIL-END OF THE RENAISSANCE.

—Andrew Nelson Lytle

"We cannot allow ourselves the luxury of lining up either with the Left against the Right, or the Right against the Left. If the Right means order, an intelligent regard for social experience, and history, then we are with the Right. If the Left means justice for the dispossessed, and a decent determination to end the miseries of the victims of industrialism, then we are with the Left.

"But there can be no conflict between Order & Justice. There is a terrible conflict between people who espouse the one and neglect the other. This is the war of ideologies. There is a terrible conflict between those who want Order but are careless of Justice, and those who want Justice but are careless of Order.

"To take sides in this war is to identify ourselves with the evils of the side we espouse and blind ourselves to the good on the other side. Distributists refuse to condone evil and condemn good in this way. They make a direct attack on the problem. They are daring enough to seek what is good and avoid what is evil in both programs."

—The Distributist League
of New England

∼ 1 ∼

A Distributist Remembers

Aidan Mackey

THERE CAN BE NO PRECISE DEFINITION OF DISTRIBUTISM, for it is organic and cannot be reduced to a formula. Human life and its society are rich and varied: what is appropriate and fruit- ful for one race, for one culture, for one family, may well be quite unsuitable for another. It is nevertheless certain that this third "thing" be- yond capitalism and socialism must be repeatedly articulated, and must be continuously pursued. In what follows, I offer my own brief thoughts on the subject as one who has merely helped, in past decades, to carry the torch that shines forth the light of the Distributist alternative to the bigness and tyranny of both sides of the political and economic spectrum.

Because we come into this world naked and helpless, and not as an indi- vidual, it is with the restoration of the family that we must make a beginning. Because of the menace of "P.C." (political coercion), and the several perver- sions currently forced upon our society, it would, I think, be wise to refer precisely to "the family under God." For during the past half century there has been a sustained and merciless attack upon family life, and our children have been increasingly taken from parental control. I write this a mere year after the politicians in Great Britain, who control our lives, decreed that a parent who smacks an unruly child risks being sent to prison – paving the way, of course, for the State to take over the "bereaved" child completely.

It is quite acceptable that I should be challenged on my own position and right to speak on this subject. My wife and I have seven children and nine- teen grandchildren. As children grow to maturity, views of life change, and not always, it must be admitted, in ways parents would wish. But we, thank God, have remained close-knit and loving to a most satisfying degree.

Additionally, as a schoolmaster and head teacher, I was for many years in close contact with hundreds of youngsters, and in the past few years have had the joy of being traced and visited by people who had been in my educational care thirty, and in one case, over forty, years earlier. Therefore, I do claim to know a fair amount about young people and their hopes and aspirations. To grow, they need a warm, secure, and disciplined home life.

In firm contradiction to today's self-indulgent and irresponsible ideas, I affirm that children need both a father and a mother, bound by an unshakeable marriage. Again, I speak from experience because my own father died when I was only six years old. I was fortunate in being the youngest of seven children, and was warmly sheltered by the older ones. My wife lost her father when she was a little older. Let no one try to tell us we suffered no loss. In our cases, it was illness that robbed us of a loving parent; we can only guess at how much more agonizing it must be for those who have a parent desert them, often in search of sexual gratification elsewhere. I have several times been involved with families devastated by being callously discarded in this way.

Most emphatically, we must first restore the family and its values. After that, in natural progression, must come the family trade or craft, and the small organic family farm. Upon these must any sane and healthy society be built, and we must destroy the grotesque combines and cartels, many of which are strong enough to dictate to governments. It is clear they exist not to produce food or furniture, but profit. We all know the euphemism "diversification," which means that in pursuit of the money-god, they will readily switch from one field to others not remotely connected, providing there is money to be harvested.

So far I have dealt with the present position, but it would be well to look briefly at the past of the Distributist movement, of which I have the distinction (the reader may judge what kind of distinction it is!) of being one of the world's oldest active members. And then – much more importantly – we consider the future.

We cannot pinpoint the birth of Distributism as such, for it is as old as mankind and, apart from slavery, is the only stable and potentially permanent way of life. It is only the name itself, and the comparatively recent movement that adopted that name, which may be described as new. In large measure inspired by the Papal Encyclical of Leo XIII, *Rerum Novarum* (popularly known as the Workers' Charter), the movement was, in the early twentieth century, brought into being by such giants as Hilaire Belloc, Vincent McNabb, O.P., and G. K. Chesterton.

One of the problems was that they were not, particularly G. K. C., men familiar with land and farming, but this in no degree lessened the rightness and sanity of their thought, firmly based on sound social philosophy and an understanding of the nature of man. Being writers and publicists, they were able to present a cogent and vivid case in various journals, notably the *Eye Witness* (later the *New Witness*, then *G. K.'s Weekly*, and, after G. K.'s death, *The Weekly Review*), and later, *The Cross & the Plough*, the organ of one of the English Catholic Land Movements.

There were also land settlements in Langenhoe, in Essex, in Northamptonshire, and the famous colony of artists at Ditchling, Sussex. Thoroughly practical men, with experience of the land, came on the scene, with an outstandingly important group in Warwickshire. And it was there that people who were unknown to fame or the public, but who were no less great men for that, planned the Birmingham Land Scheme to help unemployed and other poor families who wanted to work the soil, become established. The program was carefully thought out and costed, and could have had an enormously beneficial effect on Britain in the 1930s.

The government of the day, however, preferred people to be wage-slaves, with a waiting army of unemployed to discourage those in work from demanding a living wage. Knowing that from the start of any farming enterprise it will take at least two years before any return is made, it sank the Birmingham Land Scheme by the simple ruling that the moment the spade was offered to soil, the wielder was deemed to be in employment and, therefore, unemployment benefit ceased.

The struggle, then, was ever against enormous and dispiriting odds. I know that many of those who waged it, in the Distributist League and other groups, could very easily have become wealthy had they bent their energy and talents to the making of money. We must thank God that they did not.

Those who worked in the 1920s and early 1930s had, at least, the privilege of knowing Chesterton and the other giants, but when they departed – Chesterton died in 1936, McNabb in 1943, and Belloc, although he lived until 1953, had suffered a stroke in 1941, and had been inactive for a time before that – no laurels or rewards of any kind were on offer to those who persisted in the Distributist Cause. To my mind, the heroes of the movement were those who, in great adversity, carried on in the bleak times afterwards; from the middle 1930s through the war, when there was, humanly speaking, no hope at all. Perhaps they were sustained by those marvelous lines from the *Ballad of the White Horse*, when Mary, seen in a vision by the oft-defeated King Alfred, warns him:

> I tell you not for comfort,
> Yea, naught for your desire,
> Save that the sky grows darker yet
> And the sea rises higher.

My own involvement did not start until the late 1940s, and I must once more intrude a personal note. Several Chestertonian journals and speakers have referred to me as having carried the torch alone in those later days. This was never the case, and it would be quite unjust to make such a claim. I was about the youngest of those who, in the late 1940's, started a Distributist group in Manchester, and so I have outlived almost all the rest. In 1951, after *The Register* had apparently ceased publication, and nothing had come of the circular that Hilary Pepler and Reginald Jebb had sent out sometime later holding out the prospect of a return to publication, I visited Pepler to inquire whether or not future numbers would be forthcoming. Since it did not seem that there would be another any time soon, I launched, in January 1953, with the help of my wife and my friend Peter Diffley, the second, tiny successor to *The Weekly Review*, calling it first *The Defendant* and later *The Distributist*. It contrived to survive, without paid advertising, for six years before a growing family being raised on a schoolmaster's salary made an end inevitable.

Earlier, I mentioned the compensations gained by earlier workers in the field having over them the reassuring shadows of great men, and the bleak and dispiriting period that followed. Those of us who today work for decency and social justice have an even greater reward, for at our meetings and conferences – with an ever increasing frequency and attendance – the revival of Chesterton and Distributism is well underway. For me, late in life, to meet and talk and correspond with numbers of young, intelligent people, enthusiastically taking over the work, is a benediction higher than can be put into words.

A Chesterton Centre has even been established in Sierra Leone, under the leadership of John Kanu, not as a literary society, but as a well-organized and determined means of helping farmers and craftsmen rebuild a decent society and way of life in a country which was for years ravaged by commercial and political corruption, largely, but not entirely, from outside. Now, one-time enemies are working together on a program of social and educational reform. The effort has support from the government and the Church, and I have just learned that a recent gathering included the National Coordinator of the Sierra Leone Civil Society Movement, the President of the Sierra Leone Farmers Association, and a good number of university students. At the close, it was featured in a radio broadcast, which included an interview with John Kanu.

When a people who have grievously suffered band together to restore their society, it is to be hoped and urged that more fortunate people will want to help. There can be few worthier and more constructive causes in their own right; the fact that it is done in the name of Chesterton and Distributism is far from the essence, but to those of us who know how and for what G. K. C. and others have fought, his shadow over it is a blessing.

Things are now moving in the direction of sanity in many ways and in many places. A great deal of work is still to be done, but the outlook is better than it has been for very many years – providing that we stick at it with work and prayer.

"As far as the smallholder is concerned, Science has taken heavy payment for the service she may have rendered. She has given us mechanised farming which has made the continued existence of the smallholder more difficult by placing the apparatus of cultivation out of the reach of the man of small capital. She has reduced the production of that most healthful and soul-comforting oil, the sweat of the brow, which has hitherto been essential to farming and the simple life. She has increased the economic difficulties of the smallholder.

"But the call of the country is not easily stifled. It has a note of confidence and promise and the simple life is still possible. Its passing will not be in our generation."

—George C. Heseltine

～ 2 ～

I Fear No Peevish Master
The Romance of Distributism

Anthony Cooney

IT WOULD BE IMPOSSIBLE TO MENTION "DISTRIBUTISM" without mentioning the names of Chesterton and Belloc. Belloc's contribution to the body of ideas which became known by that name was cerebral, Chesterton's poetic. We might put it another way by saying that Belloc was a classicist and Chesterton a romantic. Nevertheless, the editing and financing of *G. K.'s Weekly* magazine fell, from its launching in 1923, upon Chesterton's broad shoulders. The value of that journal is not to be underrated. It influenced the thinking of a number of members of Parliament ranging from High Tories like Anthony Fell to honest Labor men like Simon Mahon. Perhaps the greatest success of *G. K.'s Weekly* was the exposure of the Mond-Turner plot to govern Great Britain by a cabal of bankers, industrialists, and trades-union bosses, and reduce Parliament to a committee that receives reports. A House of Commons alerted by *G. K.'s Weekly* defeated the plot.

After Chesterton's death in 1936, his paper became *The Weekly Review* and continued publication until 1948. Assigned to "expose" the "clandestine fascists" who published that paper, Douglas Hyde, the news editor of the Communist *Daily Worker*, was converted by *The Weekly Review* to both Catholicism and Distributism. Distributism also played a part in the conversion of Hamish Fraser, a member of the Communist Party's National Executive and a former commissar of the International Brigade in Spain.

Hyde's conversion in 1948 was headline news in the daily press in Great Britain. His subsequent book, *I Believed*,[1] and his nationwide speaking tour

---

1. Douglas Hyde, *I Believed* (London: Heinemann, 1951).

was not only a blow to Communist advance, but gave Distributism a new lease of life. Asked at one lecture, so the story goes, what his politics were now, he held up copies of *Rerum Novarum* and *Quadragesimo Anno* and said, "These are my politics." The conversion, in 1952, of Hamish Fraser had a similar effect. Fraser became an enthusiastic follower of Chesterton, co-operated in founding "The Anglo-Gaelic Civic Association," and edited *Approaches*, a small but influential journal, in defense of orthodox Catholic social teaching.[1]

In 1948 *The Weekly Review* became a monthly, called, in reminiscence of William Cobbett, *The Register*.[2] When that too folded, Aidan Mackey bravely launched a little monthly, first called *The Defendant* and later *The Distributist*. It became a quarterly in 1957 and ceased publication in 1960. It seemed then that Distributism had at long last been carted off to the bone yard of history.

Except for one thing. In 1954 a small group of Liverpool subscribers to *The Distributist* launched a duplicated magazine called *Platform*. They even took their Distributism to the polls, contesting seats for the Liverpool City Council. In January 1960, after the folding of *The Distributist*, *Platform* became *The Liverpool Newsletter* and has been published continuously ever since. In 1981 as editor of the *Liverpool Newsletter* I received a request from a new journal, *National Consciousness*, enquiring what exactly was this Distributism that the *Newsletter* was always banging on about? The result was a series of articles by myself, in that magazine, and in 1987 I was invited to contribute an article to the now defunct *Vanguard*, a magazine that dealt with Distributist ideas from time to time. These articles sowed the seeds of the rebirth of Distributism that we see today. That, then, is the narrative history of the few organs to date that carried an explicitly Distributist masthead: a tale soon told, which looks forward to a brave sequel.

However, Distributism is not just a series of events; it is an idea. The history of ideas is always complex; the history of this one goes well beyond the chronicle of explicitly Distributist journalism. The first thing to understand is that the idea of Distributism existed long before the word was invented. As S. Sagar, an active member of the Distributist League in pre-war days, and contributor to *G. K.'s Weekly* says:

> The immediate point here, however, is that it seemed such a normal thing that men did not think of naming it until it had been destroyed. Even then only a few men saw it so clearly as to think it worthy of a particular name.[3]

---

1. This was succeeded by *Apropos*, a quarterly edited by Fraser's son, Anthony, and still in publication.

2. Hilary D. C. Pepler (1878–1951) was the principal editorial force for the two years that the paper ran, 1948 to the early part of 1950. Pepler had been co-editor of its predecessor, the *Weekly Review*, with Reginald Jebb (1884–1977).—Ed.

3. S. Sagar, *Distributism – A Reprint of Articles Published in "The Weekly Review,"* (Croydon, Surrey,

We might claim that the first Distributist was Aristotle. Rejecting the communism of Plato's Republic, he argues in his *Politics* that:

> For while property should up to a point be held in common, the general principle should be that of private ownership – "all things common among friends" the saying goes.[1]

We could say that the first Distributist law was the decree of the Roman Senate that said that a retired Legionary should not be granted more land than he and his family could farm. We might argue that John Ball and Wat Tyler were the first English Distributists. In the Peasants' Revolt of 1381 they raised the whole of south east England against the re-imposition of feudal dues by the great magnates. However, I think that in modern times we must name William Cobbett (1783–1835) as the first Distributist. He championed rural England against industrialization. It was he whom Chesterton called "The horseman of the shires, The trumpet of the yeomanry, The hammer of the Squires."[2]

John Ruskin (1819–1900), a polymath, master of many fields of knowledge, and one of the noblest minds in the nineteenth century, also belongs to us. His Guild of St. George was the first practical attempt to establish and defend, against the encroachments of "Big Business" and "Big Money," smallholders and master craftsmen. The "Arts and Crafts Movement" of William Morris (1834–1896) had much of the same idea. Morris was a polymath, like Ruskin, and an essayist, poet, artist, and Norse scholar, who combined tapestry and cabinet-making skills of the highest order with intellectual pursuits. To these might be added those practical working men who saw that they never could be free whilst they lived in tied cottages, and who started the first "building societies" in the industrial towns of Halifax and Huddersfield. Their purpose was simple and uncomplicated – they desired to own their own homes. We may also cast our net to take in the founders of both the Consumer and Industrial Co-operative Movement which was first organized in England in the nineteenth century and then spread throughout Europe in later decades.

A. R. Orage (1873–1934) brought all these many strands together at the beginning of the twentieth century in his "National Guilds Movement." The movement, which had nationwide membership, sought to establish, with varying degrees of success, guilds of workers on the medieval model. Its platform was the London-based *New Age*, purchased by Orage and Holbrook Jackson in 1907 from Joe Clayton, a Catholic trades unionist (and

---

England: Distributist Books, n.d.), p. 2.

1. Aristotle, *The Politics*, trans. Sinclair Harmondsworth (London: Penguin Books, 1962), p. 63.

2. G. K. Chesterton, "The Old Song," in *The Collected Poems of G. K. Chesterton* (London: Methuen, 1950), p. 71.

future Distributist, according to G. K. C.'s colleague William Titterton). It was in *The New Age* that Chesterton and Belloc first expounded the ideas that were to become known as "Distributism," and it was in those pages also that the historic meeting – if not agreement – of Distributism and Social Credit took place.

Distributism, as Belloc insisted, places great emphasis upon the land; upon the widespread distribution of ownership of land. That being so, it has had, inevitably, a close association with the "Back to the Land Movement" and related ideas and programs that were especially popular in the inter-war years. Distributists were "greens" before anyone dreamed of that label. However, it must be insisted that Distributism is not just a "back-to-the-land" ideal.

Back in 1973 I was talking about Distributism to one of those superior persons who inhabit the Conservative Party. "It sounds like back to the oil-lamp age" was his superscalar response. A few weeks later, the only growth industry in Great Britain (thanks to the abominable Prime Minister Edward Heath who provoked a national miners' strike leading to a three-day working week) was candle making. People would have been glad of a few oil lamps as they sat out the power cuts! Distributism makes no secret of the fact that one of its chief objectives is the recreation of a yeomanry, and a large body of husbandmen, cultivating their own land.

Nevertheless, we must beware of so emphasizing the need for the re-population of the land that we lay ourselves open to the charge that Distributism is a scheme for driving everyone out of the towns and ordering them to grow their own cabbages. We can leave schemes for Plainer Living, Higher Thinking, and More Painful Dying to Pol Pot and the Third and Fourth Internationals!

Paradoxically, one task for Distributists is to stop city dwellers from buying cottages and smallholdings in rural areas for weekend use. In the United Kingdom, this is particularly bad in Wales and Northern England. That sort of romantic greed has put the price of even the simplest home beyond the reach of young couples who actually work the land, with the result that more people are driven from it. Scarcely less of an evil is the purchase of country homes by people who commute to work in the cities, but whose only connection with the land is the planting of a lawn and a few apple trees. The first task for Distributists today is to lobby for legislation to assist those who live and work on the land to remain there. However, politicians show little interest in this problem; after all, votes are few in rural areas! Only when we have staunched the flow from the land can we begin the real task of resettlement.

Ultimately, resettlement requires two things – training in how to live from the land whilst maintaining both its fertility and beauty, by good husbandry, and the bringing into cultivation areas now under-populated. John Seymour[1] in his many books has shown that the first is possible; he has shown it by doing it. Philip Oyler[2] has shown that the second is also possible. Broadly speaking, Oyler recommends a return to the medieval system of land ownership known as "strip farming" as opposed to the modern "ring fence" system. The ring fence system means that families live in isolated farmhouses, far from doctors, midwives, schools and entertainment. It means that some farmers have chiefly good land and others chiefly poor land. The strip system, on the other hand, means that families can be clustered together in villages, and that each farm has its share of good and poor land.

Great Britain is not an over-populated country, compared to, say, Holland, which is a food exporter. But it has a problem, as Ruskin pointed out, of maldistribution of population. For resettlement of the under-populated areas, we must look to our young people, to their idealism, and to their desire for endeavor, achievement and adventure. Taught the good husbandry that John Seymour teaches, they can bring wasteland back to fruitfulness. In the process they will, perhaps, change its natural beauty to a more human kind, the kind praised by the great pre-Distributist Charles Kingsley in his poem to Tom Hughes:

> Where's the mighty credit
> In admiring Alps?
> Any goose sees glory
> In their snowy scalps.
> Give me Bramshill Common
> St. John's harriers by,
> Or the Vale of Windsor
> England's golden eye.
> Show me life and progress,
> Beauty, health, and man,
> Homes fair, trim gardens
> Turn where'er I can.[3]

Leaving this important question of Distributism and the land, I will merely point out that there are many forms of private property – the doctor's, lawyer's or accountant's practice for example; we must defend them against government health and law centers so beloved of Marxists. There is all manner of private property proper to industry and town – from the corner shop to the family-owned factory. I would readily agree that railways owned by railmen

---

1. John Seymour, *The Fat of the Land* (London: Faber, 1961), *Self-Sufficiency* (London: Dorling and Kindersley, 1975), and *Bring Me My Bow,* (London: Turnstone, 1977).

2. Philip Oyler, *The Generous Earth* (London: Hodder and Stoughton, 1950) and *Feeding Ourselves* (London: Hodder and Stoughton, 1951).

3. Charles Kingsley, *His Letters and Memories of His Life*, ed. Mrs. Kingsley, 7th ed., Vol. 1 (London: Henry S. King & Co., 1877), p. 491.

and coalmines owned by miners, by means of a distribution of shares, would be a form of Distributism, and a form suitable for all necessary large-scale industry.

*****

What then is Distributism? First of all it is not a program or a scheme to put the world right overnight. It is not a "solution" to all our problems, like Esperanto, phonetic spelling, decimal coinage, or "comprehensive education." Distributism is a policy of a philosophy. That may not leave you much wiser at first hearing, for like all organic things, Distributism demands study before it yields understanding. We can ask three questions of any organization or group, which is pursuing an idea: What? Why? How?

> WHAT do you want to do?
> WHY do you think it is a good idea?
> HOW are you going to do it?

The answer to the question "What?" will reveal the policy – action directed towards particular objectives. The answer to the question "Why?" will describe a philosophy – a way of seeing the world, a way of seeing man, a viewpoint of reality. The answer to the question "How?" will be a specification of methods realizing the policy.

It is important to understand that every policy is derived from a philosophy. Behind every course of action we observe there is a viewpoint of reality, a belief in how things should be. If a group is dedicated to getting people to go to church, they are not doing it because they are atheists; they are doing it because their viewpoint of reality is Christian. If a group is promoting class hatred, they are not doing that because they are unpleasant people – they are doing it because their viewpoint of reality is the Marxist and capitalist viewpoint. The philosophy, which generates the policy, may be and often is, hidden. Moreover, a single philosophy may generate more than one policy, a policy may be realized by more than one method.

A policy is the application of a philosophy to the world we live in. Distributism is applied Christianity. It is for Distributists to devise the methods, in response to changing circumstances, by which the policy is realized.

Perhaps the most explicit statement of Distributism as a policy is that contained in the encyclical letter of Leo XIII, *Rerum Novarum*, which simply means "new things." Leo XIII first states that the right to property derives, not from any man-made law or human convention, but from the law of human nature. It resides in the nature of language and its future tense, that man is the only creature who is both aware of the future and who can structure it through language. Because of this a man can provide not only for his own future, but also for that of his children and his children's children. "Property," Leo is saying, "is proper to man."

Now, there are those who will say, "This is all very well, but it isn't practical. Of course there will always be the small holding, the small shop, the small business, the small wool mill, producing hand-made tweeds for precious people, but the trend is and must be towards big business, big production, and big organization. You can't stop it, it's progress, and it gives everyone cheap food, cheap clothing, and cheap shelter. Do you really think that people want to go back to scratching a living on a smallholding or working all God-sent hours in a drafty workshop with a leaking tin roof?"

My own opinion is that this frequent criticism of Distributism arises from the fact that Distributism is not couched in the "scientific" terms of capitalist and Marxist economics. Those, it is asserted in superior tones, are postulated in immutable "laws." Capitalism has its "law of supply and demand." If there is a demand for a commodity or service, then someone will supply it, for a sufficient price. There follows the "law of price" – the true price of a commodity or service is what the "market" will bear. This leads us to the "iron" laws of "rent" and "wages," and to the determination of value by "marginal utility." We may note before going on, that the economist is always careful, when stating these "laws," to add the codicil – "all things being equal." This caveat may also serve to prevent his certification by two gentlemen of another profession wearing white coats.

The Marxist, perhaps even more than the free market economist, prides himself on the "scientific" nature of the Marxist analysis and the dialectic "laws" derived from it, such as "the labor theory of value," which is always qualified by the caveat "socially useful labor." We may note in passing also, that the "scientific" nature of Marxism rests largely upon the impression created by jaw-breaking jargon, which often is simply a statement of the obvious, and more often, a statement of the untrue.

Distributism, on the other hand, seems to lack this academic apparatus. As Sagar points out:

> The root of the difficulty is that Distributism is not an "ism" in the same sense that the term is understood today. That is, it is not something men have perfected in the seclusion of a library or academy. It is not some new variation in sociology. It is an organic thing, a thing that was growing before men were under the unhappy necessity of discovering that there was a subject called sociology. It was the mark of European (and all human) life for centuries.[1]

---

1. Sagar, *op. cit.*, p. 2.

However, it is not an entirely beneficial thing to be without an academic language. From a purely practical point of view, it is difficult to debate the question without such linguistic apparatus. Men will not entirely respect something that, it may seem, is an amateur notion in conflict with the accepted, exactly stated, view of the professional. There is a passage in Belloc's *The Alternative*, which is a cogent example of the situation the Distributist finds himself in:

> What they (the Distributists) say is, if you could make a society in which the greater part of citizens owned capital and land in small quantities, that society would be happy and secure. They say (as everyone must) that such subdivision is quite possible with regard to land but they also believe it to be possible with regard to shares in industrial concerns. When they are told that a high division of this sort would necessarily and soon drift again into a congested state of ownership, with a few great capitalists on the one hand and a wretched proletariat upon the other, they answer that, as a matter of fact, in the past, when property was thus well divided, it did not drift into that condition, but that the highly divided state of property was kept secure for centuries by public opinion translating itself into laws and customs, by a method of guilds, of mutual societies, by an almost religious feeling of obligation not to transgress certain limits of competition, etc. When they are told that a state in which property was highly divided would involve more personal responsibility and personal anxiety than would the socialist state, they freely admit this, but they add that such responsibilities and anxieties are natural to freedom in any shape and are the price one must pay for it.[1]

When, many years ago, I propounded the Distributist idea to a member of the Labour Party, the latter was quick to respond that the thing was "impossible," for "it had been proven that if everyone started off with equal shares, within a generation a few families would own everything, and the rest nothing." Of course, no such thing has ever been "proven." What he meant was that it had been argued by both capitalist and Marxist economists that such a thing would happen, but argued in "sciencespeak," and therefore convincingly to the ignorant. It must be said here that Belloc has given us one of the most precise explanations of economic "laws" in his *Economics for Helen*,[2] a book no Distributist should have failed to study.

However, there is a "law" of Distributism, we might even call it a "fundamental law," and it can be reduced to a technical language. It was formulated by the late Fr. Vincent McNabb, O.P.:

The economic primaries are but two: Production and Consumption. Other activities, such as exchange, distribution, transport, market, price-fixing,

1. Hilarie Belloc, *The Alternative*, (Croydon, Surrey, England: Distributist Books, 1947; reprinted from *An Examination of Socialism* [London: The Catholic Truth Society, 1908]), p. 13.

2. Hilaire Belloc, *Economics for Helen* (Norfolk, Va.: IHS Press, 2004 [1924]).

money-value, are never primary even when practically necessary. The area of production should be as far as possible coterminous with the area of consumption. The utilitarians were wrong in saying things should be produced where they can be most economically produced. The true principle is: things should be produced where they can be most economically consumed.[1]

This statement of the Distributist "economic law" is fundamentally radical and cuts across nearly all varieties of modern economics. It places the emphasis of economic activity, of work, on consumption, and not on production, as do capitalist and Marxist economics. For both of these the object of work is material production, and for both, each in only marginally different ways, production is a variety of religious exercise, almost, in some Marxist writings, mystical activity. I would stress here that McNabb and the Distributists are stating exactly what C. H. Douglas (1879–1952), the founder of Social Credit stated: "The object of production is consumption."[2] He went on, in prose worthy of Belloc, to assert that this was the nature of work in the Middle Ages:

> How is it that in 1495 the laborer was able to maintain himself in a standard of living considerably higher, relatively to his generation, than that of the present time, with only fifty days labor a year, whereas millions are working in an age of marvelous machinery the whole year round, in an effort to maintain themselves and their families just above destitution.[3]

If we accept that the primary object of work, of production, is to consume that which is produced, and not to sell or exchange it, whether at a profit or not, the entire free-market theory is redundant. The free-market "law" is that if buyers and sellers buy in the cheapest and sell in the dearest market, the balance of supply and demand so achieved will ensure that everyone will obtain their wants at the cheapest possible price. There is a subtle fallacy in this "law" and it revolves around the codicil "all things being equal." What is the cheapest market? We have an example given by C. H. Douglas in *The Brief for the Prosecution*.[4] In the last century, Ludwig Mond formed a partnership with T. E. Brunner for the manufacture of soda ash. According to Douglas, he obtained

1. A. Cunningham, "Vincent McNabb, O.P. Primary Things: Land, Work and Sign," *The Chesterton Review* 22 (1–2), 1996, p. 73. [See the essay by Dr. Peter Chojnowski on Fr. McNabb's philosophy and vision, Chapter 6.—Ed.]

2. Major Clifford Hugh Douglas, M.I.Mech.E., M.I.E.E. was a Scottish engineer who devised and installed the London Post Office Tube, the world's first fully automatic system. He discovered that industrial production generated prices at a greater rate than it generated purchasing power. He published his findings in *The Weekly Review* and *The New Age*. Orage, the editor of the latter publication, named Douglas' proposed reforms "Social Credit." A monetary reform movement grew under this title, but, against his advice and wishes, political parties were also formed, which, as he warned, became indistinguishable from "mainstream" political parties.

3. C. H. Douglas, *The Tragedy of Human Effort* (Liverpool: K.R.P. Publishers, 1935), p. 1.

4. C. H. Douglas, *The Brief for the Prosecution* (Liverpool: K.R.P Publications, 1945).

a license to do so by the cheapest and filthiest methods. The world, more or less, bought soda ash (water-free sodium carbonate) from him at the cheapest possible price. The result was that he transformed an area, once claimed for its beauty to be the site of the Garden of Eden, into a stinking, sterile dump. We are still paying the price of cleaning it up. So, was Mond's price the cheapest possible? Plainly not, for the cost, first of dereliction and then of reclamation, was off-loaded from the price of the commodity to the taxes of the community. However, the fallacy is part of the basic assumption of free-market theory, namely that things are produced to sell. For Marxists, production is an end in itself. We can appreciate then, not only how radical the Distributist "fundamental law" is, but also how radical its application would be.

If, as the McNabb law states, the area of production and consumption should be coterminous, then everyone is assured of prices unburdened by the costs of distribution. In McNabb's view, the savings afforded by "mass production" are offset by the costs incurred by the necessary "mass distribution," which will include the costs of publicity and advertising as well as those of road, harbor and airport building, transport, spoliation, and waste.

It should not be difficult for anyone to work out how this fundamental law affects what are now called "green issues" and "alternative economics." Apply the rule to the tropical rain forests. Why are they being cleared by "slash and burn" tactics? Not because the world has an insatiable demand for ebony and mahogany, but because the land is needed for beef production. And not because the local population are insatiable carnivores, but because income from export is needed to pay the interest on debt, incurred by importing commodities on the market principle of buying in the "cheapest" and selling in the "dearest" market – instead of producing for home consumption.

What we are discovering about diet and health, not only human but also animal health, meshes with the Distributist law. We know that the healthiest food is that which is proper to, and produced in, one's native locale. We know that wheat eaters will not maintain their health and strength on rice, and vice-versa; that fish eaters cannot switch to a diet largely of muscle meat, and vice-versa. We now know that the health and fertility of the soil depends upon the return to it of the composted waste of its own product. We know that a landscape is goodliest to look at where the buildings and structures are of local stone and local timber. We know that pollution of air, water, and soil is the result of over-production, and that over-production is a necessity of the market theory of the cheapest price. In short, there is mounting confirmation of the soundness of the Distributist Law that the areas of production and consumption should be, as far as possible, coterminous.

There is a relationship and interaction between the McNabb Law of production and consumption and the Douglas analysis of the monetary system.

Douglas's basic principle, like McNabb's, was that "production is for consumption." His proposal of a "national discount" was designed precisely to eliminate from prices the detritus of past costs, so achieving the "just price" of medieval theology. His proposal of a "national dividend" was designed to equate purchasing power with production – so enabling people to buy what they produced within the national economy; i.e., "locally."

This would not, as not only his opponents but also some of his supporters, who only half understood him, supposed, result in an orgy of "consumerism" and hence production. Excess production is a necessity of the debt-money system, since it is only by selling more that the costs of the last production cycle can be recovered. For example, how do you sell people more motor cars once every family has one? Ultimately, only by manufacturing motor cars that will wear out in a few years. To this can be added changes in fashion, usually in superficial things. The result is that where the car industry might manufacture one car designed for a life of twenty years, it manufactures five cars, each designed for a life of four years. That quite simply is a waste of the earth's mineral and energy resources, which are certainly not unlimited, as Marxists and capitalists assume.

The Distributist League originally coined the term "third way" in the 1920s. And it is good to reiterate Chesterton's outline of Distributism:

> Distributism presents a social idea which nine out of ten men would in normal circumstances regard as normal.... Distributism is not merely a moderate form of socialism; it is not merely a humane sort of capitalism. Its two primary principles may be stated thus:
>
> 1) That the only way to preserve liberty is to preserve property so that the individual and the family may in some degree be independent of oppressive systems, whether official or unofficial.
>
> 2) That the only way to preserve property is to distribute it much more equally among citizens so that all, or approximately all, may understand and defend it. This can only be done by breaking up the plutocratic concentrations of our time.[1]

It will be obvious at once that this is not a statement of methods, but of aims. Distributism, and this is something generally overlooked, is therefore not an economic theory, but a political theory. Distributism describes the political aims to be realized and is, therefore, the politics of the "third way." These aims are reduced to objectives to be achieved by the "McNabb Law," summarized as making, as far as possible, the areas of consumption and production coterminous. The methods for achieving this are the business of economics and administration acting as the servants, not the masters, of the people.

---

1. Aidan Mackey, *G. K. Chesterton: A Prophet for the 21st Century* (n.p., n.d. [published 2007]), pp. 28–9.

It is beyond dispute that property can neither be widely distributed, nor remain widely distributed, in a system that issues all new purchasing power (money) as debt, repayable at interest. The chief and most obvious effect of the "fractional reserve system" of creating debt is the steady concentration of ownership. The term "Social Credit" was first used by A. R. Orage to describe C. H. Douglas's analysis of this flaw in the monetary system and his proposals for its reform. These proposals form an important part of the methods necessary to achieve the Distributist objectives. I have already referred to Belloc's *Economics for Helen*. It is plain from that text that Belloc understood the truth regarding the monetary system, and indeed his explanations and arguments are often more clearly put than those of Douglas. The truth of the debt-money system is quite simple – that widespread property cannot co-exist with usury. Or, put another way, it is impossible to draw clean water from a polluted well. Douglas, for his part, saw the necessary place of widespread property in the ethos of an authentic Social Credit:

> It is profoundly significant that what is now called socialism, and pretends to be a movement for the improvement of the under-privileged, began as something closely approaching the Distributism of Messrs. Belloc and Chesterton, *of which the financial proposals embodied in various authentic Social Credit schemes form the practical mechanism.* Socialism was penetrated by various subversive bodies and perverted into the exact opposite of Distributism, i.e., collectivism [emphasis added].[1]

Unlike Marxist utopians, Chesterton and Belloc did not specify what Distributism would be like, any more than they wished to order everyone's breakfast and approve everyone's wardrobe, much less dictate a design for everyone's home. A Distributist society would not be a utopia. It would be much larger than any such blueprint dreamed up by the will to power. It would be larger because it would be normality. It would be an escape from utopia, because utopia is a terrible place. So we may gladly admit that we do not know what it would be like. That is the romance of Distributism. Given a society, in which men, or the vast majority of men, owned property and were secure in their income, the myriad interactions of free men making empowered choices really would balance supply and demand. We would be astonished at the variety, the non-servility, and the creativity of our neighbors. In such a society men would use machines, their own machines, to make all that was necessary. They would use their hands to make all that was beautiful, or merely useful. They would, in the words of that achingly beautiful English folk-song, *On Linden Lea*: "Fear no Peevish Master."

---

1. C. H. Douglas, "Week to Week," *The Social Creditor*, January 16, 1943 (Liverpool: K.R.P. Publications), p. 3.

R.I.P. *Triumph* Magazine

A Memorial to an American Distributist Enterprise

Gary Potter

NOT MANY WHO READ THE LINES WHICH FOLLOW will have heard of *Triumph* magazine, or know much of what it was about if they have heard of it. This is natural. History really is written by the winners, and the intellectual life of Catholics in the United States has been dominated for a very long time by the thinking and beliefs that resulted in Vatican Council II, were codified by it (as with the promulgation of its Declaration on Religious Liberty), and have been regnant ever since. *Triumph* was launched in 1966 to register a Catholic dissent from that thinking and those beliefs, and then had to cease publication in less than a decade. How could it amount to more than a footnote, if that, in any Catholic history of the past half-century written today?

Its obscurity is the more assured inasmuch as its dissent was not "conservative." We understood clearly at the magazine that "conservatism" in this country, whether purely political or of a religious kind reflective of the political, represents nothing but the right wing of the national liberalism.

National liberalism?

The United States was founded, after all, as *a liberal republic*, not a Christian one. Thus there may be a recognizable body of "conservative" Catholics in America today, and perhaps best defined as those who hold that the Council's reforms were not meant to be as radical as they have proven to be. Yet it remains that the kind of ideas generally espoused by *Triumph*, including Distributist ones, were certain to be marginalized within Catholicism in the U.S. as the national liberalism developed along the lines it has during recent decades. This is to say that even so-called conservative Catholics tend to be more "conservative" (and thus more American) than Catholic. They may not be dominant, but they still represent a form of liberalism within American Catholicism. At *Triumph* we simply aimed to be Catholic.

If I say "we," it is because I was present at the magazine's founding, serving first as its assistant editor with the duties of articles acquisition, and overseeing the "back of the book" – the section where books, films, and television were reviewed. That with one exception I am now the only person present at the founding who still actively works to defend and promote *Catholic politics* testifies to the obscurity into which the magazine's point of view has fallen and, obviously, to the unattractiveness of labor in a cause that has not been a winning one. The exception – the one other person still active – is the redoubtable Dr. Thomas Molnar, but he has departed the American scene, having assumed a professorship at the University of Budapest in his native Hungary.

I just spoke of Catholic politics. They were what *Triumph* was all about. By politics I do not mean partisan ones, but simply the means by which the life of a society is regulated. At *Triumph* we self-consciously set out to make ourselves the center of what we hoped would be a Catholic political party in the U.S., but a "party" in the sense of a body of Catholic opinion, of Catholic thought, of men weighing the political and social issues of the day in the light of Church teaching – the *social* teaching as well as the religious.

We understood that acceptance of the social doctrine is not necessary for salvation, at least not in the sense that baptism and assent to the truths affirmed in the Creed recited every Sunday at Mass are. In addition to other horrors, it has unquestionably resulted in countless souls being lost. However, the history of the past two centuries, in particular, suggests how dangerous it is to ignore or reject the social teaching. Further, by "social teaching" we did not mean simply what the popes had taught in *Rerum Novarum*, *Quadragesimo Anno*, and some other encyclicals, but the politics that can be derived from the entire body of the teachings of the Church. It is hard to think of a single commandment, either of God or the Church, that is without a social dimension. In other words, when we spoke of Catholic politics, we had in mind the only sort that existed when Christendom did. (It was no coincidence that the publishing entity of *Triumph* was called the Society for a Christian Commonwealth.)

Though the magazine paid little attention to economics as such, I was misrepresenting nothing when I said a few paragraphs ago that it espoused Distributist ideas. Distributism was not explicitly the banner under which we proposed to march forth, but we were familiar with G. K. Chesterton, Hilaire Belloc, René de La Tour du Pin, Dorothy Day, the Southern Agrarians and others, and wrote about them. More to the point, if we generally ignored economics as such, it was because we knew, to put it as simply as possible, that their right ordering would follow on right politics, and this latter, right politics, depends on right morals, which in turn depends on right religion. Everybody associated with the magazine, including even those who thought of themselves as "capitalist," agreed on that, and can any notion be more Distributist? It is another way of saying that if the Catholic politics we promoted were the only kind that existed when Christendom did, we saw that the economics variously called Distributist, Solidarist, or Corporatist in this book were the only kind that existed, with local variations, in Christendom, which we hoped to help revive.

Unfortunately for *Triumph* and its larger purposes, disarray was so widespread in the Church immediately after Vatican II that we spent far more time and energy having to try to uphold right religion than some of us wanted or that would have been necessary in another time. This was for the reason that the bishops simply were not doing it.

Our preoccupation with the sorry state of the Church accounts, in part, for the magazine failing fully to exploit an historical opening as it ought.

What opening was that?

Men too young now to have a mature memory of the late 1960s may find it difficult to believe, but it really seemed, what with all the cities burning, street rioting, college sit-ins, anti-war demonstrations, assassinations, the civil rights revolution, the sexual revolution, and so on, that anything political was possible at that time – anything including introducing Catholic ideas into the national conversation, such as it then was. I would say that the election in 1968 of someone as "un-American" as Richard Nixon, a President who came awfully close to saving the Constitution by burning it, so to speak, was proof of this. A few years later came more proof with the amazing candidacy of the Southerner, George Wallace, who was on the verge of making abortion *the* divisive issue of U.S. electoral politics when he was shot. (The winners who write our history pretend now that race was his *only* issue.) Of course, on the other wing of our national liberalism there was much going on in those years, especially in the colleges and universities (the leftist professoriat now dominant on the American academic scene were students then).

In any case, no one can seriously believe that there now exists such an opening as we thought we saw at *Triumph*, not in today's consumerist society with a state more highly centralized than ever, a state whose Chief Executive is a Methodist who says he is "born again" but worships, when he does, at an Episcopalian church, thus showing himself to be the kind of putative Christian (the country is full of them) who could proclaim, as he did on September 11, 2006, that the U.S. "will lead the 21st century into a shining age of human liberty," as if that were something God must desire. If this, then, is, God forbid, a "Christian Presidency," what more genuinely Christian politician could be elected to national office today, or even nominated?

That question raises the one of what to do: how to proceed, against the day when more Americans and others elsewhere will be more interested than now in talking about what life would be like in a Christian society instead of in the one they have. The simple, and simplistic, answer is to forget the question. Just gather some tools, find a piece of land, and go work it. At least that is the answer of *some* of the purely agrarian-minded among the Distributists. The trouble with this solution is that we are not Amish. The Catholic religion is exoteric. It is not meant to be lived privately, but in society, a society larger than that of the family. I do not wish to disparage the "back-to-the-land" types, but I wish to say that *more* is needed than just this.

My own conviction is that not much more can be done for the time being towards reviving Christendom than keeping alive the *idea* of it, and that is important to do. After all, it can never exist again unless the idea of it is kept alive now. This is not to say that more should not be done if it is possible, and the very publication of the book in hand is encouraging. I cannot think of another book like it – not a reprint, but all original essays – having been published during the 40 years I have worked in Catholic journalism.

That all the essays in this book are original brings me to another matter, a political matter that bears on economics. I want to make my own "original" contribution to the volume by commenting on the most significant document having to do directly with the social teaching published by the Holy See in recent years. I speak of "Doctrinal Note on Some Questions Regarding the Participation of Catholics in Political Life" published to the world by the Congregation for the Doctrine of the Faith in January 2003. A passage of it has been widely quoted out of context as stating: "The Church recognizes that democracy is the best expression of the direct participation of citizens in political choices."

Leaving aside the reality of China today, the received wisdom is that the ideology of capitalism flourishes easiest in a democracy. Doubtless that is true. It is why, it is argued, economic liberalization in China will eventually produce political liberalization – i.e. liberal democracy. Well, let it be acknowledged that democracy *is* the best expression of the "direct participation" of citizens in political choices. That is not the same thing as saying – the Vatican document does not say it – that citizens *should* always participate in political choices or that their participation should always be *direct*.

Further, if the statement is quoted in its entirety and in context, a quite different picture begins to emerge than is given by our first impression: "The

Church recognizes that while democracy is the best expression of the direct participation of citizens in political choices, it succeeds only to the extent that it is based on a correct understanding of the human person." That person has "a duty to be morally coherent," which is to say he does not, or, rather, should not, try to lead two separate lives, a private or so-called "spiritual" one and a "secular" one (like Catholic politicians notorious for claiming to be "personally opposed" to abortion but who swear they will not seek to impose this "personal" position on others).

"In fact," we read, "every area of the lay faithful's lives, as different as they are, enters into the plan of God . . . where the love of Christ is revealed and realized for both the glory of the Father and service of others." This is the "correct understanding of the human person" on which the "success" of democracy is to be judged. "Catholic involvement in political life cannot compromise on this principle . . . . "

Those words, "cannot compromise on this principle," need to be underlined because "in this context, it must be noted that a well-formed Christian conscience does not permit one to vote for a political program or an individual law which contradicts the fundamental contents of faith and morals." Thus it is that there *are* moral principles that "do not admit of exception, compromise, or derogation," because what is at stake is "the essence of the moral law . . . . " Political programs and individual laws that concern "abortion and euthanasia," or the "rights of the human embryo," or "monogamous marriage between a man and a woman," or the freedom of parents "regarding the education of their children" and society's "protection of minors" – all these, the document specifies, touch on moral principles that "do not admit of exception, compromise, or derogation."

The Vatican document does not suggest, much less specify, what the Catholic citizen is to do when he has no choice, as likely will be the case today, except between candidates who all espouse the kind of programs and laws which "contradict the fundamental contents of faith and morals," and that question is beyond the scope of these present lines. What asks to be observed here is simply that if the Vatican document at first gives the impression that the Church now holds that a particular form of government, democracy (and implicitly the economic system usually identified with it, capitalism), is better than every other, it does not really do it. In fact, insofar as it upholds constant Church teaching, it shows itself not to differ essentially from all that was taught and upheld by such notable Catholic thinkers of the past as those who figure in the history of Distributism, and Catholic thinkers of today who draw from them.

There is another way of putting all this. Truths taught by the Church may be distorted, ignored, or neglected – they may cease to be taught by most

Churchmen for a time – *but they still remain true*. That being the case, there remains a solid foundation on which Distributism, though it would appear to most today to be a lost cause, can begin to build once again, and as the very publication of this book suggests, it has already begun to do.

Besides commenting on the 2003 Vatican document and drawing from it the point I wanted to make, there is one more matter I must see to before concluding these lines. Earlier I mentioned Dr. Thomas Molnar. I must not conclude without some remembrance of the other principals present at *Triumph's* beginning.

First of all there was L. Brent Bozell, the magazine's real founder. He was too often identified as "a brother-in-law of William F. Buckley." It made him sound as if he was nothing but another "conservative." As the man who ghosted Barry Goldwater's *Conscience of a Conservative* and once substituted for the Senator to deliver a famous speech to a "Young Americans for Freedom" rally at Madison Square Garden, he certainly had been that. Many persons – ones who were more "conservative" than they were Catholic – subscribed to *Triumph* for that reason. They thought they would be getting a Catholic version of *National Review*. When they found the magazine was not what they expected, they did not renew. That, of course, was the beginning of our end, apart from all else that worked against the magazine.

If there is a reader of these lines who loves good writing and has access to a library with some issues of *Triumph* or a collection of *National Review* from its early years, look up some articles by Bozell. Neil McCaffrey, responsible for Doubleday's line of Image Books and the founder of Arlington House and the Conservative Book Club, and my godfather when I received conditional baptism into the Church, was correct to hail Bozell as "the premier stylist of the conservative movement," when that is what he still was.

Next in importance at the magazine was John Wisner. Actually, to say that may need correction. The first of the two times he fired me from *Triumph* (I wound up being the publication's very last editor), Bozell himself said nobody was more important to it than Wisner. It was his critique of technology and what Jacques Ellul called the "civilization of technique" that was especially important to us. Wisner understood the evil of men depending on machines as once they depended on God, and much else. He was the wisest man I have ever known.

Alas, Wisner left no published books behind when he passed away some years ago. However, he carried on a vast correspondence. There must be a number of persons still living throughout ex-Christendom who cherish letters they had from him, as I do the dozens I have.

Then there was Dr. Frederick Wilhelmsen. A disciple of Belloc and also a fervent Carlist, which is to say a traditionalist in the uniquely Spanish and profoundest sense, he was also able to explain the Catholic significance of his friend Marshal McLuhan up in Canada. There is no time now I can sit drinking with like-minded Catholics and not think of how incomplete is the circle without him. As long as there are serious Catholics reading in English, his *Metaphysics of Love*, if nothing else by him, will have an audience.

I must also name Michael Lawrence as among the founding principals, though he was younger even than myself. I still mourn the fact that he abandoned apostolic work to go into public relations. But, then, my wife and I had only one child who lived. Mike had a larger family to support.

Other men came into the *Triumph* orbit after the magazine's founding. A notable example is Dr. Warren Carroll, distinguished historian and also founder of Christendom College. Who, among us, besides Bozell, could make a sentence march better than he? If I started speaking of all of them, however, the present lines would have to become a book.

Perhaps I ought to relate, if only by way of additionally proving *Triumph's* Distributist bona fides, that in 1970 when the magazine's offices were moved from downtown Washington, D.C., to rural Front Royal, Virginia, a number of the single male staffers took up residence in a house on a piece of land with a view to writing *and* growing food for themselves and others. They called the place Metternich Farm.

Unfortunately, not one of them knew anything about growing food. They suffered from the same practical difficulties to which Aidan Mackey alludes with his reference to G. K. Chesterton in his contribution to this book, so Metternich Farm did not last very long. To speak here of that failure will serve as a reminder that basic skills such as used to be possessed by almost any 4H Club[1] member are needed by anyone to whom a "return to the land" means more than driving five miles into town to buy groceries at the nearest supermarket.

If this book has nothing to do with the practical difficulties of farming, and the skills needed to overcome them, its contributors very admirably do propose remedies to numerous difficulties of a higher order. A reader may view one or another of the remedies as less than workable, but my experience is that those among Catholics who are drawn to this book's subject will be ones who understand that men sharing First Principles may disagree for prudential reasons as to their application without "excommunicating" one another. This is to say that any reader who does disagree now and then will still find this book to have been well worth the most valuable commodity he possesses: his disposable time. I feel honored that these lines of mine have formed a small part of the larger, noble whole.

---

1. For non-American readers, this would be something like a Young Farmers Club.—Ed.

In terms of these lines' organization, I ought now to have concluded. However, there is one extremely important matter which no other contributor to this volume has addressed. I shall let a brief comment on it serve as at once an additional "original" contribution to the book from me and as my real conclusion.

The native peoples of European stock in the lands of ex-Christendom have not been reproducing themselves for a number of decades. Rather, they are aborting and contracepting themselves out of existence, with others replacing them. Remaining Christians who actually practice their religion, a minority, may still be fecund, but any scheme or program of "returning to the land" must take into account that the larger lands – America, England, France, Germany, Italy, Spain, etc. – are being lost. They are increasingly being occupied by Moslems, Asians, and others to an extent that it becomes possible to envision a time not too far off when the larger lands will no longer be American, English, French, German, Italian or Spanish.

The trend of which I speak could conceivably still be reversed, but that does not seem very likely. The relevance of the trend to this book's subject is that many of the arriving occupants bring with them belief in strange gods, some conceived as benevolent, but none of whom will not finally prove inimical to our Triune One, so that in the span of a long lifetime the society will have passed from being formerly described as Christian, then as Judaeo-Christian, to Islamo-Judaeo-Christian, to something like Islamo-Buddhaeo-Judaeo-Christian. To avoid that mouthful and in typical modern style, doubtless it will be referred to as "our I-B-J-C society." The serious point here is not that our Triune God will be reduced, at best, to membership in a multicultural pantheon of deities, but that it cannot be expected the new occupants will be disposed, or even tolerant, towards economics that have Him at their center.

Accordingly, no Distributist scheme or program can possibly win future widespread acceptance and become successful – not across the breadth of society as it already exists, let alone as it soon will – unless those advancing it are also prepared to undertake a great work of evangelization, or so it seems to me.

~ II ~

PRINCIPLES
HISTORICAL AND THEORETICAL

For centuries now opportunism has encroached upon
essential right until certitude has been all but banished. We are looking
for a place where a successful stand may be made for the logos
against modern barbarism. It seems that small-scale
private property offers such an entrenchment . . . .

—Richard M. Weaver

"[A]t root, I'll Take My Stand *was an attack on the 'business civilization' of America and, in this, the Agrarians were very much in the mainstream of social criticism. A dissatisfaction with the callow hedonism, crass consumerism, and spiritual shallowness of the years between 1910 and 1930 was articulated by a variety of thinkers, whether conservatives, such as Irving Babbitt, Paul Elmer More, and George Santayana; radicals, such as the 'Young Intellectuals' Randolph Bourne, Van Wyck Brooks, Lewis Mumford, and Waldo Frank; or independent critics such as H. L. Mencken . . . .*

"The Agrarians, however, rejected any program of cultural liberation as firmly as they did the shallow and destructive capitalist culture such a program was designed to negate. They proposed, instead, the preservation of the cultural tradition of leisure and order that they believed characterized the South. This they considered a radical idea, for it entailed going to the roots of American culture and restructuring the American economy."

—Paul Murphy

~ 4 ~

Part of This Complete Breakfast

G. K. Chesterton's Distributism

Dale Ahlquist

I REMEMBER A CERTAIN KIND OF TELEVISION COMMERCIAL that I vaguely saw about a million times when I was growing up. It was for some breakfast cereal. It would always end with a quick parting shot of the bowl of cereal surrounded by a lot of other food with the announcer's voiceover urgently telling us, "Part of this complete breakfast!" The unconscious message was that the cereal alone was the complete breakfast. The "part of" was the part we missed. In order to achieve that elusive standard of completeness, we really had to have all that other stuff too. I can't remember what it all was. It went by too fast. I know there was a glass of orange juice. There might have been a side of baked beans for all I know. And maybe some liver steaks. It is quite possible, in fact, that the breakfast shown would have been just as complete without the cereal. At any rate, the cereal alone was not enough, even though most people bought it thinking it was.

Most of our modern ideas suffer from being no more than breakfast cereal. Most of the energy and attraction in them is in the packaging. Inside there is very little substance. A lot of it is fried air with sugar coating. There may be a few grains of truth, but not enough, not the whole truth. Yet the world feeds on these light and snappy ideas and on nothing else. The rest of the complete breakfast is completely missing.

Even those ideas which are profound and practical for our world still suffer from incompleteness. We can have the right ideas about politics and economics, but life is more than politics and economics. The affliction of specialization is myopia. As specialists we are under the delusion that our small area of expertise informs us about everything else. We know more and more about less and less. Truth has been carefully compartmentalized. Colleges and universities have been carefully departmentalized. We are all specialists, and none of us are generalists, and there is no glue to hold all our fragmented truths together. There is thinking, but no thought, as in a complete understanding that is comprehensive and coherent.

G. K. Chesterton had a word for all the specialists of the modern world. It is a surprising word. A jarring word. The word is "heretics." The problem is not that the specialist – or heretic – is wrong, but rather narrow and incomplete. The heretic is someone who has broken himself off from a wider view of the world. The heretic, says Chesterton, has locked himself in "the clean, well-lit prison of one idea."[1] Another way Chesterton puts it is that the heretic has one idea and has let it go to his head.[2] It is a case where myopia leads to madness.

Chesterton was one of the last of the great generalists. He wrote about everything. Everything: history, current events, art, literature, politics, economics, social theory, science, philosophy, and religion. But his dozens and dozens of books and his thousands of essays were not simply random observations and disconnected thinking. His writing was all part of one very consistent and coherent and complete system of thought. We could argue that Chesterton really wrote only one book, but it was in many chapters, many volumes. In one of those essays, he says, "There is only one subject."[3] Elsewhere, he writes,

> Men have always one of two things: either a complete and conscious philosophy or the unconscious acceptance of the broken bits of some incomplete and shattered and often discredited philosophy.[4]

To try to sum up Chesterton's "complete and conscious philosophy" is a good exercise. Like any good exercise, however, it is not easy. Chesterton saw the world as a wonder, a miracle that does not explain itself. He saw life as a gift, the best kind of gift – a surprise, and something undeserved. Thus, gratitude and joy informed his perspective of everything. He believed in the dignity and liberty of the human person, made in God's image, but sullied by sin. He believed that we generally want happiness but often pursue pleasure in the mistaken sense that it is the same thing as happiness. He saw morality and civil order as safeguards against sin and utter selfishness. He

---

1. G. K. Chesterton, *Orthodoxy*, from *The Collected Works of G. K. Chesterton* (San Francisco: Ignatius Press, 1987–2005), Vol. 1, p. 225. All further citations are from G. K. Chesterton; volume and page numbers are from the *Collected Works* unless otherwise indicated.

2. *The Catholic Church and Conversion*, Vol. 3, p. 104.

3. *Illustrated London News*, February 17, 1906, Vol. 27, p. 126.

4. *The Common Man* (New York: Sheed and Ward, 1950), p. 173.

saw the home and the family as the centerpiece of society because they are the centerpiece of living. Home and family are the normal things. Trade and politics are necessary but minor things that have been emphasized out of all proportion. He saw that proper proportion was the key to art as well as the key to justice. And sanity.

As a young man, Chesterton flirted with socialism, but he soon realized that it was mostly a reactionary idea. The rise of socialism and its attendant evils was a reaction against industrial capitalism and its attendant evils. The danger of fighting injustice is that if the battle is misguided, even a victory is a defeat. Good motives can have bad results. This is the point Chesterton makes when he talks about how the "virtues wander wildly"[1] when they are isolated from each other and wandering alone. In a broken society where we have this seemingly endless battle between the left and right, the virtues on either side are doing war with each other: truth that is pitiless and pity that is untruthful.

The conservatives and the liberals have successfully reduced meaningful debate to name-calling. We use catchwords as a substitute for thinking. We know things only by their labels, and we have "not only no comprehension but no curiosity touching their substance or what they are made of."[2]

It is interesting, it is fitting, that the philosophy which Chesterton embraced as the only real alternative to socialism and capitalism (as well as to liberalism and conservatism) goes by a name that is utterly awkward and misunderstood. As a label it is so useless it cannot even be used as a form of abuse. Its uselessness as a label demands that it be discussed. To say the name immediately requires explanation, and the explanation immediately provokes debate. The troublesome title is "Distributism." It has to do with property. It has to do with justice. And it has to do with everything else.

The word "property" has to do with what is proper. It also has to do with what is proportional. Balance has to do with harmony. Harmony has to do with beauty. The modern world is out of balance. And it is ugly. We have only glimpses of beauty, glimpses of things as they should be. These glimpses are our inspiration.

The word "economy" and the word "economics" are based on the Greek word for house, which is *oikos*. The word "economy" as we know it, however, has drifted completely away from that meaning. Instead of house, it has come to mean everything outside of the house. The home is the place where the important things happen. The economy is the place where the most unimportant things happen. The backwardness of the situation is something constantly pointed out by Chesterton: "There is nothing queerer today than

---

1. *Orthodoxy*, Vol. 1, p. 233.

2. *William Cobbett* (London: Hodder and Stoughton, 1925), p. 125.

the importance of unimportant things. Except, of course, the unimportance of important things."[1]

There is another rather neglected meaning to the word "economy": the idea of thriftiness.

> The best and last word of mysticism is an almost agonising sense of the preciousness of everything, the preciousness of the whole universe, which is like an exquisite and fragile vase, and among other things the preciousness of other people's tea-cups. The last and best word of mysticism is not lavishness, but rather a sublime and sacred economy.[2]

Chesterton points out that inside the word thrift is the word thrive.[3] We can only thrive within our means, just as we can only be free within the rules. The modern understanding of the word economy is, once again, just the opposite. It is about accumulation instead of thrift. Even worse, it is about mere exchange. It is about trade, and not even about the things that are traded. It is about figures in a ledger. It is about noughts. It is about the accumulation of zeros. It is more about nothing than it is about something.

Our separation of economy from the home is part of a long fragmentation process. Each of the modern ideas that might have once been part of this complete breakfast have come to claim that they are complete all by themselves. We have separated everything from everything else. We have accomplished this by separating everything from the home. Feminism has separated women from the home. Capitalism has separated men from the home. Socialism has separated education from the home. Manufacturing has separated craftsmanship from the home. The news and entertainment industry has separated originality and creativity from the home, rendering us into passive and malleable consumers rather than active citizens.

There is more to Distributism than economics. That is because there is more to economics than economics. Distributism is not just an economic idea. It is an integral part of a complete way of thinking. But in a fragmented world we not only resist a complete way of thinking, we do not even recognize it. It is too big to be seen. In the age of specialization we tend to grasp only small and narrow ideas. We don't even want to discuss a true Theory of Everything, unless it is invented by a specialist and addresses only that specialist's "everything." In reality, everything is too complicated a category because it contains, well, everything. But the glory of a great philosophy or a great religion is not that it is simple but that it is complicated. It should be complicated because the world is complicated. Its problems are complicated.

---

1. *Illustrated London News*, January 3, 1914, Vol. 30, p. 17.

2. *Daily News*, March 23, 1907, from microfilm.

3. *William Cobbett, op. cit.*, p. 212.

The solution to those problems must also be complicated. It takes a complicated key to fit a complicated lock.

But we want simple solutions. We don't want to work hard. We don't want to think hard. We want other people to do both our work and our thinking for us. We call in the specialists. And we call this state of utter dependency "freedom." We think we are free simply because we seem free to move about.

Chesterton's opening line in his book about his visit to America was this: "I have never managed to lose my conviction that travel narrows the mind."[1] As with all his paradoxes he points to a truth that is the opposite of what we expect. The man in his field, the man in his garden, thinks about everything. The man who is traveling thinks about only a few things. He is distracted not just with details but with destinations. He thinks the thing he has come to see is the only important thing and this makes him narrow. The real purpose of traveling is to return. The true destination of every journey is home. That is the main idea behind Distributism.

The Distributist ideal is that the home is the most important place in the world. Every man should have his own piece of property, a place to build his own home, to raise his family, to do all the important things from birth to death: eating, singing, celebrating, reading, writing, arguing, story-telling, laughing, crying, praying. The home is above all a sanctuary of creativity. Creativity is our most Godlike quality. We not only make things, we make things in our own image. The family is one of those things. But so is the picture on the wall and the rug on the floor. The home is the place of complete freedom, where we may have a picnic on the roof and even drink directly from the milk carton.

We will stop here a moment and address the feminists who recoil in horror as they read this use of the male pronoun and the warlike word, "man." Chesterton's view of women is not that they are chattel but that they are queens of their own realm.

> Women were not kept at home in order to keep them narrow; on the contrary, they were kept at home in order to keep them broad. The world outside the home was one mass of narrowness, a maze of cramped paths, a madhouse of monomaniacs.
>
> It is not difficult to see why . . . the female became the emblem of the universal . . . . Nature . . . surrounded her with very young children, who require to be taught not so much anything as everything. Babies need not to be taught a trade, but to be introduced to a world. To put the matter shortly, woman is generally shut up in a house with a human being at the time when he asks all the questions that there are, and some that there aren't. It would be odd if she retained any of the narrowness of a specialist.

---

1. *What I Saw in America*, Vol. 21, p. 37.

Now if anyone says that this duty of general enlightenment . . . is in itself too exacting and oppressive, I can understand the view. I can only answer that our race has thought it worthwhile to cast this burden on women in order to keep commonsense in the world. But when people begin to talk about this domestic duty as not merely difficult but trivial and dreary, I simply give up the question. For I cannot with the utmost energy of imagination conceive what they mean. When domesticity, for instance, is called drudgery, all the difficulty arises from a double meaning in the word. If drudgery only means dreadfully hard work, I admit the woman drudges in the home, as a man might drudge at the Cathedral of Amiens or drudge behind a gun at Trafalgar. But if it means that the hard work is more heavy because it is trifling, colorless, and of small import to the soul, then as I say, I give it up; I do not know what the words mean. How can it be a large career to tell other people's children about the Rule of Three, and a small career to tell one's own children about the universe? How can it be broad to be the same thing to everyone, and narrow to be everything to someone? No; a woman's function is laborious, but because it is gigantic, not because it is minute. I will pity Mrs. Jones for the hugeness of her task; I will never pity her for its smallness.[1]

*****

CHESTERTON COULD BE very specific at times, but in general, he was a generalist. His critics always rush in with objections to his generalizations forgetting that they are generalizations, and generalizations by their nature allow for exceptions. The problem in the modern world is that the exceptions get all the attention. The generalizations get none. The exceptions have become the rule. It is now an exception for a woman to raise her own children. But Chesterton's Distributist ideal not only called for mothers to stay at home, it called for fathers to stay at home as well. The home-based business, the idea of self-sufficiency would not only make for stronger, healthier families, but a stronger, healthier society. If everything in a society is based on nurturing and strengthening and protecting the family, that society will survive centuries of storms.

A home-based society is naturally and necessarily a local and de-centralized society. If the government is local, if the economy is local, then the culture is also local. What we call culture right now is neither local nor is it culture. It is an amorphous society based on the freeway off-ramp and tall glowing signs that all say the same thing. Convenience is our culture. We all convene at the convenience store, where we get our gas and our munchies and our magazine and we are careful not to look anyone in the eye, not even the Pakistani clerk who waves our credit card across the laser beam. This is a

---

1. *What's Wrong with the World*, Vol. 4, pp. 117–19.

revealing snapshot of our fragmented society: passive, restless, shutter-eyed, lonely, not at home.

It would take "a clear and conscious philosophy" to build a Distributist society, not a philosophy of broken and leftover ideas. The first clear and conscious idea would be to recognize that money is not the most important thing. It is the means and not the end. The end is a quiet, happy home. It is many small places with many local heroes.

So. How does this all happen? That is the grand question when it comes to Distributism. Chesterton argues that the main thing about Distributism is that it is voluntary. If we are not creatures of free will, if everything is predetermined by God or by Fate or by Biology or by Birth Order or by the Big Bang, well, then I suppose it is not worth wasting energy talking about how we can bring about a Distributist society. Let's just kick back and pop open a beer.

Though Chesterton would argue that a Distributist society would be most fully realized if it were based on a Catholic worldview, he would not insist upon that basis as essential for achieving such a society. In fact, he would argue that such a society is more congenial to the different religions than any other societal plan. Freedom of religion, as it now supposedly exists under a huge centralized government, actually needs to be "enforced" by that government. The result, as we have seen, is that religion has actually been stifled where the government watchdog is there to "guarantee" the freedom. But local-based governments (supported by local-based economies) are more conducive to religious freedom because people of the same religion would naturally gravitate together. The main reason that people of the same religion tend to scatter in our society and that people of different religions tend to mix uncomfortably is that our society is not based on the home. It is based on the opportunities outside the home. The better jobs are always elsewhere. It is not their religion that makes people chose a place to live; it is their job. It is convenience. It is not philosophy.

The dilemma of Distributism is the dilemma of freedom itself. Distributism cannot be done *to* people, but only *by* people. It is not a system that can be imposed from above; it can only spring up from below. It can only come from what Chesterton calls "the non-mechanical part of man, the sacred quality in creation and choice."[1] If it happens, it seems most likely that it would be ushered in by a popular revolution. In any case, it must be popular. It would at some point require those with massive and inordinate wealth to give it up. In most popular revolutions, this has been achieved by means that are not always soft and cushy. In order to avoid a lot of blood and

---

1. *George Bernard Shaw*, Vol. 11, p. 441.

breaking glass, religion can provide a very practical solution. It usually does. The Christian argument, if taken seriously, should be more terrifying to a rich man than a mob with axes and torches. The Christian argument has to do with eternity and not just immediate creature comforts. The central figure of the Christian religion said quite unambiguously that it is easier for a camel to go through an eye of a needle than for a rich man to enter heaven. No matter how the rich man may try to breed smaller camels and manufacture larger needles, no matter how hard he snorts and stomps, he cannot get around the reality that to cling to his riches is to put his soul in peril. Although there are commentators who rush to soften the interpretation of this passage, the message is unfortunately backed up by the rest of the New Testament, most notably in St. Matt. xix:16–22, where a very good man is told to sell all he has and give to the poor, and in St. James v:1–6, where the description of the eternal scenario for the rich is not very soft at all. The implication is clear. As Chesterton says, "The obligation of wealth is to chuck it."[1]

But the rich are a small part of the problem – only because there are so few of them. The larger part of the problem is the mentality that drives so many people to chase after money. Again, religion provides a practical solution. There is a commandment that states, "Thou shall not covet." This little known commandment would have to be rediscovered and re-emphasized in order to build a Distributist society.

Most people have never heard of Distributism. They know only about socialism and capitalism and favor one or the other while they suffer under a combination of both. Our schools have ill-served us, for the idea has never been taught. If more people were exposed to the idea they would realize that it makes sense. They would at least realize that there is an alternative to the two ideas that they claim polarize them but which in fact unite them in despair. The big schools right now tend to teach the smallest ideas. But Distributism is, like any secret, something that cannot be kept secret forever, in spite of institutionalized censorship. It will be taken seriously in spite of those who sneer at it. It will be stumbled on by those who try to avoid it. To quote Chesterton in reference to something else, Distributism "has not been tried and found wanting; it has been found difficult and left untried."[2]

It is quite possible to defend Distributism as the best system with which to build a fair society and a solid economy. We can have the discussion, if we must, by confining ourselves to the subjects of law and labor practice and ownership policy and taxation and the rest of the textbook and news-

1. *New Witness*, Oct. 14, 1915, from microfilm.

2. *What's Wrong with the World*, p. 61.

paper stuff. We can provide answers for all the arguments and objections that come from either the socialists and the capitalists. It would be a fertile and provocative discussion to be sure. But it would always be incomplete. Distributism is only part of this complete breakfast. There is more to it than commercial breakfast cereal to be sure. There is more to it than state-issued gruel. We can make the argument that it is daily bread. But it needs the other staples of human life to supplement it. It needs the milk of morality, the meat of meaning, the juice of joy. We must have a code to guide us, a purpose to push us, a philosophy to fill us. Man cannot live by bread alone.

"The city worker is apt to consider farming under any conditions as being beneath him – an inferior occupation all the way round. The tenant farmer of long standing may regard independent landownership as a status utterly beyond his attainment. Both of these attitudes must be changed if the general redistribution of farm property is to become a fact. The bringing about of such a change constitutes a challenge to every one who holds such an ideal dear . . . .

"There must be, in effect, a spiritual rebirth of the mass of the people. There must be a general departure from the social and economic objective of money-making. 'Progress' must cease to be the national fetish that it is. Discontent must cease to be 'divine' in the popular estimate and come to be regarded as the generally undesirable thing that it is. There must be a new system of social values.

"It will be argued that all of this is impossible, that the whole trend of history is to the contrary, that one cannot 'turn back the hands of the clock.' Critics offering these arguments may be correct, but they must support their arguments with something more solid than a mixture of Hegelian metaphysics and Marxian economics, or the mysticism of 'Progress,' before their contentions are to be taken as finally true."

—TROY J. CAULEY

~ 5 ~

Un Homme de Tradition

René de La Tour du Pin and the
Principle of Association

Christopher Blum, Ph.D.

RANCE IN THE 1880s GROANED UNDER THE DISMAL rule of the Third Republic, which was, as one Catholic writer of the day put it, "but Freemasonry organized into a government."[1] This regime of fiery anti-clericals and hardened capitalists understood itself as the child of the French Revolution and, accordingly, prepared to celebrate its centennial in 1889 with great éclat. Finding this sort of festivity offensive, a "group of men of tradition" planned and staged a counter-centenary that would, as René de La Tour du Pin, its principal organizer, explained, "oppose these declarations by taking up the movement of 1789 through the reunion of provincial assemblies similar to those that had preceded the convocation of the Estates-General."[2] The ensuing series of assemblies has generally been seen as a quixotic failure that merely underscored the distance between orthodox Catholics and the rhythms and habits of modern French society. From the perspective of the development of Catholic social theory, however, the counter-centenary, coming as it did during the crucial preparatory period before Leo XIII's *Rerum Novarum*, reminds us that the first principles of an authentic Catholic understanding of society are not the same as the principles of the Revolution of 1789. According to the men of 1789 and their *Declaration of the Rights of Man*, the rights and liberty of the

---

1. The Catholic journal *L'Univers* for April 20, 1884, quoted in Geoffrey Cubit, "Catholics versus Freemasons in Late Nineteenth-Century France," in Frank Tallett and Nicholas Atkin, eds., *Religion, Society and Politics in France Since 1789* (London: Hambledon, 1991), p. 121.

2. René de La Tour du Pin, *Aphorismes de politique sociale* (Paris: Beauchesne, 1930), p. 7.

individual take *absolute priority* within society, and every human associa-tion is to be judged on the basis of its relation to those individual rights. For René de La Tour du Pin, for Leo XIII, and for countless other Catholic voices then and since, individual rights cannot be given this absolute priority and must not be allowed thereby to dissolve the bonds of society, so necessary for man's perfection and happiness.

The Roots of a Social Catholic

IN 1895, René de La Tour du Pin wrote to his long-time associate in the Catholic social apostolate, Léon Harmel, to explain the nature of his commitment to their common endeavor. His long years of work for "the emancipation and the moral and material prosperity of the working classes," he explained, had not necessitated that he forget "anything of the traditions of the home, nor learn from modern schools."[1] As a Catholic social theorist, he was a "man of tradition," and family tradition at that.

Charles Humbert René de La Tour du Pin Chambly de la Charce (1834–1924) belonged to a noble family of the Champagne region of northeastern France whose earlier members included a veteran of St. Louis's Crusade and a victim of the Terror. The family had remained faithful to France's ancient Catholic piety, with that sternness that characterized the French nobility at its best. La Tour du Pin liked to repeat his father's admonition about the re-sponsibilities their 750-acre estate would one day convey to him: "Remem-ber that you will only be the administrator of this land for its inhabitants."[2] Like many conservative nobles, La Tour du Pin headed for a career in the military as the only avenue of public service open to those who considered the rule of Napoleon III to be illegitimate. Captured by the Germans during the Franco-Prussian war, and held prisoner in Aachen, he and his fellow prisoner Albert de Mun were befriended by a German Jesuit who put into their hands Emile Keller's fiercely Catholic *Encyclical of December 8 and the Principles of 1789.*[3] The encyclical in question was Pius IX's *Quanta Cura* (1864), the one to which the *Syllabus of Errors* had been attached as an ap-pendix. In *Quanta Cura*, Pius IX affirmed that "human society, when set

---

1. La Tour du Pin's letter to Harmel is reproduced in Elisabeth Bossan de Garagnol, *Le Colonel de La Tour du Pin d'après lui-même* (Paris: Beauchesne, 1934), pp. 264–66.

2. *Ibid.*, p. 32.

3. Emile Keller, *L'Encyclique du 8 Décembre et les principes de 1789* (Paris: Poussielgue, 1865). A sec-ond edition was published in 1866. Selections of Keller's book in English translation may be found in *Critics of the Enlightenment: Readings in the French Counter-Revolutionary Tradition*, ed. C. O. Blum (Wilmington, Delaware: ISI Books, 2004).

loose from the bonds of religion and true justice, can have, in truth, no other end than the purpose of obtaining and amassing wealth" (§4). Keller agreed, and argued forcefully that the lot of the suffering working classes would be improved only when Europe had rejected the unbridled cupidity enshrined in the principles of 1789 and again embraced the spirit of association that had animated Europe's Christian past. This argument profoundly shaped René de La Tour du Pin's thinking, inspiring in him a life-long questioning and elaboration of what he called the "traditions of the hearth."

After their release from internment, both Mun and La Tour du Pin went to Paris, where they saw firsthand the horrors of the Paris Commune and the intense hatred and destructiveness of class warfare. Moved by this experience, both dedicated themselves to the cause of the worker and to an authentically Catholic response to the social problems of the day. The two collaborated fruitfully in the foundation of the *Oeuvre des Cercles Catholiques des Ouvriers* (The Organization of Catholic Workingmen's Circles) in the 1870s, after which Mun went on to become the great parliamentary spokesman of Catholic social thinking in France, while La Tour du Pin pursued studies in Catholic economics and politics.[1] Through his participation in what has come to be known as the *Union de Fribourg* – annual meetings of leading Catholic social theorists held in the Swiss university town of Fribourg in the 1880s – La Tour du Pin is numbered among the architects of *Rerum Novarum*. The results of his thinking were published as essays in *Association Catholique*, the journal of the *Oeuvre de Cercles*, the best of which were in 1907 collected into one volume, *Towards a Christian Social Order*. The volume enjoyed modest success in European Catholic circles.[2] These essays bear the imprint of the German tradition of Catholic social thought, and particularly of the writings of Bishop Wilhelm Emmanuel von Ketteler (1811–1877), who had insisted that the plight of the worker was not merely due to a lack of almsgiving, but resulted from detrimental structural changes in society.[3]

La Tour du Pin saw that the social and legal changes wrought by the revolution in France and extended throughout Europe by Napoleon had left the working classes at the mercy of the owning classes. Like Ketteler, he held that the workers were in need both of voluntary associations, or unions, that

---

1. On Albert de Mun's parliamentary activity, see Parker Thomas Moon, *The Labor Problem and the Social Catholic Movement in France: A Study in the History of Social Politics* (New York: Macmillan, 1921).

2. *Vers un ordre social chrétien* (Paris: Beauchesne, 1907). For an English translation of La Tour du Pin's essay on the corporate régime, see Blum, ed., *Critics of the Enlightenment*.

3. For an English version of Bishop von Ketteler's most important texts see *The Social Teachings of Wilhelm Emmanuel von Ketteler*, trans. Rupert Ederer (Washington, D.C.: University Press of America, 1981).

would strengthen their position within society, and of legal and institutional changes that would make these associations permanent and truly oriented towards the common good. For La Tour du Pin, these associations were not to be composed merely of workers, for that would be to widen, not lessen, the breach and the strife between the owning and the working classes. Instead these unions should be modeled upon the guilds of old, which had combined owners and workers into associations that protected both their economic interests and their communal way of life. To protect these associations from the corrosive effects of unlimited competition, La Tour du Pin held that the state would need to guarantee their legal and social standing. Such a state would also recognize the rights of individuals, but would do so within a context of pre-existing common rights and needs. La Tour du Pin once described this kind of corporate state as "a return not to the form but to the spirit of the institutions of the Middle Ages."[1] He rightly saw that such a corporate organization of society would necessarily involve a rejection of the legacy of the French Revolution.

The Counter-Centenary

WHILE THE FRENCH Revolution is perhaps most commonly remembered for its bloody events, its lasting effects were in the field of law: it destroyed the complex society of orders and corporate bodies that constituted the Old Regime and instituted a society in which associations of any kind were either suspect or illegal. The law of June 14, 1791 (named after its principal author Isaac Le Chapelier), which made illegal any association of workers, declared that it was "contrary to the principles of liberty" for any group of citizens to "make agreements among themselves tending to refuse by mutual consent or to grant only at a determined price the assistance of their industry or their labor." It further added that any such assemblies of workers would be considered seditious.[2] Coupled with article 17 of the *Declaration of the Rights of Man and of the Citizen* declaring property to be "an inviolable and sacred right," the Le Chapelier law ensured that the Revolution would lead to the rise of Socialism by rendering the situation of the worker far more unstable than it had been under the previous regime – however onerous it may have been in its final days – of

1. La Tour du Pin quoted in Philippe Levillain, *Albert de Mun: Catholicisme francais et Catholicisme romain du Syllabus au Ralliement* (Rome: École Française, 1983), p. 671.

2. Isaac Le Chapelier, "Law of June 14, 1791," in *The Old Régime and the French Revolution*, ed. Keith Michael Baker, in the *University of Chicago Readings in Western Civilization* series (Chicago: University of Chicago Press, 1987), p. 249.

guilds and masters. And though the Le Chapelier law was at last set aside in 1884 with the belated legalization of trade unions, much of the judicial legacy of the French Revolution remained. By the 1880s, religious congregations in France and in much of the rest of Europe were only allowed to exist if they ministered to an obvious need such as nursing. In France, the 1884 legalization of trade unions came in the same parliamentary session as the legalization of divorce, and thus was not a change in the first principles of French law so much as a concession to socialist political movements. To La Tour du Pin, therefore, the Revolution was inherently opposed to Catholic civilization, and its upcoming centenary an appropriate occasion to reject its individualism once and for all.

The counter-centenary of 1889 was a project of the *Oeuvre des Cercles Catholiques des Ouvriers*, then having a modest but real effect upon French society thanks to a membership approaching 50,000 people. When Albert de Mun announced the plan of a counter-centenary to the leadership of the *Oeuvre* in 1887, he described it as "a great Christian demonstration in which we shall together proclaim the rights of God over and against the rights of man."[1] The situation of the Church in France in 1887 was perilous, particularly with respect to education. Some Catholic schools – those run by the Jesuits, for instance – were officially outlawed, and others were merely tolerated. Mun, therefore, saw the counter-centenary as an opportunity to galvanize France's many nominal Catholics, and to encourage them to support the rights of God and of the Church through political action. For La Tour du Pin, however, a short-term political goal, laudable though it was, remained insufficient. He wanted the celebration of the counter-centenary to be a declaration against individualism.

It was La Tour du Pin's model that the *Oeuvre des Cercles* adopted in its planning. The counter-centenary would have as its goal the demonstration of the parallels between French society in 1789 and in 1889 so as to show that the Revolution had not solved France's social problems but only compounded them. To do this, the leadership of the *Oeuvre* would prepare a study of some of the hundreds of *Cahiers de Doléances* (Notebooks of Complaints) that had been prepared in 1789 so as to inform King Louis XVI and the Estates General of the needs of the French people. The *Oeuvre* would also commission surveys of the current social conditions of France. The results of both studies were then to be combined in documents sent around the country to members and friends of the *Oeuvre*, to prepare them to ratify demands for political reform at regional assemblies held in the Spring of 1889. The assemblies themselves, in La Tour du

---

1. My account of the counter-centenary is primarily indebted to Robert Talmy, *Aux Sources du Catholicisme social: l'École de La Tour du Pin* (Tournai: Desclée, 1963).

Pin's eyes, would take up the unfinished work of reform where it had been derailed in 1789; they would do this primarily through their very constitution, which would be based upon his conception of the three different social functions within a State, and patterned roughly upon the three estates of the Old Regime. The first function, as La Tour du Pin explained in a letter to one of his collaborators, was the "moral service" provided by ministers of religion and teachers; the second was "public service" in the government, the military, or the field of law; the third was the "economic service" performed by all those engaged in agriculture, industry, or trade. Within each of these three "estates" or social functions, representatives to the counter-centenary assemblies would be recruited from whatever associations or groups existed at the time. By bringing together groups constituted by social function, these assemblies would, La Tour du Pin thought, embody the corporate regime and be a first step towards its concrete realization.

La Tour du Pin's program was an ambitious one, and it is not surprising that it met with only limited success. The *Oeuvre* did hold seventeen regional assemblies in the Spring of 1889, and these in turn sent delegates to a national assembly in Paris, held in late June of that year. Yet the 346 delegates to the Paris assembly were nearly all drawn from the privileged ranks of society, including a large number of the nobility, and the confessional nature of the *Oeuvre* meant that most existing French workers' associations were left unrepresented. What can be said, at least, is that the demands of the various assemblies were very much in line with the most common ones of the day: a maximum length to the working day, limits to the work of women and children, insurance to provide for accidental injury and old age, and international treaties to protect these provisions. There were, in addition, demands for reforms that had a more distinctively Catholic inspiration, such as protests against the recent legalization of divorce and work on Sundays, and a call for liberty of instruction for Catholic schools. Most importantly, however, from La Tour du Pin's perspective, was the call for the reorganization of society into a corporate regime. In his concluding address to the assembly, Albert de Mun excoriated the Revolution for having created a "social order that may be summed up in two words: stock-jobbery and poverty." The proper response to the crass regime of liberalism was to reject it in favor of a corporate regime. "In bygone days," Mun explained, "there were Orders in the State; today, they no longer exist. But there are and there will be more and more professions. It is upon them that, henceforward, the social organization may repose."[1]

---

1. Albert de Mun, quoted in Talmy, *op.cit.*, p. 246.

Thanks to Mun's fiery oratory, the counter-centenary enjoyed a certain notoriety. A writer in *Le Temps* warned the French bourgeoisie that "if they want to save liberalism in this country, and if they want to save themselves and not be crushed between two enemy armies ready to join against her, between those two socialisms which would act together to overturn the society issued from the principles of 1789, now is their time to act."[1] The various assemblies, however, did not lead to any permanent change in French internal politics. The *Oeuvre* itself was soon riven by the controversies of the *Ralliement*, Leo XIII's policy of encouraging French Catholics to participate in and support the French Republic instead of continuing to hope for a restoration of the monarchy. Many French Catholics, La Tour du Pin among them, were not able to abandon a tradition they had so long struggled to uphold. "It is precisely because my faith in this program and love for this cause," wrote La Tour du Pin to Léon Harmel, "are not the fruit of a conversion, but are the legacy of fidelity, that it is not fitting for me to serve them under different colors."[2] René de La Tour du Pin's active role in French Catholic politics, therefore, came to a premature end with the counter-centenary, but the principle for which he had contended, the principle of association, was soon after accepted as one of the bulwarks of Catholic social doctrine.

Rerum Novarum & the Principle of Association

ONE REASON FOR the failure of the counter-centenary to generate much support for significant changes in French society is that La Tour du Pin's ideas were not warmly received within Catholic circles. It would not be an exaggeration to say that he was outside the mainstream of Catholic thought in France, which was defined by a kind of conservative liberalism critical of the secularism of the French Revolution but less so of its individualism. The chief exponent of this conservative liberalism was the Belgian economist Charles Périn. Like La Tour du Pin, Périn saw association as a potent means of bettering the condition of the workers; unlike him, he insisted that the corporations be entirely voluntary and that the State not support them with regulation. "As soon as you admit that the State had the right of regulation in questions of production," Périn wrote, "you are heading straight toward Socialism."[3] Périn, his followers, and his friends, were quick to brand La Tour du Pin's Corporatism as Socialism. The reac-

1. *Le Temps*, quoted in Henri Rollet, *L'Action sociale des catholiques en France (1871-1901)* (Paris: Boivin, 1947-1958), Vol. I, p. 134.

2. La Tour du Pin to Harmel, quoted in Bossan de Garagnol, *op. cit.*, pp. 265–66.

3. Quoted in Moon, *op. cit.*, p. 63.

tion of Leo XIII when presented with a sketch of La Tour du Pin's ideas in 1885 was rather different: "But, my son, this is not Socialism, this! This is Christianity!"[1] Popes are traditionally hesitant to enter too strongly into contemporary debates, and the debates among Catholics over social theory in the 1880s were no exception. *Rerum Novarum* did not, therefore, whole-heartedly embrace La Tour du Pin's corporatism. It did, however, respond to the French Revolution's heritage of liberalism with a ringing endorsement of the principle of association.

The principle of association had been explicitly rejected by the leaders of the French Revolution. In 1791, in the midst of the Constituent Assembly's debate about the nature of the liberal society it was creating, Isaac Le Chapelier had said that "there are no powers except those constituted by the will of the people expressed by its representatives," and that "to preserve this principle in all its purity, the Constitution has abolished all corporations, from one end of the state to another." He concluded, on a chilling note, that henceforth the Constitution "recognizes only the social body and individuals."[2] In *Rerum Novarum*, Leo XIII responded to this withering liberalism by affirming the right of "private societies" to exist and to pursue the private advantage of their members. Such private societies as trade associations or religious confraternities "exist within the State" as "parts of it," formed from "one and the same principle" as the State itself, "namely, that men are by nature inclined to associate." Should such private societies act in such a way as to jeopardize the "justice or the welfare of the State," then they should be corrected or perhaps even suppressed by the State, but, Leo XIII warned, the State "must use the greatest precaution lest it appear to infringe upon the rights of its citizens" (§72). Such statements were close to La Tour du Pin's conception of a corporate regime. Leo XIII, however, stopped short of deciding whether labor associations should be composed of both workers and employers or of workers alone (§69), and he offered in support of the political standing of associations only the careful prescription: "Let the State protect these lawfully associated bodies of citizens" (§75).

In the twentieth century, La Tour du Pin's theory of the Corporate State received its warmest welcome in Austria, where it had home-grown precursors, and in Spain, Portugal, and Vichy France. Corporate theorists such as the Spaniard Victor Pradera and the Austrian Baron Karl von Vogelsang, and corporatist political leaders such as Engelbert Dollfuss and Antonio de Oliviera Salazar, are now almost entirely unknown in the English-speak-

---

1. Leo XIII quoted in Bossan de Garagnol, *op. cit.*, p. 250.

2. Isaac Le Chapelier, "National Assembly Debate on Clubs," Sep. 20, 1791, in Baker, *op. cit.*, pp. 279–280.

ing world, even among well-educated Catholics.[1] In the 1930s, however, it appeared that some variety of La Tour du Pin's corporatism would emerge as the primary expression of Catholic social thought – so much so that Pius XI's *Quadragesimo Anno* could be described as a kind of dialogue with corporate theory.[2] The 1930s, sadly, were not a time for fruitful experiments in European politics, and the various Catholic corporate regimes were either overwhelmed by Nazi Germany, as in the case of Austria and Vichy France, or compromised through their political actions.

What, then, remains of value in a theory of society seemingly born only in protest against the French Revolution and since cast aside amidst the seemingly relentless tide of globalization? Certainly, at the very least, La Tour du Pin's theory serves as a salutary reminder that the liberalism of 1789 is by its nature corrosive of human associations of all kinds. The motive force of the French Revolution, as François Furet has memorably said, was hatred for the aristocracy. In the attempt to rid French society of what they perceived as the dead hand of feudal institutions, Isaac Le Chapelier and the other leaders of the Constituent Assembly used as their tool a conception of society devoid of all privilege whatsoever – at least in theory. Liberty, to Le Chapelier, meant a perfect equality under the law and a consequent absence of privileges. Membership in a community, he knew, directly *implied* privilege, and therefore, the political and legal standing of communities and associations had to be denied, beginning with the Church and ending with the communes and guilds. It was the very logic of the Revolution at work.

Man cannot live without association and community, and so the nineteenth and twentieth centuries saw revivals of communal living and work, among which La Tour du Pin's *Oeuvre des Cercles* figured prominently. In our day, however, it is the fragility of community and other intermediate associations before the onslaught of an activist civil rights jurisprudence, on the one hand, and the cancerous growth of multinational corporations such as Wal-Mart, IBM and Halliburton on the other, that is most obvious. Among the contemporary voices protesting the baleful effects of liberalism, few have been as eloquent as Wendell Berry, the Kentucky farmer and poet. In "Does Community Have a Value?"[3] he has defended a doctrine remarkably similar in its outlines to La Tour du Pin's. And like the French counter-revolutionary landowner, Berry sees that while fruitful human association

---

1. A useful though unsympathetic survey of Catholic politics in early-twentieth century Europe is Tom Buchanan and Martin Conway, eds., *Political Catholicism in Europe, 1918–1965* (Oxford: Oxford University Press, 1996) [to which may also be added Martin Conway, *Catholic Politics in Europe* (London and New York: Routledge, 1997)—Ed.].

2. See especially §§82–7, 91–5.—Ed.

3. Wendell Berry, *Home Economics* (San Francisco: North Point Press, 1987), pp. 179–192.

should ultimately be protected by wise legislation, it must initially be created by voluntary act. "The only preventive and the only remedy" to the centripetal forces tearing apart community in our day, he explains, "is for the people to choose one another and their place, over the rewards offered them by outside investors." La Tour du Pin might have us substitute "way of life" for Berry's "place," but he would doubtless agree. The counter-revolution, as Joseph de Maistre taught, must be the contrary of revolution, and nothing could be more contrary to the principles of 1789 than to choose the fellowship of the City of God over the rugged and self-centered individualism of the boundless frontier.

~ 6 ~

Father Vincent McNabb's "Call to Contemplatives"

Peter Chojnowski, Ph.D.

There is a little hope of saving civilization or religion except by the return of contemplatives to the land.

—Fr. Vincent McNabb, O.P.

I F CATHOLICS ARE GOING TO CONFRONT THE WORLD with the idea that they have the answers to the fundamental *problems* of human life and society, they must also provide our neo-pagan world with concrete and principled *solutions*. It is my contention that these answers will not come from "partisan" quarters: they are not the province of thinking by the "left" or the "right"; by "Republicans" or "Democrats"; by "liberals" or "conservatives." Rather, they will come from a wholesale reconsideration of our political, social, and economic goals, priorities and practices, and the principles that such an examination need be based upon.

The Catholic Church is, indeed, an essentially spiritual institution. Nevertheless, it has, in a manner of speaking, made its own the famous dictum of Terence – "Nothing human is alien to me." It can adopt this motto without artifice or disingenuousness precisely because, it seems to me, the problems that confront us today are not questions of mere technique or policy but rather fundamental questions of social philosophy and vision.

The vision of which I speak was put forward persuasively and with precision by Fr. Vincent McNabb, O.P., an English Dominican priest and one of the leading lights of the Distributist school in England during the 1920s and 1930s. His biting, penetrating criticisms of urban industrial society and his constant teaching and writing about its perils unjustly earned him the title of a "dangerous and holy crank" with those who would not, or could not, follow the intrinsic logic of Catholic social teaching. But his perseverance

in the face of both unrelenting hostility and abject ignorance merely under-
lines his strength of character and his commitment to the truth that his life
and work articulated.

Life and Work: A Brief Sketch

HE WAS BORN Joseph McNabb to a sea captain and a peasant mother
in Portaferry, near Belfast, Ireland in 1868. The tenth of eleven children, his childhood, and the unstinting religious and communitarian example of his capable parents, was to mark McNabb's social criticism indel-
ibly. In the joys and sorrows of his own family, he saw an image of the Holy
Family of Nazareth - for him the archetype of a real Catholic social order.
McNabb's earliest memories of his family life were of his mother's love for
her own children, as well as the truly poor of the parish. His defense of family life, which grew, presumably, from his own experiences as well as from
prayer and reflection, was set down particularly in *Eleven, Thank God!*

His father's work dictated a family move to Newcastle-upon-Tyne, England, while McNabb was a young man. Moved by the life and spirituality of
the Dominicans who ran the local parish, he entered the Order of Preachers
in 1885. From 1885 to 1891 he studied in the English Dominican novitiate
at Woodchester, taking the name Vincent. Following his ordination, he was
sent to Louvain, Belgium, for further studies, but he spent most of his life,
subsequently, as a parish priest at St. Dominic's in London.

He spent his entire life and being living out the statement in the *Summa
Theologiæ* of St. Thomas Aquinas – almost a second bible for Dominican
clerics – that the most perfect form of human life is the one in which the
contemplative channels his own attained wisdom into action, both through
teaching others and among the society of men to achieve the common
good.

One of the most recent short examinations of Fr. McNabb's life and work,
the introduction of Prof. William Fahey to the new edition of McNabb's *The
Church and the Land*, tells us that from very early on after his ordination
and taking on duties at the priories where he was assigned, McNabb had
farmed small plots of land. Through farming, Fahey writes,

> McNabb's spiritual life and the social teachings of the Church united. The
> act of farming gave him an insight into what England had lost and what
> Christendom might gain. The centrality of the rural life was, of course, im-
> portant in any Thomistic analysis of politics and society; and in medieval
> England Dominicans were accused, at least, of stirring up the landed peas-

antry against the unbridled powers of their day. Nevertheless, few Dominicans have ever shouldered the plough.[1]

In support of his broad contention that Catholics should leave the in-
dusrialized and mechanized cities, Fr. McNabb was an uncompromising
sponsor of the Catholic Land Movement that encouraged urban Catholic
families to "flee to the fields" in search of a natural, family-friendly life of
co-existence with fellow men and fellow creatures. His published works deal,
of course, with his social philosophy and his own particular articulation of
the general Catholic moral truths that bear on society, politics, and economics. Most outstanding of these works, aside from pamphlets, articles, and
numerous sermons are *The Church and the Land* (1925), *Nazareth or Social
Chaos* (1933), and *Old Principles and the New Order* (1942). Beyond social
criticism, McNabb's well-rounded vision produced monographs on literary
figures such as Chaucer or Francis Thompson and historical notables like Ss.
Mary Magdalen, Elizabeth of Portugal, and John Fisher. He also produced
apologetic works such as *Meditations on St. John*, *The Doctrinal Witness of
the Fourth Gospel*, and *Did Jesus Christ Rise form the Dead?* Other titles – like
the *Oxford Conferences on Faith*, *Oxford Conferences on Prayer*, and *The Craft
of Suffering* – stemmed from his extensive and tireless preaching.

The wisdom that Fr. McNabb drew upon as the basis for his thinking was
common fare for many Catholics prior to the twin disasters of World War
II and Vatican II. The three works that McNabb speaks of as being his well
of inspiration are the Bible, the *Summa* of St. Thomas, and *Rerum Novarum*,
the encyclical on the condition of the working class issued in 1891 by Pope
Leo XIII.

The coherent social teaching of the Catholic Church, formally beginning
with that encyclical, was for Fr. McNabb simply Thomism in action. And *action* – the realizing of "the good of the true" – was clearly the primary objective of all of McNabb's writing on the social order. He argued that if we can
see the concrete, lived problems of the age and we know the Catholic moral,
doctrinal, and social principles which are meant to be remedies for any human problems, we cannot but desire to implement those truths in the lives
of real men, women, and children in order to ameliorate the evils that beset
us in the life of the modern system – or the "liberal" system, as we might say
in the classical and historical sense – and to assist these same people at the
same time in their movement towards their ultimate end, God.

---

1. William Fahey, Ph.D., "Introduction," *The Church and the Land* (Norfolk, Va.: IHS Press, 2003), p.
11. Sources for Fahey's biographical sketch are identified as, besides McNabb's own works, Ferdinand
Valentine, *Father Vincent McNabb, O.P.: Portrait of a Great Dominican* (London: Burns & Oates, 1955)
and the McNabb issue of *The Chesterton Review* (22 [1–2], 1996).

Aside from his writing on social issues, he frequently engaged the listening public in London on Sundays near Marble Arch in Hyde Park, over the many Sundays between 1920 and 1943. Additionally, there were his frequent appearances at meetings of the Distributist League. Indeed, one witness, present at League functions and activities during its heyday, goes so far as to say that McNabb was not just one of the main inspirers, but perhaps *the* main inspirer, of the Distributist movement founded and championed by Hilaire Belloc and G. K. Chesterton.[1] The tribute to Fr. Vincent offered by this witness, Fr. Brocard Sewell, when writing of his memory of the great Irish and English Dominican, reveals, from the distance of some 30 years, a bit of the "veneration" in which McNabb was held by the Distributists:

> [Fr. McNabb] went as far as he could to reject [machinery's] use in his own life, and urged others – especially those engaged in Distributist back-to-the-land ventures – to do the same. Living in London, he walked everywhere, and never used any form of mechanical transport if he could avoid it. One of the busiest of men, he received a large post every day. Normally he answered every letter on the day he received it, and in his own handwriting. People marveled at the amount of work he got through; but part of the secret was that he never wasted time, as he used to put it, in taking holidays, going to the cinema, listening to the radio, or reading novels. He had long been one of the sights of London – "a piece of old London walking about," as he described himself – since he was unique among his brethren in always wearing publicly the striking black and white habit of the Friars Preachers. In the end he became a national figure; largely on account of the success of his broadcast talks and meditation. He did not enjoy broadcasting, but did this work "under obedience."
>
> Father McNabb was held in great veneration by all Distributists, and no session at The Devereux was complete without a talk by him. When he entered the room everyone rose – a tribute paid to no other speaker except Mr. Chesterton on his rare appearances – and it was the same at the end of the evening, when he left to walk the four miles back to his priory in Hampstead.[2]

Notwithstanding Fr. Vincent's passionate defense of Distributist principles and vision, and the clear embrace that the men in the movement gave him as "one of their own," McNabb frequently – like his contemporary, A. J. Penty – offered the reminder that he was not nearly as keen on labels as he was on principle.[3]

---

1. See Michael Sewell (later Fr. Brocard Sewell), "Father McNabb, the Writer," *The Very Reverend Father Vincent McNabb* (Oxford: Blackfriars, n.d.), p. 25.

2. Fr. Brocard Sewell, "Devereux Nights," in John Sullivan, ed., *G. K. Chesterton: A Centenary Appraisal* (New York: Barnes & Noble Books, 1974), p. 147. [NOTE: The Devereux was where the talks and meetings of the Central London branch of the Distributist League were held on Friday nights.—Ed.]

3. "You must let me withhold either approval or disapproval," McNabb wrote to Sewell on July 11, 1932,

Notwithstanding his fierce intellectual independence, one circle McNabb could not help intimate association with was the community of craftsmen who surrounded Hilary Pepler and Eric Gill at Ditchling, from about 1917 to 1927. The village community of Catholics was, for Fr. Vincent, a living embodiment of the kind of simplicity he saw as characteristic of Nazareth, and it would have had, therefore, the "approval of heaven as the norm for all mankind."[1] In spite of his later regrets that those at Ditchling had been not fully successful at putting "first things first" – one of McNabb's bywords, as we shall see – he nevertheless envisioned it as at least a kind of attempt to put into practice his vision of the importance of the land, of rural life, and of the family liberated, rescued, and sheltered from the materialism, the dehumanization, and the sinfulness of either pampered or cramped urban industrialism. Though the development of life at Ditchling ultimately turned more towards the "hand work" of craftsmanship, and not as much towards the "land work" of sustaining family life on subsistence farm plots, there was the Land Movement of the late '20s and early '30s to accept McNabb's support and spiritual and philosophical patronage.

Msgr. Ronald Knox said McNabb was "the only person I have ever known about whom I have felt, and said more than once, 'He gives you some idea of what a saint must be like.'"[2] Chesterton referred to him as "one of the few great men I have met in my life."[3] Belloc's testimonial to his holiness was concluded with the simple statement: "Never have I seen or known anything on such a scale."[4]

The "Old Principles"

In his introduction to Fr. McNabb's authoritative statement – for a 1932 Catholic Truth Society pamphlet – of the motives of the Catholic Land Movement of the 1920s and '30s, G. K. Chesterton sums up perhaps the whole of

---

"because I am not a Distributist. How often have I said that I am not a *politician*, nor an economist? I have, therefore, no competence to say what is or is not compatible with Distributism. The settling of that question must be left to the Distributists" (Valentine, *op. cit.*, p. 138). This of course had no effect on the Distributists' appreciation for and perception of Fr. McNabb as "one of them," as Sewell's retrospective following McNabb's death so eloquently attests.

1. Hilary Pepler, "Handwork or Landwork," *The Very Reverend Father Vincent McNabb* (Oxford: Blackfriars, n.d.), p. 27.

2. Michael Hennessy, "Father Vincent McNabb: a Voice of Contradiction," http://www.vincentmcnabb.org/contradiction.html, accessed December 1, 2007.

3. "Introduction," *Francis Thompson and Other Essays* (Ditchling: Pepler & Sewell, 1936), p. viii.

4. "To the Undying Memory," *The Very Reverend Father Vincent McNabb* (Oxford: Blackfriars, n.d.), p. 5.

McNabb's approach to the social ills of his day with a reference to his well-known motto:

> Father Vincent McNabb, who has helped innumerable individuals in innumerable ways, has helped his own generation and the whole world especially by fixing and affirming and reaffirming the view which he expresses as putting first things first.

Thus, Chesterton goes on to write, it was eminently suitable that in expounding the motivation of the movement to settle Catholics on the land in family-owned, subsistence farms he expound the issue "in primary or spiritual terms." Not because McNabb was a cleric and should only speak of clerical and therefore spiritual matters, but – and this is the crucial point – because the first fact is "that men are spiritually unhappy, which comes before the fact that they are now economically and materially unhappy."[1] It is clear from this simple assessment that McNabb's approach – spiritual because the spirit is primary, not because of his spiritual office – offers precisely what we are looking for: an articulation of a thorough-going critique of the modern world with its political, social, and economic assumptions, "radical" and fundamental enough to strike at the root of what needs fixing, bypassing and avoiding the useless partisan polemic which keeps the political machine running but does little to affect real change in people's lives.

The aptitude of Fr. McNabb's thought to provide this framework of "radical" critique is further confirmed by his rootedness in the philosophy of St. Thomas: for that philosophy considers, above all, *ends* or purposes, and it is only by understanding the hierarchy or relative importance of purposes that one can properly orient the means used to pursue them.

This, indeed, is the tribute offered by fellow English Dominican Fr. Gerald Vann, O.P., in his brief reminiscence of Fr. Vincent. The tribute is a useful introduction to the underlying ideas of all of Fr. McNabb's social philosophy.

> "In the beginning was the word . . . . In the beginning is always the word. And we know the importance of getting the *right* word. One year's newspapers contain more words than were written in the whole century of St. Thomas. Most of them are useless. Some are diabolical." They are the expression of a world which is wrong, often enough, from the beginning because it is seeking the wrong *end*. "All means are measured. Only the end is unmeasured. External things must be measured by their purpose." Material things are means for human purposes; and human purposes themselves are measured by the ultimate purpose, which is God. The world against which Father Vincent argued reverses this order of values. "The world is going to

1. G. K. Chesterton, "Foreword," *The Catholic Land Movement* (London: The Catholic Truth Society, 1923), p. 3.

pieces because it is seeking things." It is seeking the wrong end; and all its care and benevolence is misplaced as long as it remains the wrong end. This was his great criterion of plans for social reform. "Nowadays the wrong thing is so disguised that people are at pains to do it the right way. A lot of modern energy is spent thus. Things are camouflaged – 'dainty margarine.' Whenever you find a man highly perfumed there's something the matter with him . . . . The Church used to be accused of making the end justify the means. Now the world makes the means justify the end." We must – it was a favourite slogan of his – put first things first. That was just what our civilisation was not doing: it was putting first things last. And it was only towards the very end of his life that the world began to realise it. It took a war to make people realise, as he had long realised, the folly of an economic structure built up on the principle of waste – the corollary of production only for profit instead of for use. (It took a war to make people re-use their envelopes; though for years Father Vincent had been re-using them.) But things done under pressure of war conditions may not outlive the war. Father Vincent was concerned about economics because he was concerned about men's souls. He was concerned about the economics of waste because sooner or later material waste involves the wasting of the spirit. He was concerned with modern commercialised and industrialised urban conditions because often enough they make it impossible for the poor to live a Christian life without heroic virtue – and that is putting an outrageous burden on men and women. He was concerned about the world's attitude to material *things*, because it leads inevitably to subhuman conditions of living and so destroys *human beings*. And so he knew that a social revolution was necessary; but he knew also that a revolution could only do more harm than good, even if the end it aimed at was good, unless it used the right means. "We must do the right thing in the right way. Justice is doing just things justly."[1]

Beginning, then, with this premise – that priorities must be in order; that spiritual happiness must precede material and economic happiness; that, from an explicitly Catholic point of view, spiritual health and the salvation of souls must come before material convenience and the amassing of gadgets; that first things must be put first – we offer the following enumeration of principles neatly and succinctly packaged into a 12-point manifesto which Fr. McNabb called simply "Exodus" – in the spirit of the exodus from the city to the land that he promoted among Catholic families for at least the last thirty years of his priesthood.

1. The "flesh pots of Egypt," which must be given up, are to be left not for the milk and honey of Palestine but that "the people may go and worship God." (Exodus 5.1)

---

1. Fr. Gerald Vann, O.P., "Memior," *An Old Apostle Speaks* (Oxford: Blackfriars, 1946), pp. 4–5.

Here the priority – first things first – becomes clear. The flight from urban life, in our time suburbia – must be motivated by the most sublime of callings, or it is wrongly founded. The flight to the land, so passionately called for by Fr. McNabb as part of a wholesale reconstruction of the social economy, is based primarily on carving out a space for the family to worship God, and, in a more all-encompassing way, we might say to fulfill its duties towards God.

In the same vein we note that Fr. Vincent's pronouncements were never offered as solemn economic or political judgments, but in the best tradition of Aristotle and the thinkers who inherited and built upon his wisdom, as *moral* judgment. His introductory remarks to the last of his major works of social criticism, *Old Principles and the New Order*, offer a rather impregnable defense of this approach, unarguable for Catholics and at least logically coherent for those of good will but not of the Faith:

> The Church is not primarily interested in politics or economics, because neither politics nor economics are primary.
>
> Yet the Church is necessarily and greatly interested in politics and economics because both politics and economics are moral.
>
> This book, therefore, has been written by a priest-teacher of the Church, not as a politician nor as an economist seeking the civil well-being of the State. But it has been written by a theologian whose concern must be for those moral principles which are the necessary root of the civil well-being of the State.[1]

The second point, along with the fourth and eighth, which are related to it:

> 2. To cease to live in the town while continuing to live on the town may be serving Mammon rather than God; indeed may be serving Mammon under the guise of serving God.
>
> 4. Farmers should farm primarily for self-support. They should sell as little and buy as little as possible.
>
> 8. The natural defense of Freedom is the Home; and the natural defense of the Home is the Homestead.

Here McNabb makes an implied reference to the perspective of Catholic social thinkers on the balance and relationship between city and country that has so many profound consequences on the health of the state. To cite even a fraction of the references in this regard is well beyond the scope of this essay, but it should be enough to point out that, dating back to Homer, Cicero, and Aristotle, thinkers in the mainstream Western tradition have considered agriculture to be the primary of the arts. Similarly, that state in which the occupation of citizens in raising the food and primary goods required for the state as a whole has long been considered the most stable

---

1. New York: Sheed and Ward, 1942 (p. xv).

and well constituted. This applies in the broadest sociological way, and in the narrowest, personal way. So we find English Distributists, such as Penty, and other English and American ruralists such as Montague Fordham, H. J. Massingham, and those of the Catholic Rural Life Movement, arguing for national self-sufficiency as opposed to national dependency in agricultural products. And we find Catholic economists and thinkers such as C. S. Devas considering the problem – as Mc Nabb does – on the level of the family, pointing out the importance for individual families, as well as the stability of the state, of a social order consisting predominantly of families owning and inhabiting their largely self-sufficient homesteads.[1] Thus McNabb argues for a network of families in the country on their own homesteads as constituting the essential social fabric: capable of providing a spiritual environment where the virtues are able to flourish; part of a self-sufficient nation where the products required for it come from within it, rather than without, thus supporting local farmers and industries and not sacrificing them to outsourced labor and foreign multinationals.

This approach is also the key to rectifying man's economic maladies and dislocations. The dedication of the greater part of human manpower to the production of "primary goods," the food, clothing, fuel, and shelter that man needs to sustain life will help to focus craft know-how upon the basic means of human sustenance, so that the nation, the local community, or even, in a certain way, the family can attain a level of self-sufficiency that would establish them as stable and coherent communities. Problems of employment also take on a new perspective when we consider that Fr. McNabb, with Penty and other of the Distributist thinkers such as Kenrick and Robbins, were arguing for the employment of men and families on the land, making primary goods, as an alternative to keeping them on the dole or letting them starve as part of the unemployed masses.

Always the Dominican, McNabb elsewhere cites the political teaching of St. Thomas, from *De Regno*, to advance this view that the self-sufficient society and local community, especially in regard to the production of "primary goods," is the best form of human society. Citing from Chapter III of the *De Regno*, McNabb quotes St. Thomas:

> The more a thing is found to be self-sufficient the better it is; because what needs another is clearly wanting . . . . Therefore it is better for a city if it has a sufficiency of things from its own lands, than if it should be exposed to commerce.

To this St. Thomas himself adds the authority of Aristotle who stated that "it is more fitting that the citizens should be occupied outside cities, than that

---

1. Charles S. Devas, s.v., "Agrarianism," *Catholic Encyclopedia* (New York: Robert Appleton Company, 1907–12; online edition K. Knight, 2003).

they should dwell always within the city walls." Here we see how McNabb, in advocating a flourishing agrarian life of self-sufficient agricultural, predominantly family units, adopts and applies the Aristotelian-Thomistic social, political, and economic tradition.

Further, essential principles that form further bases for the discussion of self-sufficiency are the following:

3. The area of production should be as far as possible coterminous with the area of consumption. The utilitarians were wrong in saying "things should be produced where they can be most economically produced." *The true principle is: things should be produced where they can most economically be consumed.*

5. "Big" farming is mass production applied to the land. Agricultural mass production is based on the Market, depends on Transport and, together with these is controlled by Finance.

Here we have one of the McNabb observations that is rather priceless. Production is not for profit: it is for consumption. A fundamentally different way of considering economic activity than that to which we are accustomed. The lynchpin of the effort towards self-sufficiency. If middle men, markets, and elaborate exchange mechanisms are taken out of the basic wealth-generation, exchange, and distribution mechanisms; if the eggs can come from the henhouse into the kitchen rather than from the mechanized dairy farm via the refrigerated truck into the hyper-market, this will be a true victory for the simple, sane, and spiritually healthy life. It is this to which Fr. McNabb dedicated his life, and this to which we must return if we will know true peace and spiritual health – and even physical health as well, as the modern organic and health foods movements are finally learning, even if they are behind Fr. Vincent by several generations.

We also find here an echo of the "anti-machinery" position that Fr. McNabb was thought to have adopted by some of his Distributist colleagues, though to over-simplify it in that fashion would be to fail to put "first things first." For him the question wasn't an abstract one of pro- or anti-machine, but of whether additional mechanization and mass-production would help to keep individual families on the largely self-sufficient homestead, or whether it would facilitate their flight to the cities. He wasn't the only one with this concern. We've already referred to A. J. Penty, who was *the* thinker on the machine question within Distributist circles. And from among the Southern Agrarians, for instance, we are reminded by Dr. Fahey, in his recent introduction, just how similar McNabb's concern was to that of Andrew Lytle, a respected, if somewhat neglected Southern Agrarian thinker, as expressed in his essay, "The Hind Tit," for the celebrated anthology *I'll Take My Stand*:

How is the man who is living on the land ... going to defend himself against this industrial imperialism and its destructive technology? One common answer is heard: industrialize the farm; be progressive; drop old-fashioned ways and adopt scientific methods . . . . Such admonition coming from the quarters of the enemy is encouraging to the land-owner in one sense only: it assures him that he has something left to steal . . . . *A farm is not a place to grow wealthy; it is a place to grow corn* [emphasis added].[1]

Additional points of the "McNabb Manifesto" emphasize simple truths of traditional and Catholic social thought, dating back to the Fathers of the Church and to Our Lord himself. All of these are consistent with, and support, his vision of the independent family on the land. They need little comment, but they are essential philosophical underpinnings for the social order that he advocates.

6. A man's state is not measured by his wealth; but a man's wealth is measured by his state. Hence, as state is social position based on social service, it follows that a man's wealth is measured by his social service.

9. As Political Economy is the child of Domestic Economy, all laws that weaken the Home weaken the nation.

10. The Family, not the individual, is the unit of the nation.

I have singled out the following principle for special mention because of its importance today among self-styled "conservatives" who are quite prepared to pay lip service to the institution of property while sacrificing its application to the God of competition on the altar of *laissez faire.*

7. The divine right of Property means not that some men shall have all property, but that all men shall have some property.

The consistency of this statement with the teaching of the Popes, particularly in encyclicals such as *Quadragesimo Anno,* may be surprising, but if so it is not because the teaching is not one approved by the Church but because the approved teaching is so little known and heeded. Some might find the statement to be revolutionary, but, if it is, it is in the sense that Fr. Vann and the writers in *Integrity* magazine called for a social revolution to subordinate economic conditions to the needs of the common man. A plan that would doubtless be welcomed by the masses but potentially unpalatable to those wishing to hang onto more than their fair share.

The remaining two points of Fr. Vincent's twelve are the following:

11. There are only Things and Tokens. The world-wide economic crisis, if it exists, is a dearth of things, not of tokens.

12. Now a dearth of things cannot be met by the creation or redistribution of tokens. A dearth of things can be met only by a creation or redistribution of things.[2]

---

1. *I'll Take My Stand: The South and the Agrarian Tradition* (Baton Rouge and London: Louisiana State University Press, 1977), pp. 204–205.

2. *Francis Thompson & Other Essays* (Ditchling: Pepler & Sewell, 1936), p. 74; cf. an earlier version in

These two, it will be clear, focus upon the distinction, made by St. Thomas and others, between "real" and "artificial" wealth; between things that are immediately useful to us, and things (tokens) that are useless except insofar as they can be exchanged for the former. Without an understanding of that distinction, and an application of it to policy, no human-scale and healthy economic and social restructuring is possible.

. . . And Their Application

The problems Fr. McNabb was addressing in the 1920s and 1930s were real; for example, the rapid decline of Catholic cultural life and practice in the urban milieu of England and America, along with the lower birthrates which were causing the Catholic portion of the citizenry in Britain and America to plummet relative to the overall growth in population. In support of this, he cited, for instance, American Archbishop Edwin O'Hara, who documented the demographic fact that the general population of the United States had increased by 17% from 1906 to 1916, while the Catholic Church increased its numbers by only 10% during the same period. This was compared to a 19% increase in membership in Protestant churches. Fr. McNabb's answer to these very concrete problems was simple: Catholic families must return to the land if they are to serve as the building blocks of a restored Christian Order. This advice to the Catholics of the 1920s, '30s, and early '40s was not merely a matter of demography, but a grave moral concern, since he continually asserts that modern urban life is a proximate occasion of sin.

It is, once again, in the informative introduction by Dr. Fahey to the modern edition of *The Church and the Land* that we find an answer to the question that continually surrounds the agrarian answer to many of the modern world's problems: "How can this pleasing vision of the way society ought to be, be realized in the lives of real men and women in our own age?" In answer to this question, Fahey provides us with a summary of the concrete results of the agrarian Catholic Land Movement as it really existed both in Britain and the United States prior to World War II. Between 1926 and 1930, 14,000 men formally applied for smallholding grants with the British Ministry of Agriculture. Confronted with the economic catastrophe of 1929–30, some 26,000 men took advantage of temporary government subsidies to move from urban areas to farming properties. According to the statistics he cites, some 73% of these transplanted city-dwellers remained on the land as successful small-holding farmers. The efforts in England, Wales,

---

From a Friar's Cell (New York, 1924), p. 117.

and Scotland were encouraged by Popes Pius XI and Pius XII and a host of Catholic intellectuals. The race to the rural was even more impressive in the United States. Here, between the years 1930 and 1932, some 764,000 moved from the city to the countryside to take up life on the land.[1]

By quoting from St. Thomas Aquinas's *De Regno* and by continually citing Pope Leo XIII's statement in *Rerum Novarum* that "The law should favor ownership. Its policy should be to induce as many as possible of the humbler classes to become owners," Fr. McNabb firmly sets his agrarian vision within the intellectual tradition of the Catholic world. The palpable and enticing goals set by Fr. McNabb, the American Catholic Rural Life Movement, the British Catholic Land Movement, and the Distributist League were instrumental in reviving an appreciation, in the first half of the 20th century, for the traditional political outlook of the Catholic Church that emphasized subsidiarity (i.e., a decentralized political and economic order)[2] and the common good. Understanding himself to be only following a path cut by the great doctors of the Catholic past and, specifically, responding to the cry in *Rerum Novarum* that "a remedy must be found, and found quickly," we are not surprised that, in this context, Fr. McNabb explicitly denies that he is a part of any political movement. Rather, he understood himself to be a pastor of souls who was urging families to find a life in harmony with nature, a life where work, worship, intellectual leisure, and family life were all of a cloth, for the good of their bodies and their souls. As he noted in *The Church and the Land*:

> If the thoughts and hopes that have inspired [this book] do not inspire some of our readers, the book will have been written in vain. Indeed, not only will the writing of the book, but even the many years of life and thought behind the book, will have been in vain. To find no one answering our Call to Contemplatives will seem to give the lie to one of our deepest and most mature convictions.[3]

In this quotation from the first chapter (which he insists should also be read as the last chapter), entitled "A Call to Contemplatives," of his first important, book-length work outlining his social vision, Fr. McNabb states that what he is calling for is an exodus, an exodus from the modern techno-urban versions of the "flesh-pots" of Egypt to the land "flowing with milk and honey." (Hence the title for his 12-point manifesto.) In order to clarify for his reader what he intends by this "call" and his reasons for drawing this comparison between the flight of the Israelites from captivity in Egypt to the "wilderness" of Sinai and the back-to-the-land movement that he cham-

---

1. Ralph Borsodi, *Flight from the City: An Experiment in Creative Living on the Land* (New York, 1933), p. xxii.

2. See also my essay in the present volume, Chapter 12.—Ed.

3. *The Church and the Land, op. cit.*, p. 31.

pioned, McNabb emphasizes that it is, ultimately, only for a religious motive
that anyone would desert the cities for the difficult life of the country or remain on the land in spite of the financial enticements of the suburbs or the
city. We might expand that description of motive, today, to include a broader
philosophical, ideological, and sociological sense – particularly for those not
of the Catholic faith – of the crusade to preserve humane values and traditions in an increasingly materialistic and mechanized world. In pointing out
that the Israelites left Egypt not to inherit a land of "milk and honey," but to
"worship God," McNabb preached in 1925 what other Catholics would have
heard at a much later date from another "uncompromisingly" traditional
cleric. In his Priestly Jubilee Sermon on September 23, 1979, Archbishop
Marcel Lefebvre stated, in addressing the lay faithful:

> And I wish that, in these troubled times, in this degenerate urban atmo-
> sphere in which we are living, that you return to the land whenever possible.
> The land is healthy; the land teaches one to know God; the land draws one
> to God; it calms temperaments, characters, and encourages the children to
> work.[1]

Throughout his writing, Fr. McNabb provides examples of the moral
compromises that almost inevitably follow from life in the urban/suburban
world of contemporary cities. What we see in McNabb's advocacy of the back-
to-the-land movement in England was not merely a practical moral solution
to real human problems, but a general questioning of the progressive nature
of our contemporary liberal, consumerist, and technology-dominated world.
In his "Attempt at a Social Balance Sheet," included in *The Church and the
Land*, McNabb challenges us by forcing us to look at the damage done to
normal human life by industrialism and urbanization. How many families
have their own homes? How many workers live over their work? How many
mothers go out to work? How many children are in the average family?

These are questions which the modern manipulators of mass opinion insist do not matter. But they do matter, not only for depression-era urban
workers, but for ourselves in this micro age. Are we not continually saying
that milieu matters? Is it not the case that the whole reason for re-establish-
ing Christendom, other than to make everything a footstool of Our Lord
Jesus Christ, is to make the external society more conducive to living the
life of virtue, both natural and supernatural? Does the technology-based
urban system, which is expanding every day, incline us and ours to the life
that God wishes us to live? Does it provide us with the daily food for contemplation from which a stable life of human nobility and meritorious acts
of natural and supernatural virtue flow?

---

1. Fr. François Laisney, preface and ed., *The Collected Works of His Excellency Archbishop Marcel Lefebvre* (Dickinson, Tx.: The Angelus Press, 1985), p. 10.

Fr. McNabb's answer is clearly "No." It is a "No" that has the potential to shake the inhuman economic system which daily forces men and women to sacrifice the normal so that a few rich men may increase their profits. The way in which McNabb's critique throws into question the foundations of the current economic system is by focusing on the fact that the modern capitalist industrial economy, and certainly all of the socialist economies that have been known, concentrate human effort and manpower on the production of what Fr. McNabb calls "secondary goods." Insert into the equation the elaborate mechanism of middle-men; proxy trading, derivatives, and elaborate exchange mechanisms that must be managed by computer rather than men; corporate takeovers; the infrastructure of not just the welfare state but the welfare corporation; the outsourcing of jobs, production, factories, and services to lands far from their areas of primary consumption; the decline of quality and personal service and its substitution by cheap, plastic junk and impersonal and uncaring "interaction"; and the widespread, nay, the pervasive non-owning status of people in terms not just of productive property but even the major consumption good, i.e., the home – and with all this you have a clear picture that the principled critique made by Fr. McNabb was, to use an apt metaphor, "right on the money," and if its relevance has changed at all since it was first made, it has only increased. Indeed it was precisely the "relevance" of St. Dominic to McNabb's life and thought that earned him praise from editor of the English Dominican journal *Blackfriars*, for having shown how St. Dominic was still "up to date" in his lifetime. "The true contemplative is always contemporary," he noted; for "the contemplative preacher applies eternity to his own times."[1]

Why encourage "contemplatives," then, to rediscover the land in the first decade of the 21st century? Shouldn't we leave them alone lest they hurt themselves? Does it help the advancement of the perennial philosophical tradition of the Church, that thinking men and women know what feed grain is needed for a ewe in her last period of gestation? Yes, it does. If the realism of St. Thomas is to be more to us than a system of remote abstractions, no matter how true, we must continually refer back to the natural realities that generated the concepts in the first place. It is not to be forgotten that the primary referent for Aristotelian philosophy is *organic* being. In the farm yard there is no Cartesian "pure extension."

---

1. "To the Undying Memory," *The Very Reverend Father Vincent McNabb* (Oxford: Blackfriars, n.d.), p. 5.

"*I believe we would now be justified in defining the so-called Agrarian Movement not only in terms of its first gropings and tentative beginning, but also in terms of its ultimate broader direction and general fruitfulness of application. For brevity, I might call it the cause of civilized society, as we have known it in the Western World, against the new barbarism of science and technology controlled and directed by the modern power state. In this sense, the cause of the South was and is the cause of Western civilization itself.*"

—DONALD DAVIDSON

~7~

Capitalism and Distributism

Two Systems at War

Thomas Storck

> Capitalism no more means the affirmation of an individual, or a
> family's right to possess land, machinery, housing, clothing, reserves
> of food and the rest, than fatty degeneration of the heart means the
> normal function of the heart as the circulator of the blood in a healthy
> human body.
>
> —Hilaire Belloc, *The Crisis of Civilization*

WHAT IS THE DIFFERENCE BETWEEN **D**ISTRIBUTISM and capitalism? To approach this question we must first know what Distributism and capitalism *are*. Usually those who favor capitalism, and who simply assume that it is the most desirable, or even the only, economic system, do not bother to *define* it. Perhaps they think it is co-extensive with private ownership of property, or that anything that is not socialism is therefore capitalism.

I

ECONOMISTS AND ECONOMIC historians have often struggled to define capitalism precisely. Robert Heilbroner wrote, "*What is capitalism?* That is the profound and perplexing problem . . . . "[1] Other writers, such as Amintore Fanfani, have struggled to evaluate the many and varying attempts to define it.[2]

But without tracing all these efforts in detail, let us turn instead to a definition that is given by a preeminently authoritative source, and which meets

---

1. Robert Heilbroner, *The Nature and Logic of Capitalism* (New York: W.W. Norton, 1985), p. 14.

2. See Amintore Fanfani, *Catholicism, Protestantism, and Capitalism* (Norfolk, Va.: IHS Press, 2003).

the criteria for precision and historical accuracy. This is the definition given by Pope Pius XI in his 1931 encyclical *Quadragesimo Anno* (§100): "[T]hat economic system, wherein, generally, some provide capital while others provide labor for a joint economic activity."[1] In other words, capitalism is the economic system in which, *for the most part*, some people provide the capital – i.e., the financing or the productive property or both – for an enterprise, and others provide the labor, in exchange for wages paid to them by the former.

This definition of capitalism gets at its essence as an economic arrangement in which ownership is separated from work. A few brief and somewhat random thoughts under this subhead will illustrate a few of the evils that have arisen, and in my view always will, from any capitalist form of the economy, where work and ownership are separated.

In essence, it is my contention that these evils revolve around a single defect, flowing directly from the work-ownership divide. And that defect is this: the separation between work and the ownership of productive property (or simply the ownership of financial wealth in lieu of physical property) tends to liberate the appetite for amassing wealth from the natural limits attached to it when that wealth is acquired by an individual with his own labor applied to his own productive property. Further, because human work of its very nature tends not to the production and amassing of unlimited riches, but towards the production of specific goods in order to satisfy given human needs, it is limited – or given a defined purpose – by those needs that it aims to fulfill. The creation or amassing of wealth accomplished by ownership and manipulation alone of factories, businesses, and financial instruments, because they are separated from the labor that makes the possession of such things productive, is of its nature virtually without limit. For these things can be, and tend to be, manipulated, traded, managed and operated for the single purpose of amassing ever-greater financial wealth. The satisfaction of particular material needs is only an incidental or even trivial by-product of this kind of activity, and as such there is no "natural" or built-in limit to this kind of wealth creation. If the purpose is simply to make money, and amass wealth, there is no automatic and objectively verifiable point – as there is with personal labor coupled with a modest share of productive property jointly engaged in a specific enterprise to meet a real and specific need – at which this purpose can be said to be fulfilled and the operation therefore cease. Thus, both the different means employed and the different ends pursued by these two kinds of "wealth creation" necessarily give rise to radically different outcomes.

---

1. Translations and paragraph numbers of these and future citations from papal encyclicals are from the Vatican editions, http://www.vatican.va.

The propensity of ownership divorced from labor to seek after an unlimited accumulation of wealth constitutes what some have called the "spirit" or "essence" of the capitalist system. Let us explore a few of the related concepts here, before contrasting the drawbacks and dangers of this system and its spirit with its modest, natural and healthy Distributist alternative.

We see this spirit at work most clearly in the business corporation, which is the most perfect kind of capitalism. Here ownership is entirely separated from work, for the stockholders are often unaware of the activities of the firms they legally own, of their products, labor policies, political activities, or foreign ventures. As long as stock prices are rising or dividends are satisfactory, most have no desire whatsoever to know about these things. The managers – theoretically hired hands, like the shop workers – actually run the organization. But, like the stockholders, they are not really focused on the product. That is why manipulation of stock prices, buyouts, takeovers, and such behavior is so attractive to them – it is an easier and faster way of making money than the tiresome work of manufacturing and selling a real product. And what of the firm's product? Yes, that is necessary, but these stockowners and managers do not focus primarily on producing useful and well-made products to fulfill a human need, but merely upon products that can be sold. Put succinctly, if a product is badly made and serves no real and useful purpose, *but sells*, then it will be pushed for all it's worth.

Contrast this attitude with that of a traditional craftsman. It is true that he hopes to make a living by selling his product, but he usually also has concern for its quality, a love for his material, and a feel for his art. A corporation does not. The product is necessary only because of the money it produces. The corporation does not ask, "Is this something useful and good that people need?" but rather, "Can we convince people to buy this and thus make money?" For if one accepts that the inherent purpose of economic activity is to produce the goods and services necessary or useful for a truly human life, then it is *production* that is of the *essence* of economic activity. But if my chief concern is not production for use, but simply *moneymaking*, then my whole focus changes. I no longer care what is made or how much of it, as long as it is profitable.

If a society sees economic activity as a human activity directed towards the specific end or purpose of fulfilling its need for goods and services, then it will tend to erect safeguards – legal, social, customary – to channel economic activity towards those ends. As soon as a society forgets that economic activity has such an end, then the mere acquisition of wealth implicitly and automatically takes its place.

Of course, a necessary and important by-product of production is the support of the producer. Everyone who understands that economic activity exists for the provision of necessary and helpful goods and services also recognizes that the producer must make a living by the use or sale of the thing that he makes. So there exists another end or purpose of economic activity: the maintenance of the producer. Yet there is a limit inherent in all this, namely: how much one needs to support oneself and one's family in a human fashion, in the "frugal comfort" of which Leo XIII spoke in his 1891 *Rerum Novarum* (*RN*).

However, capitalism has its own spirit, one that regards wealth not as a necessary means to supply our earthly needs, but as something to be increased beyond measure. By "beyond measure" I mean, as noted above, something precise, for the correct measure of a man's earthly needs is man himself. Thus, for example, a man can eat only so much food in a day. If he wanted three times as much food every day as he could properly eat, he would be desiring to multiply his possession of food beyond the proper measure. Every man needs a dwelling. Perhaps some few could argue that they need more than one. Yet undoubtedly at some point any *legitimate* need for more houses would be passed. A man who desires, say, four houses, is in most contexts obviously asking for more than he really needs. And so with the rest of our property. Material things exist to satisfy reasonable human *needs*, not unlimited human *wants*. Or as Saint Thomas Aquinas put it, "[T]he appetite of natural riches is not infinite, because according to a set measure they satisfy nature; but the appetite of artificial riches [i.e., money] is infinite, because it serves inordinate concupiscence . . . . "[1] Fanfani summarizes Catholic teaching on wealth acquisition as follows:

> Man has necessities, needs that must be satisfied, and, if temporal goods can satisfy them, it is a duty and legitimate to seek to acquire such goods, bearing in mind two rules, first that they must be acquired by lawful means, secondly that the amount acquired must not exceed the need.[2]

Thus, as soon as we divorce ownership from work, given fallen human nature's propensities, we create a society in which wealth no longer is seen as having a purpose other than itself, and the real economic needs of society are subordinated to the pure freedom to engage in limitless and socially useless *wealth acquisition*. These results, whether one considers them positive or negative, are inevitable, and many conceive them to be part of the essence of capitalism. This limitless acquisition of abstract wealth was one of Belloc's main concerns:

> [W]ealth obtained indirectly as profit out of other men's work, or by exchange, becomes a thing abstracted from the process of production. As the

---

1. See St. Thomas Aquinas, *Summa Theologiæ*, II, I, Q. 2, A. 1, ad 3.
2. Fanfani, *op. cit.*, p. 128.

interest of a man in *things* diminishes, his interest in abstract wealth – money – increases. The man who makes a table or grows a crop makes the success of the crop or the table a test of excellence. The intermediary who buys and sells the crop or the table is not concerned with the goodness of table or crop, but with the profit he makes between their purchase and resale. In a productive society the superiority of the thing produced is the measure of success: in a commercial society the amount of wealth accumulated by the dealer is the measure of success.[1]

Nor is it only those who own the means of production who exemplify the effects of capitalism, for the separation of ownership from work creates a permanent class of non-owning workers, a circumstance frequently deplored by the popes,[2] and one that inevitably exacerbates class conflict. This situation produces men alienated from their work and dulled in spirit. For under capitalism some men become mere tools of those who are the owners of capital.

The *Wall Street Journal* carried an article on the growing practice of factories operating 24 hours a day, seven days a week. The article spoke of a Mr. Herman Lea, a part-time Protestant preacher, who had hoped to become a regular pastor, but whose schedule and life were entirely disrupted by the factory's new work schedule.[3]

Mr. Lea and his co-workers at Goodyear have inadvertently discovered the unspoken reality of manufacturing: increasingly it is structured around the machines, rather than the people who run them. The reason is said to be "economics." Every hour a costly plant sits idle is a drain on the company's bottom line, something no one can afford in the face of today's sharply slowing domestic economy and the aggressive competition of many foreign countries.

Compounding the new schedule is Goodyear's move to 12-hour shifts, which is common when companies go non-stop. Mr. Lea gets more days off with the longer shifts, but the longer workday is far more grueling for the 50 year-old. Moreover, his days off vary each week, further complicating his life. He had a stroke in February, which he blames partly on the stress of juggling his schedule.

The making of economic activity into a relentless pursuit of riches – i.e., the "bottom line" – clearly and unavoidably has deleterious effects on work-

---

1. Hilaire Belloc, *An Essay on the Nature of Contemporary England* (New York: Sheed & Ward, 1937), p. 67.

2. Leo XIII stated "The law . . . should favor ownership, and its policy should be to induce as many people as possible to become owners" (*Rerum Novarum*, §46). See also *Rerum Novarum*, §13; *Quadragesimo Anno*, §§59–63; *Mater et Magistra*, §§112–115; *Laborem Exercens*, §14.

3. Timothy Aeppel, "Juggling Act: More Plants Go 24/7, and Workers Are Left at Sixes and Sevens," *The Wall Street Journal*, July 24, 2001, p. A1.

ers and illustrates capitalism in action: not only the frequent financial exploitation of workers, but the insistence that they structure their entire lives, and that of their families, around the economic process.

I am not suggesting that the separation of labor from capital, of ownership from work, is *in itself* and in the abstract unjust. Pius XI says, in the very next paragraph, "the system as such is not to be condemned." If such separation were in itself wrong, then an elderly woman would do wrong were she to hire the teenager next door to mow her grass or paint her porch with *her* lawnmower or *her* paint and brush. For in this case she supplies the capital and he the labor. Any society always includes some economic activity of this type, where one party supplies the capital and the other the labor. This separation of capital and labor, however, does present a difficulty when it becomes the dominant form of economic activity, setting the tone for the whole of society, and when the separation is rigid, i.e., where instead of *a portion* of the capital necessary for an enterprise is supplied by an individual or firm other than the laborers, *all* of the capital is typically provided by one entity, and the laborers provide *only* their labor.

If what I have said is accepted, then we can better understand capitalism's effects in practice, or what is sometimes called the "spirit of capitalism." Here is Fanfani's pertinent description:

> Modern man, who is capitalistic, regards wealth as the best means for an ever more complete satisfaction of every conceivable need; he also regards it as the best means for improving his own position. He considers goods as instruments to be used *ad libitum* by their possessor. He does not recognize any claim on them on the part of third parties not their possessors, still less does he think it unlawful for their possessor to use them so as to obtain an unlimited increase or their reproduction at ever diminishing cost.[1]

To regard it as lawful or even laudable to increase wealth without measure flows naturally from the separation of ownership and work. For work, as the production of goods and services, is naturally oriented toward the fulfillment of human needs, whereas the accumulation of wealth has no natural orientation except the satisfaction of potentially unlimited desires. *Gain has no natural limit.* But to allow moneymaking to assume such a prominent place in human life and society is to divorce man from any inherent limits and ultimately to allow his culture to become permeated with a commercialism that subordinates everything to economic activity. A capitalist economic system will invariably result in the commercialization of the entire society, not merely in the economic field but in every conceivable field – social, moral and religious. Why? Because the economy will be focused not on

---

1. Fanfani, *op. cit.*, p. 22.

the production of goods and services for use, something inseparable from man's life on earth, but increasingly on the mere acquisition of wealth. Moneymaking becomes the keynote of society. As has been truly noted, "society itself becomes an 'adjunct' of the market."[1]

It is no surprise that capitalism and the commercial order that it brought about has changed more than the economic system. Like a leaven working its way through dough, the separation of ownership from work allows society to turn its almost exclusive attention toward economic gain. Fulfilling human needs via economic activity is now important only since it produces gain, for gain itself has become the sole social good. But a society in which the principle of limitless gain was not victorious would look very different.

Seen from the vantage point of our habits engendered by our thoroughly industrialized society, it is hard even to imagine life in countries not yet industrialized, at least to the same degree. Spain is a good example of the latter. Holidays, saints' days, local fiestas lasting for several days, family celebrations, and so on, have at least as great an impact on the course of life as work and "efficiency-mindedness." Next to work rhythm there is also a leisure rhythm, not in the sense of "rest from work," but as a characteristic of the outlook on existence.[2]

But America is a society shackled to work, in that it knows no other purpose for human existence.[3] Contemplation is no more characteristic of it than it was of Soviet labor camps. The very justification for private property in our society and in a traditional society differs. Consider the famous statement of Leo XIII about private property:

> Men always work harder and more readily when they work on that which is their own; nay, they learn to love the very soil which yields in response to the labor of their hands, not only food to eat, but an abundance of the good things for themselves and those that are dear to them (*RN*, §47).

But we would try in vain to discover how an owner of stock could ever "learn to love the very" shares which yield, not "an abundance of good things," but a dividend check or a capital gain, in response to the labor of someone else's hands. Instead of an economy devoted to meeting real human needs, we have an economy devoted to making money in any way possible, with ownership, control, and labor separated to the detriment of all three.

---

1. Ellen Meiksins Wood, "From Opportunity to Imperative: the History of the Market," *Monthly Review* 46 (30), 1994, p. 20.

2. Thomas Molnar, *Authority and Its Enemies* (New Rochelle, N.Y.: Arlington House, 1976), p. 76.

3. See Juliet B. Schor, *The Overworked American: the Unexpected Decline of Leisure* (New York: Basic Books, 1992) and John de Graaf, ed., *Take Back Your Time: Fighting Overwork and Time Poverty in America* (San Francisco: Berrett-Koehler, 2003).

When ownership and work are joined, many evils are reduced or eliminated, while many good things flourish more easily. Property is seen for what it is, a means of support for men and their families, not something whose aim is to facilitate financial speculation that results in the disruption of the stability of neighborhood, parish, and family. Property is simply not synonymous with money. No one who looks at his land as potential cold cash could ever "learn to love the very soil which yields in response to the labor of their hands . . . an abundance of the good things for themselves and those that are dear to them." These are fundamentally different ways of viewing property, and in fact of viewing life as a whole.

The remedy, then, for this dysfunctional system, ultimately productive of instability, is simply the reconnecting of ownership, control, and work as much as practicable. For that we need the Distributist order that Chesterton, Belloc and many others labored to bring about.

II

THE WORD *DISTRIBUTISM* is unfamiliar to most people, as is the notion that there is any alternative to capitalism except socialism or communism. There are many reasons for this supposition. The major extrinsic reason is that in our public discourse it has been not merely assumed but actively propagated for decades that capitalism and socialism (or communism) are the only choices available to peoples and nations. There is a major intrinsic reason as well. Both capitalism and socialism (or communism) inhabit the same economic world. They have roughly the same goals, at least in theory: productive efficiency and equity. As regards efficiency, they differ greatly about means; as regards equity, they differ about means and to some extent about ends. But the upholders of each system understand each other. They are after the same things in different ways. This truth is brought out fully in these words of Msgr. Fulton Sheen:

> The Church agrees with some of the protests of communism. In fact, there is a far better critique of the existing economic order based on the primacy of profit in two Encyclicals of Leo XIII and Pius XI than there is in all the writings of Marx. But the reforms of communism are wrong, because they are inspired by the very errors they combat. Communism begins with the liberal and capitalistic error that man is economic, and, instead of correcting it, merely intensifies it until man becomes a robot in a vast economic machine. There is a closer relation between communism and monopolistic capitalism than most minds suspect. They are agreed

on the materialistic basis of civilization; they disagree only on who shall control that basis, capitalists or bureaucrats.[1]

Both socialism and capitalism are products of the European Enlightenment (at least in their overt forms) and are thus modernizing and anti-traditional forces. In contrast, Distributism seeks to subordinate economic activity to human life as a whole, to our spiritual life, our intellectual life, our family life. It does not regard the mere production of goods, still less the acquisition of wealth, as ends in themselves. Such a traditional view regards society neither as an "adjunct of the market" nor as the embodiment of the Marxist workers' paradise. As a result, from a traditional Christian standpoint, both socialism and capitalism are reductionist attempts to subject all human life and society to an essentially economic principle of organization.[2]

Traditional societies did not look upon something from a purely economic standpoint just because it generated material wealth. Contrast this with the economic tradition stemming from Adam Smith in the case of, e.g., property. That tradition has not asked many questions about what property *is* apart from its use in exchange. Land, real property, movable goods, as well as such intangible surrogates for real economic goods as currency, shares of stock, futures contracts, stock options, etc., are all considered property and *equally so*. None is primary. None is the paradigm for property. Since each can be legally owned and exchanged according to their monetary value, they are basically equivalents. Land is nothing special. An ancestral home or farm has no more worth than stock options of equal monetary value. Property is nothing except a form of money-value embodied in any of various objects.

What follows from this? Since property is interchangeable, it comes to be seen as existing for the sake of exchange, and exchange is facilitated by having no emotional, familial or social attachment to any particular piece of property. Attachments like this are considered uneconomic, and therefore causes of economic inefficiency. If I am unwilling to sell my farm at an excellent price, because my grandfather is buried on it, or because I do not wish to subject the neighboring farmers to a suburban housing development, I am, it is claimed, clearly acting against my own economic self-interest and thus against the rationale of capitalist economic thinking. When property is seen as a collection of things of different types that we

---

1. Fulton J. Sheen, *Communism and the Conscience of the West* (Indianapolis and New York: The Bobbs-Merrill Company, 1948), pp. 80–1.

2. This is akin to what John Paul II calls "the error of economism," that is, "of considering human labor solely according to its economic purpose." See *Laborem Exercens*, §13.

may use to enrich ourselves, why does it matter who owns it, provided that it does its job? Thus capitalists do not blush when property becomes concentrated largely in the hands of the rich,[1] and communists do not blush when property becomes concentrated largely in the hands of the government. Property in both systems has no meaning except its cash value, so the only questions about ownership are questions of so-called efficiency: how to get the most wealth or equity out of it, how to prevent poverty or redistribute wealth. Capitalists and communists differ about which system best produces efficiency and equity, but they agree that these are the only relevant questions. According to its exponents, capitalism makes as much of an equity claim as socialism, in that it sees itself as the best means for eliminating poverty and raising the general level of wealth.

But if we look at property differently, we see that there are alternatives to these terrible twins. If we see property as existing not merely to facilitate exchange and wealth-creation, but as part of a society where other things, such as worship of God, love of family, cultivation of the intellect and the fine arts, are paramount, and where material goods and services are seen as something that is *for the sake of* those more important goods, we will see that property must be looked at as *more than economic*. Then we might begin to make distinctions about different sorts of property based on something other than monetary values.

For example, there are many reasons for thinking that land is not simply another form of property, but a *special* form of property. On the purely economic level, the amount of land is essentially fixed. Secondly, if land is rendered useless or harmful, for example, by ruining it with chemicals or toxic waste, although theoretically it can be cleaned up, often this process is extremely difficult and expensive, and in the case of nuclear waste, might take centuries. Thirdly, land is the precondition not only for almost any other economic activity, but for any kind of human activity. Moreover, farming, and any work directly dependent on the land, like raising animals, does not fit the capitalist free market paradigm which is based on commercial activity. For example, farms cannot be moved to cheaper locations like factories, and they are heavily dependent on non-economic factors, like weather. Thus Leo XIII's famous statement that "the earth, though divided among private owners, ceases not thereby to minister to the needs of all; for there is no one who does not live on what the land brings forth" (*RN*, §8).

---

1. Between 1980 and 1999 the "percent distribution of aggregate income" received by the lowest 20% of the U.S. population fell from 5.3% to 4.3%, while the percentage received by the top 5% rose from 14.6% to 20.3%. During the same period the percent received by the highest 20% rose from 41.1% to 47.2%. *Statistical Abstract of the United States* (Washington: Government Printing Office, 2001), table 670.

Thus looking only at economic arguments, land is not the same as, say, stock certificates. This is confirmed for us if we look beyond economic considerations. Nor, in doing so, are we moving from the realm of facts or reason to that of "values" or emotions. Only if we regard man as purely an economic being who realizes his true self in producing and consuming alone, can we think that it is solely economic motives which a hard-headed person ought to attend to, and that everything else is simply the subjective province of poets or dreamy clerics.

What is man's life for? A Christian can hardly say that it is for the amassing of goods. On the contrary, Our Lord said, "A man's life does not consist in the abundance of his possessions" (St. Luke xii:15). Rather, it is our spiritual life, our intellectual life, our family and community life, in which human good really consists. But if this is so, then the external goods that mankind undoubtedly needs ought to facilitate these. For instance, family life is easier if a family can stay in one place, if its extended family can grow up naturally around it, if it can be part of the same parish and community. If land is simply seen as one among other economic goods, to be sold at will for the greatest gain, then the likelihood of such stable communities and neighborhoods is greatly reduced.

Moreover, what is true of land is true of all property that directly subserves a truly human life. Just as we are all dependent on the land, we are all dependent on the products of the land and on many of the products of human art, such as clothes, dwellings, etc. Property must serve man, and since this is true, it follows that the arrangements that mankind makes for managing property are properly the concern of the community as a whole.[1] Society should control economic activity to make it a servant, not a master.

Now the notion of controlling economic activity makes many people think of socialism or state-run economies, but this is not what I mean. Rather, I am describing an economy in which, as much as possible, economic activity performs its natural (and naturally limited) role of providing man with the goods and services required without dominating his life. This is, I contend, best accomplished by what is called *Distributism*.

Distributism is an economic system in which private property is no longer regarded primarily as something to be manipulated, sold, resold, exchanged and transformed for gain *alone*, but for the production of necessary goods and services, which, supported by legal and social systems, serves human life and society. A farm is for producing food, and a farmer is a food-producer, not someone who is hoping for a good price when he

---

1. It is clear from papal teaching that property rights are not absolute and are subject to reasonable regulation by the civil authority. See *Quadragesimo Anno*, §§44–49 and *Populorum Progressio*, §§23–24.

is able to subdivide his land and sell it to housing developers. Moreover, the farmer is part of a rural way of life which has important benefits for society, and by raising his family on his farm the farmer is contributing to the health of the nation. Nor are factories or workshops to be looked at primarily as means of making money, but as existing for the production of real goods. Of course, producers must earn enough by their work to support themselves and their families, but they must see this as a by-product of their productive activity. There is an immense difference between a man making a living by producing shoes, and a man making a living by selling his shoe factory to a large corporation which will promptly close it and ship production overseas. Or between someone who makes his living selling books and someone who makes his living speculating on the stock market. It is my contention that Distributism is the best means of creating the kind of economy I have suggested, because well-distributed private property, legally safeguarded to prevent it being again concentrated in the hands of a few, tends to create conditions in which economic activity is for production for use rather than for gain alone, and in which the intangible goods which the human community requires, such as stability and prosperity, are also fostered.

What then is Distributism?[1] It is that economic system or arrangement in which the ownership of productive private property, as much as possible, is widespread in a nation or society. In other words, in a Distributist society most heads of families would own small farms or workshops, or in the case of entities which are necessarily large, such as railroads, they would either be jointly owned in some manner by the work force (be it noted: workers of hand *and* brain) themselves, or, more exceptionally, by the government.[2] Thus, another name for Distributism might be the system of micro-property.

Let us now discuss some of the objections to Distributism that are raised. It is often assumed that Distributism necessarily entails a lower level of technology than we have today, or even a reversion to the technology of the Middle Ages. Neither of these is true.

Although there may well be reasons to question the rapid technological changes characteristic of our culture, and to wonder how much modern technology has really benefited man, still Distributism is incompatible with no particular kind or level of technology. It is true that the *direc-*

---

1. Much of this description of Distributism is taken from Belloc's *An Essay on the Restoration of Property* (Norfolk, Va.: IHS Press, 2002 [1936]). The last chapters of his *The Crisis of Civilization* (Rockford, Ill.: TAN Books and Publishers, Inc., 1992 [1937]) as well as G. K. Chesterton's *The Outline of Sanity* (Norfolk, Va.: IHS Press, 2001 [1926]) are also helpful.

2. Belloc, *Restoration*, p. 66. It is worth noting that in *Quadragesimo Anno* Pius XI sanctions state ownership of certain industries in appropriate cases. See §114.

tion of technical research might change towards inventing devices that are more useful to smaller enterprises, as well as avoiding those which encourage immorality, but this would not necessitate a slowing down of invention.

Secondly, when people hear the word Distributism, it suggests to some a situation where government takes away people's property and gives it to others. They fear that the government will expropriate the property of the rich, or even the middle class, and distribute it to the poor, so that those who have worked hard to accumulate something will find it taken away and given to those they consider lazy and envious. This, too, is not the case. Rather, the chief method that Belloc suggests to establish Distributism is through taxation, which would induce a steady sell-off of concentrated property. For instance, if I own one or several stores (say pizza restaurants) I would have a reasonable and normal rate of taxation, but as soon as I begin to assemble a chain of such businesses, then my rate of taxation would rise so sharply that no one of a normal disposition would seek to continue to own such a chain.

There must be a differential tax on chain-shops, that is, on the system whereby one man or corporation controls a great number of different shops of the same kind. To control two such may involve but a small tax, to control three a larger one in proportion; and so on, with the curve rising steeply until the ownership of, say, a dozen in the territory over which the Government has power and the ordnance specifies becomes economically impossible.[1]

A similar scheme of taxation would attack "multiple shops," that is, stores selling many lines of goods, such as mega or "box" stores, and stores with "large retail turnover."[2]

Of course, a suitable period of time would be necessary to complete an orderly sell-off of property from excessively large owners to small owners before the new tax system came into full effect. Moreover, if this is instituted at a very reasonable pace, with tax rates on concentrations of property increasing gradually each year, this would give owners more time to prepare and help to prevent a "firesale" of their property. Similarly some form of guaranteed loans would have to exist to allow those without property or money to purchase the excess property that was being sold.[3] Although, naturally, every difficulty cannot be anticipated, the main outline of how to proceed is clear.

---

1. *Ibid*, p. 58.

2. *Ibid*, p. 59.

3. Belloc touches on this point, pp. 60, 99. For a more developed theory that could be adapted to Distributism, see John H. Miller, ed., *Curing World Poverty: the New Role of Property* (St. Louis : Central Bureau/*Social Justice Review*, 1994), pp. 133–49.

Since this tax structure is to persist after a Distributist economy has been established, this will answer the objection that property will inevitably become concentrated once again, since all men are not equal in intelligence, strength or energy, nor for that matter, in ruthlessness or deceitfulness.[1] Moreover, one key but often overlooked point of Distributism is the demand for the formation of occupational groups or "guilds" by small owners, after the manner of their predecessors, the medieval producers (that is to say, adopting the principles and values of the Middle Ages, but not the structural forms) and after the teaching of the twentieth century popes who championed this mode of organizing production, especially Pius XI and Pius XII.

> The principal structure for safeguarding the small unit – which is the seedling of our economic reforestation, our delicate experiment in the reconstruction of property – must be the Guild: not the unprotected guild arising spontaneously (for that would soon be killed by the predatory capitalism around it), but the Guild *chartered and established by positive law.*[2]

The role of the guilds or "vocational groups" will be to provide a measure of organization to the small owners, whether urban retailers, manufacturers, or farmers. These self-governing bodies can concern themselves with assuring a supply of raw materials, making technological knowledge available to the entire membership, ensuring equitable prices and fair market share, training and apprenticeship programs, and helping to make sure that no one firm or owner enlarges his business or farm so as to begin anew the concentration of property. Occupational groups might own cooperative banks to provide financing to their members. They could also provide health and unemployment insurance as well as benefits for their widows and orphans. One can see that the state's role would actually be reduced in a Distributist society, as many matters handled by the government would be transferred to occupational groups. In a Catholic society the Guilds – as they did in the Middle Ages – will have Masses said for deceased members and celebrate the feast of the patron saint of their trade or occupation. Overall, they will seek to foster a fraternal spirit, so that the members look upon each other as brothers in Christ serving the common good, rather than as economic rivals.

Of course, no one will be forced to become an owner under Distributism. Some men will still prefer to be employees, and doubtless some

---

1. Compare this to Pius XI' statement in *Quadragesimo Anno*, §107: "This accumulation of power, a characteristic note of the modern economic order, is a natural result of unrestrained free competition which permits the survival of those only who are the strongest. This often means those who fight most relentlessly, who pay least heed to the dictates of conscience."

2. Belloc, *Restoration, op. cit.*, p. 95, emphasis in original.

will remain so necessarily, notwithstanding their ultimate desires. But the point is that society will tend to look upon property and economic activity differently than it currently does, and this will result in a fundamental shift away from our commercialized society.

Conclusion

I HAVE ARGUED THAT capitalism, the separation of ownership and work, necessarily leads to economic exploitation and dislocations. Distributism is an alternative, a serious and viable alternative founded on man's real need for external economic goods, but recognizing that man is not simply a worker or consumer, and that the economic apparatus must be firmly subordinated to the totality of man's life. Capitalism is able to maintain its hold on our minds chiefly because most people think that its only rivals are socialism or communism. But if we do not allow the preconceived categories of modern thought to blind our economic thinking, then perhaps we can look at new and different options. If we do this, the alternative that Distributism offers looms large as a very attractive possibility, a possibility that can become a reality by first capturing our minds, our imaginations, and then our wills.

"Despite the fact that ours is a decreasingly rural society, and despite the reality that a shrinking portion even of rural society resembles the image romantic agrarians portray, theirs remains a vital and important point of view. It is important in part because it has played a role in stimulating some new and promising developments in agriculture and agricultural research, such as organic farming and low-input sustainable agriculture. And it is important because it forces us, in an uncompromising fashion, to confront ourselves and what we have become, to take stock of our values, and to consider seriously the nature and purpose of life."

—David B. Danborn

~ 8 ~

Heinrich Pesch and the Idea of a *Catholic* Economics

Rupert Ederer, Ph.D.

EING A PRACTICAL AND NOT A SPECULATIVE SCI-ence, economics does not purport simply to describe economic phenomena and their interrelationships. It involves human actions and therefore also a definite moral dimension. The purely descriptive part may be termed neutral so that it is not specifically Catholic, whereas human economic actions, and the systems of economic thought, with the prescriptions, norms, judgments, and philosophical approaches that inspire them, may or may not be consistent with, or inspired by a social philosophy conformable to, Catholic moral teachings. When treating, therefore, of an approach to economics where the doctrines, systems, and philosophies espoused conform to these Catholic morals, we may be permitted to speak of *Catholic* economics and *Catholic* economists, but *only* if such is indeed the case. It is the same with philosophy, which, since it confines itself to the light of natural reason, is Catholic only in the sense that its outcomes do not conflict with Catholic teaching entailing supernatural revelation also. To suggest that one's interpretation of the complex and important reality that is economic life does not reflect also one's philosophical and, for that matter, theological orientation is absurd, as was pointed out by the exemplary Jesuit economist Heinrich Pesch.[1]

Pesch was born in 1854 in Cologne, Germany, and died in 1926 in Valkenburg, Holland. He was trained as a priest in England (because of Bismarck's

---

1. Heinrich Pesch, S.J., *Lehrbuch der Nationalökonomie*, Vol. II, Book 1, trans. Rupert J. Ederer (Lewiston, N.Y.: Edwin Mellen Press, 2002–3).

laws against the Jesuits), and later as an economist in Berlin, and his work gave special meaning to what is sometimes termed *Catholic* economics. Accused of "theologizing" economics, he remonstrated that there is no such thing as a neutral economic science. He insisted that economics is and has always reflected one *Weltanschauung* or another. Pesch indicated that from the beginnings of the modern world, this worldview was a materialistic Enlightenment one, and later, a positivistic and naturalistic one.

Other leading builders of economic systems like Adam Smith and Karl Marx were anything but value-neutral. Smith was a moral philosophy professor who passed judgment on the old mercantile system and guild restrictions, as well as on "those affected to trade for the public good."[1] In *Kapital*[2] Marx indicted the capitalists and their system for what he saw as institutionalized exploitation of the working class. Classical economists, like Thomas Malthus and John Stuart Mill, were also consummate ideologues – this word being understood as proponents of a particular ideological view of the world that was *necessarily subjective*. In his 1798 essay, *On Population*,[3] Malthus, a one-time Anglican minister, urged "moral restraint" to avert the consequences of unrestrained population growth. Mill, whose 1859 essay *On Liberty*[4] made him a champion of libertarians, was one of the first to use the expression "social justice" in his economic texts,[5] and to propose positive programs like profit-sharing between employers and workers. And John Maynard Keynes gave rise to what came to be termed the "new economics."[6] Among other things, Keynes decried the persistent tendency to underemployment and stagnation, which he perceived to be due in part to the absence of governmental interference in economic affairs according to the canons of the "old economics." So the idea of economists outside the Catholic pale operating in strictly explanatory and "value-neutral" terms is easily and quickly seen to be impossible to sustain.

During his theological studies at Ditton Hall in the industrial heartland of Victorian England, Heinrich Pesch was in a position to observe first

---

1. Adam Smith, *Wealth of Nations* (New York: The Modern Library, 1937), p. 423. Smith's expression of disdain for those who affect to act for the common good comes along with his profession of faith in the "invisible hand" to make things come out right in the economy.

2. Karl Marx, *Kapital: A Critique of Political Economy*, Vol. 1, "The Process of Capitalist Production," trans. Moore and Aveling (Chicago: Charles H. Kerr and Co., 1918).

3. Thomas Malthus, *On Population* (New York: Random House, 1960).

4. J. S. Mill, *On Liberty* (Indianapolis: Hackett, 1978).

5. J. S. Mill, *Principles of Economics with Some of Their Applications to Social Philosophy*, ed. W. J. Ashley (New York: Longmans, Green and Co., 1909), p. 818.

6. John Maynard Keynes, *Theory of Employment, Interest, and Money* (New York: Harcourt, Brace & Co., 1935). Keynes did not oppose capitalism, only its *laissez-faire* manifestation. In fact, he proposed to save capitalism from itself.

hand the condition of the working class under free-market capitalism. It was the same economic landscape that Karl Marx and Friedrich Engels surveyed a few decades earlier, but with radically different conclusions! The experience, reinforced by the Leo XIII encyclical, *Rerum Novarum (RN)*,[1] which appeared four years after Pesch was ordained a priest, prompted him to devote his life to trying to improve the conditions of the workers. Like Marx and Adam Smith, he too was a serious student of philosophy. Before turning his attention specifically to economics, Pesch developed *Solidarism*, which is a social philosophy that goes beyond the two notionally opposed systems – capitalism and socialism, the former already then a longstanding and grim reality, while the latter still but an academic scheme – and which bases its tenets upon three essentials: the necessity of conforming economic life to justice and charity, subsidiarity, and the organization of employers and employed into vocational groups according to the function they perform in society.

Pesch formulated this social philosophy during the years between his return to Germany and the publication of his major work, the *Teaching Guide to Economics*[2] *(Lehrbuch der Nationalökonomie)*. In the meantime, he wrote several articles for the prestigious journal *Stimmen aus Maria Laach* (now *Stimmen der Zeit*), of which his renowned and published philosopher brother, Tilman Pesch, S.J., was the long-time editor. A number of these articles were revised and arranged into the nearly two thousand page, two-volume *Liberalism, Socialism, and Christian Social Order (Liberalismus, Socialismus, und Christliche Gesellschaftsordnung)* that appeared between 1898 and 1901. Therein were contained the foundations of Pesch's Solidarist philosophy as juxtaposed to capitalist liberalism and socialist collectivism. Pesch saw the former as the root of the social problems of the time, and as the original incitement of the growing socialist attacks against it and the existing social order overall. It is worth noting that throughout his work, he always used quotation marks around the "laws" of supply and demand that were supposed to produce optimum economic results automatically under free market capitalism. He used them also when referring to "scientific" socialism. This indicated the extent to which he regarded both as spurious in their pretensions.

Socialism was still several years from becoming a social reality, but it was recognized by Pesch and by the Church, as indicated in *RN*, as a serious threat. In retrospect the six-hundred-page *Modern Socialism*,[3] published

---

1. The papal encyclicals referred to in this essay use translations and paragraph numbers of the Vatican editions (http://www.vatican.va).

2. Elsewhere the book's title is rendered as the *Compendium of the National Economy.*—Ed.

3. Heinrich Pesch, S.J., *Liberalism, Socialism, and Christian Social Order*, Book 4, *Modern Socialism*,

before the fact, therefore represents a masterful *a priori* critique of the entire socialist phenomenon. It includes the attempts by revisionist socialists like Eduard Bernstein to cover up and back away from the blatant flaws that critics had even then noted in the Marxian theoretical schema. By the time the last editions of the *Lehrbuch* were competed, Marxian socialism had become a reality in Russia in 1917, with results that substantiated the critique by both Pesch and Leo XIII before him.

The Jesuit began his economics studies at the University of Berlin in 1901, where his professors included Gustav Schmoller (1838–1917), leader of the so-called younger school of economics, and Adolf Wagner (1835–1917), a member of the Christian Socialist Party. The first edition of the first volume of the *Lehrbuch* was published in 1905. The fifth volume appeared in 1923; and by 1926 when Pesch died, the first three volumes had come out in revised second editions. It is the only economics text I am aware of that bears an imprimatur of the Ordinary, or local bishop, as well as the *imprimi potest* of his superior in the Jesuits. This indicates that there are weighty moral aspects involved in economic reality, since the imprimatur has no application to purely descriptive economic analysis or to morally "neutral" policies. Accordingly, in any discussion about Catholic economics, the *Lehrbuch der Nationalökonomie* deserves profound consideration.

Its author presented what actually involved a revision of many basic economic concepts within a descriptive framework of the turbulent German economy during the first quarter of the twentieth century. More importantly, Pesch wove his description around the social philosophy *of Solidarism*, according to a methodology that involved the *Seinsollen* (what-ought-to-be) along with the *Sein* (what-is). The title of the opening section provides an indication of a significant difference between this exhaustive economic textbook and those that preceded and came after it. We find "Chapter One: Man as Lord of the World According to God's Omnipotence."[1] That is followed by "Chapter Two: Work as the Means to Exercise Dominion Over the World." Thus we have the opening chapters of Genesis laying the foundations for an economic system that puts the critical factor of production – human labor, not capital – in the first place for developing the wealth of a nation. Adam Smith and Karl Marx both recognized this primacy. But neither was able to follow up this fact consistently because of his flawed philosophy. Smith, therefore, went on to propose that national wealth would be maximized if each individual were allowed to pursue his self-interest freely (liberalism). Marx, on the other hand, perceived the need to subject human labor, as well

trans. Rupert J. Ederer (Lewiston, NY: Edwin Mellon Press, 2005).

1. Pesch, *Lehrbuch, op. cit.*, Vol. I, Book 1, p. 1.

as all other factors of production, to the state that was allegedly controlled at the outset by a proletarian dictatorship (collectivism).

Between these two positions Pesch interposed his principle of solidarity and certain concomitant obligations. Accordingly, he perceived the wealth of a nation, along with the actual welfare of the individual, as stemming from "social interdependence, the actual mutual dependence of people on one another."[1] A moment's reflection will surely affirm that our well-being depends on the massive and ubiquitous, even if unwitting, cooperation with others that is implicit throughout all economic activity.[2] It takes only another moment to make us aware that there are consequent moral obligations (in justice and charity) on the part of individuals who benefit from the largesse, i.e., the common good, which results from the cooperation implicit in all stages and processes of economic life. This contrasts sharply with Adam Smith's cynical observation that he never knew much good done by those who affected to trade for the public good. Needless to say, it also stands directly opposed to the virtue of social justice defined by Pius XI, which of its "very essence" demands "from each individual all that is necessary for the common good" (*Divini Redemptoris* [*DR*] §51).[3] Accordingly we are faced with a choice between governance according to virtuous behavior on the part of free human beings, singly and in occupational groups, or by an "invisible hand" that ends up historically as institutionalized greed, or else by a band of commissars, also judged by history as becoming avaricious "insiders."

With these basic components in place, Pesch presented, in his second volume, an outline of what an economic system based on solidarity involves. He applied the principle to three different levels of society where economic interdependence plays its critical role. These extend from the "universal solidarity of all mankind," to "citizens of the same state," and to "those who work at the same occupation."[4] The first of these appears to be even more relevant in our contemporary world, now grown so much "smaller" than it was when the second volume of the *Lehrbuch* first appeared in 1909. However, when Pesch published the second edition of that volume in 1925, he had already observed the attempt at establishing the short-lived and ineffectual

---

1. *Ibid.*, p. 36.

2. Such interdependence is apparent in the division of labor on which Adam Smith put great emphasis in his *Wealth of Nations* (Chapter One). It is also present, even in one-sided fashion, in Marx's class solidarity.

3. The Vatican's English translation seems to have a typographical error, for it has substituted "for" where "from" is clearly intended, based upon the non-English editions and authoritative texts, such as that included in Oswald Von Nell-Breuning, S.J., *Reorganization of the Social Economy*, trans. Bernard W. Dempsey, S.J. (Milwakee: The Bruce Publishing Co., 1936).

4. Pesch, *Lehrbuch*, *op. cit.*, Vol. II, Book 1, pp. 241–243.

League of Nations. That prompted his warning: "Without God at the center of society, without charity which goes along with all obligations in justice, that noble idea of the League of Nations remains sheer fantasy, or a horrible idol to which nations would only pay homage under physical duress."[1] At a time when the national individualistic spirit was regnant, and now retrospectively in the light of what happened afterwards, the words seem not just appropriate, but prophetic. We have here in fact an insightful statement by a Catholic economist.

Solidarity among citizens of the same state is a concept with which contemporary globalists may have some difficulty. Pesch insisted throughout his work on a definite practical primacy of the *national* economy, as opposed to internationalist currents then becoming fashionable. He indicated here too that the economy is also a working community. As such, the economic process is not an open arena of opposing interests, but instead a place where individual economic units and forces work *with* and *for* one another. That expression of *national solidarity* foreshadowed the third level in the application of the principle of solidarity.

For contemporaries, guild-like solidarity among those who work at the same occupation presents what is perhaps the most alien if not the least palatable application of the principle. The organization of parties on the two sides of the labor market – in opposition to each other – is recognized and accepted as probably inevitable, given the bellicose conditions existing between the "classes" which the capitalistic system generated, and upon which the socialists based their own opposing ideology. Organization for the overall benefit of one's specific occupation, trade, or industry is now regarded pretty much as a relic of the medieval guild system. That received a sound thrashing, from Adam Smith, among others, as he crafted liberal capitalism in his *Wealth of Nations.* To a certain extent such castigation was valid then inasmuch as the guilds in the late Middle Ages often lost sight of the higher level of solidarity that entailed the common good of all citizens of the same state, partly as a consequence of the influence of a human nature wounded by original sin, and partly by the surreptitious – if documented – rise of the capitalist spirit during the last phase of the medieval period. Unfortunately, the proverbial baby was once again thrown out with the bath water. Nevertheless, the concept itself is even now not entirely out of fashion. We do in fact still have occupational organizations of a sort in the medical and legal professions as well as in professional sports. These provide wide-ranging regulation with regard to matters like the conduct of members, remunerations, guidelines of competition, and other rules of self-governance of the respective occupations, not unlike what the medieval guilds established for

1. *Ibid.*, p. 242.

craftsmen and merchants. Among other things they set limits to the much-vaunted free competition of the labor market, since they discourage members of certain of these professions from undercutting each others' fees in the market for services. Now, as then, there may not always be the proper regard for the broader common good, which is where the higher authority – the estates entrusted with the overall common good – would be obliged to intervene. Nevertheless their survival in what are specifically modern contexts suggests that occupational organizations are perhaps, indeed, a "natural" concept, as Pius XI suggested in 1931 (*Quadragesimo Anno* [QA], §83). That brings us to the intriguing relationship of Heinrich Pesch's scholarly work to the social teachings of the Catholic Church.

*****

I N *SOLLICITUDO REI SOCIALIS* (*SR*), his second encyclical addressing the economic order, John Paul II stated:

> The Church does not propose economic and political systems or programs, nor does she show preference for one or the other . . . provided that human dignity is properly respected and promoted, and provided she herself is allowed the room she needs to exercise her ministry in the world (§41).

Those who are discomfited by certain Church teachings about the economic order typically delete the latter provisos. A solid case can certainly be made that both the socialist and capitalist programs respectively have failed to live up to the stated qualifications. In the case of the socialistic system, as it came to prevail in the vast Soviet empire, this is obvious. In addition to the abolition of the natural right to own productive property, individuals were persecuted for their religious beliefs, and the churches were harassed to the point of virtual extinction. Meanwhile, in the prevailing capitalist system, the very real lack of worker rights, including especially the right to a just wage, represented precisely the kind of lack of respect and promotion of human dignity that John Paul II mentioned. The labor of human beings came to be regarded and treated as any other commodity on the market in accordance with the "laws" of supply and demand. That would explain why popes since Leo XIII, speaking for the "Mother and Teacher of Western Civilization," have not shied away from pointing out time and again the errors in existing systems and proposing correctives. Indeed, the English title of Pius XI's QA was *On Restructuring the Social Order*, corresponding to the purpose stated in its preamble.

Since liberal capitalism and collectivist socialism have both been scored as failing the test, the Church has at times been misrepresented as favoring a centrist type of system retaining what is acceptable, while rejecting what is not, in existing social systems. Actually the proposed corrections have less to do with the position on some imagined socio-political spectrum, than what is in conformity with principles stemming from the natural law that has been perverted or fallen into disuse. For example, failure to pay just wages is objectively theft, which is why the matter is presented in the *Catechism of the Catholic Church* under the Seventh Commandment (§2434). The impact on human society, including grossly distorted income distribution patterns, has bordered on the catastrophic in the temporal dimension, spilling over also into the spiritual one. The anti-life attitude, with birth prevention and contraception backed up by abortion, as it prevails in the wealthiest nations, is an example of such "spillover." Hence the Catholic Church has felt *compelled* to involve itself in the discussion over the past century.

Thus it was that the learned Jesuit Heinrich Pesch, with excellent schooling in philosophy and theology as well as economics, became one of the Church's leading lights and inspirations in the preparation of encyclicals dealing with the economic order. This is obvious with regard to *QA*, issued by Pius XI just five years after Pesch died, as it is also in the trilogy of social encyclicals issued by John Paul II a half-century later. A fellow Jesuit, Oswald von Nell-Breuning, who had been Pesch's understudy, is widely acknowledged as having written *QA*; he was in any case the primary *peritus*. Subsequently, Pius XII relied on the Jesuit Gustav Gundlach, another disciple of Pesch, for the social teaching contained in many of his addresses throughout his nineteen-year pontificate. Indeed, it was Pius XII who first began using the expression "solidarity" with great frequency and in a completely relevant sense in his many allocutions and messages. Later, John Paul II spoke of "solidarity" almost reflexively. It was he who explained the principle in great detail, declaring it to be "undoubtedly a Christian virtue" (*SR*, §40), and identifying it later as social charity (*Centesimus Annus* [*CA*], §10).

The Peschian imprint is clearly present in the main principles proposed in *QA*, Pius XI's blueprint *for restructuring the social order*. These include the aforementioned organization according to *occupational groups*, the concept that Pesch had adapted to modern industrial society when he established it as one of his three specific applications of the *principle of solidarity*. The translation was sometimes awkward, and rendering it with terms that contemporary readers were unfamiliar with turned out to be at times even more awkward. Pius XI intended these groups as a means to de-emphasize and eventually to overcome the existing situation where he saw workers and employers divided "into two camps . . . where the two armies are engaged in combat . . . . " He proposed the occupational groups, variously called "functional groups" and "vocational groups" as, "if not essential to civil society, at least a natural accompaniment thereof" (*QA*, §83). Such guild-like groups would include all persons across each trade or industry: workers, managers, and owners. Payment of the minimum wage would be aided by such an organization, for example, because it would prove difficult unless all competitors were held to the same minimum standards.

A second principle for social order included in *QA* is the *principle of subsidiarity*, which is likewise set forth in Pesch's Solidarist schema. It defines the subsidiary relationships and roles that obtain between various social bodies, up to the level of the government of the state itself. The principle proposes that "it is an injustice and at the same time a grave evil and disturbance of right order to assign to a greater and higher association what lesser and subordinate organizations can do" (*QA*, §§79). In the Pius XI encyclical it is presented for the first time with this specific name. It appears in various points in Pesch's schema, even though he did not originate either the term or the concept, which actually represents a commonsense (i.e., natural-law) principle. Not surprisingly, therefore, it is indicated throughout history by various persons. As just one example, in 1854, Abraham Lincoln stated:

> The legitimate object of government is to do for the community of people whatever they need to have done but cannot do at all, or cannot do so well for themselves in their separate and individual capacities. In all that the people can individually do as well for themselves, government ought not to interfere.[1]

The third element common to both Pesch's Solidarist schema and the papal plan for reconstructing the social order is represented by the critical importance of the twin virtues of *social justice* and *social charity*. Here we are squarely in the realm of moral theology that deals with the virtues in their specific social dimensions, i.e., having the common good as their objective. Pius XI first mentioned the two as required to replace both "free competition," which "cannot direct economic life," and the "economic dictatorship which has recently displaced free competition" (*QA*, §88).

Pius XI did not directly offer precise definitions of these two virtues, and in retrospect that may be seen as unfortunate. "Social justice" came to represent for some less a virtue than a catch-all slogan for a kind of vague, feel-good reformism. Meanwhile, for the more militant it became more like a battle cry, as in the case of liberation theology. The definition of it followed, however, in a subsequent encyclical in 1937. We find in *DR*: "Now it is of the very essence of social justice to demand from each individual all that is necessary for the common good" (§51). Clearly then, it involves an *action*: giving what is due; a *subject*: each individual; and, finally, an *object*: the common good, from which each individual in turn benefits to a greater or

---

1. Don E. Fehrenbacher, *Abraham Lincoln Speeches and Writings 1832–1858* (New York: Literary Classics of the U.S., Inc, 1989), p. 301.

lesser degree. The Pope was distinguishing this application of the virtue of justice from *commutative justice* that has the good of specific individuals as its object in their relations with one another (as opposed to their individual or collective relations with society).

Here we have a clear example of the Church's special teachings as being in the realm of moral theology. The cardinal virtue of justice, in its various applications, was already in theology texts at the time of St. Thomas Aquinas' *Summa Theologiæ*, where we find the distinction between *commutative*, *distributive*, and *legal* justice. These are now also included in the *Catechism of the Catholic Church* where *legal* justice "concerns what citizens owe in fairness to the community," while *distributive* justice "regulates what the community owes its citizens in proportion to their contributions and needs" (§2411). Both directly and intimately involve the common good.

Heinrich Pesch had already included social justice among the principles for his Solidarist system, indicating, then, that it was a "relatively new" concept.[1] It originally involved both *legal* and *distributive* justice. On the assumption that a system of positive legislation may well be imperfect and incomplete, he added another dimension not found in theology texts: *contributive* justice. That calls for contribution by members of society of whatever the common good may require, yet always in accordance with their various capacities. It approximates, therefore, the definitions of social justice presented by Pius XI in *DR*. An example of its application would be the requirement in *QA* (§71) that "changes be introduced as soon as possible whereby . . . a [just wage] will be assured to every adult workingman." In non-socialist societies wages are not legislated, which would make their payment an obligation in legal justice; often, in fact, the conditions enabling private employers to pay them are not present. It was the restoration or establishment of such conditions in society, by the collective actions of its members on both a small and large scale, that Pius XI was calling for. Pesch's indication of "justice and charity" as the "ethical principles of the objective regulation of social life"[2] is especially relevant for this discussion. It corresponds precisely with the Pius XI proposal for social justice and social charity as "true and effective principles" for guiding economic life.

While Pesch did not yet employ the specific term, *social charity*, it was certainly implicit inasmuch as charity appeared in this context along with social justice. In any case, as an illustration of a continuing kind of development in Catholic social teachings, John Paul II identified the *principle of subsidiarity* as social charity in the third of his trilogy of social encyclicals,

1. Pesch, *Lehrbuch, op. cit.*, Vol. II, Book 2, pp. 296–9.
2. *Ibid.*, p. 296.

CA (§10). That principle is precisely the dominant motif of the entire Peschian system.

Finally, as a decisive indication that Heinrich Pesch was completely synchronized with the Catholic Church's social teaching, so that he was in a sense proposing what may be termed *Catholic* economics, there is the just-wage doctrine as emphasized by popes from Leo XIII through John Paul II. The latter affirmed most emphatically the doctrine first presented ninety years earlier (*RN*, §§44–45). In *Laborem Exercens* (*LE*) we find: "It should be noted that the justice of a socioeconomic system and, in each case, its just functioning, deserve in the final analysis to be evaluated by the way in which man's work is properly remunerated in the system." As if wishing to leave no doubt about the urgency of the matter, there was this follow up statement in the same paragraph: "Hence, in every case, a just wage is the concrete means of *verifying the justice* of the whole socioeconomic system and, in any case, of checking that it is functioning justly" (§19; emphasis in original).

The doctrine was developed extensively by Pius XI in *Quadragesimo Anno* (*QA*, §§64–75). He attested there to its extreme urgency by the statement: "[I]f this cannot always be done under existing circumstances, social justice demands that changes be introduced as soon as possible whereby such a wage will be assured to every adult workingman" (*QA*, §71). That is precisely why Pius XI had set forth the concept of *occupational organizations* which constituted a basic reform of existing structures where the "hiring and offering for hire in the so-called labor market separate men into two divisions, as into battle lines . . . " (*QA*, §83). The urgency that John Paul II attached to this matter of the just wage indicated clearly that the reforms that his predecessor called for in 1931 are far from accomplished!

John Paul II, like Heinrich Pesch before him, based the primacy of the just wage ultimately on Aristotelian-Thomistic metaphysical principles. The Pope singled out the factor of production, labor, as the central one. It is not merely the subject of economic action, but also its purpose. In speaking of the "priority of labor over capital" as "a principle that has always been taught by the Church," he referred to labor as "always a primary *efficient cause*" of production. This he juxtaposed to capital that "remains a mere *instrument*, or instrumental cause" (*LE*, §12; emphasis in original).

Pesch established the just-wage principle on the basis of the primacy of labor, also referring to it in Aristotelian-Thomistic terms as the "primary efficient cause" of economic production.[1] He thought it devastating and wrong that the independence of capital during the period of free-enterprise capitalism elevated capital so much so that it was put on a par with

---

1. Pesch, *Lehrbuch*, *op. cit.*, Vol. IV, Book2, p. 354.

the original factors of production. The latter were for Pesch human labor and nature, which he called *causae principales* of production, whereas capital remains but a *causa instrumentalis*.[1] As an economist, Heinrich Pesch perceived the just wage also as the economically correct wage.[2] He did so proceeding on purely practical economic grounds. Since economic activity is destined for the well-being of all persons and not for the enrichment of the privileged and perhaps aggressive few, and since the vast majority of persons must earn their livelihood mainly by their work, i.e., from wages, and since an economy can ultimately only be termed prosperous if those who constitute the vast majority enjoy relative prosperity, and finally, since only a just wage can ensure such prosperity, ergo: for the economy overall to prosper, all who work for their living are *entitled* to just remuneration for their work. That includes all full-time adult workers even at the unskilled levels.

What is more, the just wage in our post-industrial era is more than a mere subsistence wage as characterized in earlier times. The technological marvels which that revolution wrought in industry and throughout the economy, including agriculture and transportation, brought about an economic abundance such as the world never before experienced. As Pius XII pointed out, "It is undeniable that technological progress comes from God, and so it can and ought to lead to God."[3] By uncanny coincidence, Adam Smith's manifesto on liberal capitalism was first published in the same year (1776) as James Watt made the first practical use of his steam engine by pumping water from a coal mine. Accordingly, in the years that followed, the great potential from this providential benefit was unduly restricted by the workings of Smith's "invisible hand." It is important to note here that his disdain for affecting "to trade for the public good" stands diametrically opposed to the concern for the actions promoting precisely that good, i.e., the common good, as indicated in Pesch's Solidarist system and in Catholic social teachings. In any case, it turned out during the course of history that keeping a large part of mankind from full access to the bounty afforded by the industrial revolution was not only morally reprehensible but also economically self-defeating. One result was the want-in-the-midst-of-plenty associated with the recurrent cycles of prosperity and depression that came to characterize the modern capitalistic era.

That represents a position that has also been arrived at by other economists, even those that may wish to shy away from the particular moral

---

1. *Ibid.*, p. 359.

2. Pesch, *Lehrbuch, op. cit.*, Vol. V, Book 2, pp. 77–114.

3. Pope Pius XII, *Christmas Message*, 1953, in Vincent A. Yzermans, ed., *The Major Addresses of Pope Pius XII* (St. Paul: North Central Publishing Co., 1961), Vol. II, p. 174.

component that is a part of Pesch's Catholic economics. For example, they would include supporters of the so-called "under-consumptionist theory" of business fluctuations, such as the Swiss economist Jean Sismondi[1] and more recently the British economist John Maynard Keynes (1883–1946). Of course, Karl Marx used this historic economic anomaly for his own ideological purposes, i.e., in outright opposition to private ownership of the means of production. Pesch countered by proposing that it is man that needs to be "socialized," not the material means of production.[2]

Within the purview of Catholic economics, valid scientific truth cannot conflict with philosophical and theological truth. Therefore, from a Catholic point of view, virtuous conduct effecting justice in the matter of wage payment cannot be assumed as somehow the automatic outcome of so-called economic "laws," for such a result indeed requires *purposeful* human effort, and decisive moral action. But there has been a substantial neo-liberal revival of the disproved economic theory that if the contending parties are allowed to compete freely on the market, the "laws" of supply and demand will automatically deliver a wage that is just. This once again reflects Adam Smith's "invisible hand," with its intimation that self-interest pursued without external restraint will result in the maximization of national economic welfare.

Pesch was of another mind. He likened self-interest to a powerful steed that needs to be reined in by the coachman. The "coachman" is threefold. First there is the *correctly informed individual conscience* that recognizes what the virtues of justice and charity entail in economic life, and which prompts individuals to act accordingly. This informed, individual conscience is then strengthened in its sense of obligation, and its virtuous decisions are encouraged, supported, and confirmed by the structure of *occupational organizations* that must also themselves operate in accordance with the broader common good. In the event that these fall short in their responsibility, there is in the last instance, in accordance with the principle of subsidiarity, the *state* entrusted with the important and sacred task of protecting the overall common good. Implicit throughout are the virtues of *social justice* and *social charity* which alone can assure that the individuals by themselves, and then in their performance as members of intermediate organizations, will operate in conformity with the common good at all levels of the social order.

---

1. The Swiss-born economist Jean Charles Leonard de Sismondi, although not a socialist, was an early critic of the *laissez-faire* approach of classical economics and of the kind of income distribution he perceived as resulting from it. He envisioned a role for government to bring about a better sharing of wealth and property in his work *Nouveaux Principles d'Economie Politique* (Paris: Chez Delaunan, 1819).

2. Pesch, *Lehrbuch, op. cit.*, Vol. II, Book 1, p. 241.

Thus, what the Catholic Church proposed in 1931, elaborating on themes that coincide with the economic vision and work of Pesch, represents an *integral* blueprint for the reconstruction of the social order, and specifically the economic order. There is far more involved here than merely the size or structure of business enterprises or the revival of forms inappropriate to the post-industrial revolution world. Ultimately, Pesch offers a sterling example both of what it means to be a *Catholic* economist and of what such an economist can offer to the world. In the period since the Second Vatican Council, many experts have betrayed the trust of the faithful. Pesch was a man cut from a different cloth. True to the solid training and faith that characterized Jesuit formation during the late nineteenth and early twentieth centuries, he was not befuddled by inordinate ecumenical distractions from his basic Christian and specifically Catholic orientation. Thus we find his social and economic teaching permeated with an unshakable faith and rooted in the highest of truths. As he notes in concluding the second volume of the *Lehrbuch*,

> In the re-creation of the truly human person by Christ, we have the most important contribution of Christianity to the social question. From the Christianity of the soul, we arrive at the Christianity of the world.[1]

---

1. Pesch, *Lehrbuch, op. cit.*, Vol. II, Book 2, p. 358.

~ 9 ~

Distributism and "Modern Economics"

Edward McPhail, Ph.D.

> Property is like muck, it is good only if it be spread.
>
> —G. K. Chesterton, quoting Francis Bacon

I **PROPOSE IN THIS CHAPTER TO EXAMINE SOME ASPECTS** of the broad school of thought known as Distributism in light of several of the various trends in today's textbook economics. My examination will show, I think, that many of the newest trends in "alternative" economics parallel quite notably the strains of thought running through the Distributist ideas of Hilaire Belloc, G. K. Chesterton, and other supporters of that movement in England who were writing almost a century ago. From a certain narrow perspective, Distributism has often been attacked as *"un*economic," impractical, and simply a fantasy. Contemporary economics, however, has much to learn from Distributism, and their direction is frankly a positive one in view of the current openness to including, in economic analysis, emphases on the person, improvement of the quality of life, and the role fulfilling work – emphases that have been central concerns of Distributist thinkers from its foundation. An incorporation of these concerns into modern economic thinking might also enhance the explanatory and predictive power of the economic models relied on for policy making. On the other hand, a systematic exposure of Distributism to these more recent trends in economic reasoning will help to produce a compelling reconstruction of Chesterton's and Belloc's Distributist ideas for academics and professionals used to traveling in specifically "economic" circles.[1]

---

1. For those seeking a fuller discussion of Distributism please see the other chapters in this book and the catalog of IHS Press. In future work I will expand on the themes that I raise in this chapter.

For the purposes of what follows, I take Distributism to mean an economic system broadly characterized by widespread ownership of productive property. Chesterton thought that Distributism would benefit from the discipline that theoretical analysis imposes, and that Distributism is best seen as a big tent, not a small one, inside of which any number of interpretations and perspectives can fit. As the philosopher of common sense, Chesterton was unwilling to specify an explicit program of action beyond some general economic reforms that would aid small businesses. Rather, he wanted to make the abstract case for the principle of widespread ownership. How that would actually play out in the world could not be foretold but was to be discovered, rather, by actually doing it. Through experiment and trial and error we would see what worked and what did not. No matter the actual form that Distributism would take, the different types would be unified by Distributist principles. Hence in his *Outline of Sanity* Chesterton stresses the *concepts* which give unity to the Distributist movement, without dogmatically fixing the specifics:

> Now this outline is an outline; in other words, it is a design, and anybody who thinks we can have practical things without theoretical designs can go and quarrel with the nearest engineer or architect for drawing thin lines on thin paper. But there is another and more special sense in which my suggestion is an outline; in the sense that it is deliberately drawn as a large limitation within which there are many varieties.[1]

The time is ripe for reevaluation of Distributist principles in light of recent advances in experimental and behavioral economics. Religious and ethical beliefs, behavioral norms, conventions, and institutions – all are accepted as having a part to play in economics today, given the new perspectives and theories that have come to the fore. These new developments in economic theory offer tools that can actually be used to address Distributist concerns, which were not accounted for or explicable within neoclassical economics. The tools of today's economics are well suited to examining the modern applications, within economic thought, of the theory of Distributism.

Post-WWII Economics

SINCE WORLD WAR II, the conventional account of economic behavior has held that people act as rational agents pursuing their own self-interest.[2] This model, notwithstanding its degree of relevance to the lives

---

1. G. K. Chesterton, *The Outline of Sanity* (Norfolk, Va.: IHS Press, 2001), p. 90.

2. For discussions of the strengths and weaknesses of this approach see Samuel Bowles and Herbert

of real people and their experiences, has been maintained and used for its explanatory power in academic and professional economic work: the model makes definite predictions, and it is elegant because of its simplicity, i.e., it does not have too many moving parts. Some of the results of these models and the properties of the state of the world that they predict – put forward as presumably desirable – are based upon rather strong assumptions and have, therefore, significant consequences when they are employed.[1]

For example, the fundamental theorem of economics states that all competitive equilibria are "Pareto efficient." This means that no agent can be made better off without making another agent worse off.[2] This provides one normative defense of the market. If markets give rise to competitive outcomes in the real world that tend to approximate competitive equilibria, then it is inferred that these outcomes would also tend to be Pareto efficient.[3]

There are, of course, other motives neglected by this model that help to explain human behavior as well. Distributists would note that a failure to keep this in mind would lead to serious error. Ignoring the connection between economics and religion, for example, or the role that ethics must play in economic theory is a mistake. Human behavior is certainly more complex than an explanation by self-interest alone will allow.

But because these models are based on theories that seem powerful and elegant, they have greatly influenced other academic disciplines like sociology, political science, and the law. This one-way transfer of the economic toolkit was dubbed "economic imperialism." Alternative models were discouraged because the economic method discounted what other disciplines

---

Gintis, "Walrasian Economics in Retrospect," *Quarterly Journal of Economics*, 115 (4), 2000, pp. 1411–39; Samuel Bowles, *Microeconomics: Behavior, Institutions, and Evolution* (New York: Russell Sage, Princeton, N.J.: Princeton University Press, 2004); and Amartya Sen, "Rational Fools," *Choice Welfare and Measurement* (Oxford: Basil Blackwell, 1982), p. 99. In Edward A. McPhail, "Introduction," *An Essay of the Economic Effects of the Reformation* (Norfolk, Va.: IHS Press, 2003) and "Introduction," *Economics for Helen* (Norfolk, Va.: IHS Press, 2004), I consider additional criticisms.

1. By assumption, for example, a motive such as altruism is reinterpreted, in this context, so that it can be seen as a manifestation of self-interest: the behavior is undertaken because sympathy for others leads to an increase in the altruist's own welfare.

2. Competitive markets give rise to surpluses or gains from trade that go to both the consumer and the producer. The difference between what an agent would have been willing to pay and the price they pay is a surplus that goes to the consumer. The difference between what a supplier must receive to induce them to provide the good or service and the price they actually receive is a surplus that goes to the producer. These gains from trade are exhausted in a competitive market and are "Pareto efficient."

3. As I discuss below, one problem is that, if people are in part shaped by the economic games they play, then markets, in effect, satisfy the preferences that they help to create. To rely solely on the normative criteria of Pareto efficiency to justify market allocation evades the issue of institutional evaluation, since other institutions may more fully satisfy the preferences that they create. For an economic system such as Distributism that values democratic decision making, a key question is "How do we devise institutions that will not only allow people a say in how their economic lives are governed but also to help to encourage the development of people that thrive within democratic institutions and that will enable those institutions to flourish?"

had to offer. As the phrase connotes, economic methods were employed as weapons to "conquer" academic territory. As a result, economic imperialism acted as a firebreak isolating conventional economic "wisdom" both from the facts of human behavior and from insights offered by competing perspectives in other disciplines.

Homo Economicus

> What is remarkable about the standard model [of economic behavior] is that it is at once vacuous and wrong.
>
> —attributed to Nobel laureate Kenneth Arrow

TODAY IT IS widely recognized that employment of the assumptions of a self-contained, "rational" system such as the self-interest approach to economic reasoning can produce misleading policies that lead officials to take actions that produce results contrary to their original aims. Unforgiving federal sentencing guidelines, Robert McNamara's infamous policy of raising the cost of participation in the Vietnam War, and the misuse of "game theory" during the first Gulf War and its application to the current conflict in Iraq[1] are three examples of what happens when the assumptions of the *homo economicus* (i.e., consideration of man's behavior as driven solely by economic motives of self-interest) are brought to bear on policy decisions without an understanding of the weakness of the models and the assumptions they contain that may or may not actually be true in the situation under consideration. To give another example, self-interest may offer a possible explanation of why people vote the way they do, but it fails to explain why they would even vote at all.[2]

This model has had, in fact, little success explaining the features that are common to most economies. For example, as Distributists have stressed, people are inherently social, yet sociality poses problems for the *homo economicus* model. It is unable to explain why people help strangers, why they make anonymous donations, and why they are willing to punish others who violate norms of fairness even when to do so is costly to them. People engage in "collective action": they fight for freedom, democracy, religious rights, justice for persecuted groups, etc., even when they would benefit by *not* doing

---

1. A Rand study (Paul K. Davis and John Arquilla, *Deterring or Coercing Opponents in Crisis: Lessons from the War With Saddam Hussein*, 1991) notes that almost every prediction about Saddam Hussein's reasoning before and during the first conflict proved wrong.

2. The probability that a vote will change the outcome of an election is vanishingly small, yet there are costs of going to vote. Hence *homo economicus* would not vote unless the election involves small numbers.

so. *Homo economicus* takes little account of the human capacity for moral actions, beyond the conventional concepts of personal and immediate gain, and cannot explain the level of honesty that we see in the world. It excludes non-consequentialist action such as commitments. Some even point persuasively to its dubious consequentialist morality: "to teach the principle (of *homo economicus*) as unconditionally valid . . . is to offer an education in the corruption of character."[1]

While economists and social scientists continue to document the limitations of conventional economics, the literature on alternative approaches has steadily grown. As a leading economist put it "*Homo economicus* is dead, but whose *homo behavioralis* will replace him?"[2]

One response to these criticisms relies on an amended version of the conventional model; one that explains human behavior as the product of "enlightened" self-interest. With this model economists reinterpret anomalous behavior – i.e., behavior that doesn't fit in the standard self-interest model – as if it were just another case of self-interested action. By and large, attempts to extend the conventional model by assuming that disparate actions are actually instances of "enlightened" self-interest are not persuasive either. One cross-country study took account of a variety of different societies from hunter-gatherer, nomadic-herding, and other small-scale societies, all of which exhibited a wide *variety* of economic and cultural conditions. The enlightened self-interest model was not supported in any of the societies studied.[3]

These narrow models are, however, pervasive throughout conventional economic textbooks. From these policy makers learn the economic ideas that are the basis of public policy, and they are thus trained to employ narrow models that seriously limit how policy issues are framed, objectives articulated, and alternatives assessed. Their economic reasoning, therefore, often embodies limited conceptions of personal well-being and the public good. The problem lies not so much with the *practice* of policy economics itself, but with incorrect economic *beliefs* and the preference for formal, abstract models, which are employed *at the expense of substantive economic analysis.* The problems with the academic environment in economics simply make matters worse. Professional advancement in economics is often seen to come by way of mastering mathematical and statistical techniques

1. Elizabeth Anderson "Some problems in the Normative Theory of Rational Choice," working paper, University of Michigan, Economics Department, March 1990.

2. Ken Binmore's jacket blurb for Bowles's *Microeconomics*.

3. Joseph Henrich, Robert Boyd, Samuel Bowles, Colin Camerer, Ernst Fehr, Herbert Gintis, and Richard McElreath, "In search of *Homo Economicus*: Behavioral Experiments in 15 Small-Scale Societies," *The American Economic Review* 91 (2), Papers and Proceedings of the Hundred-Thirteenth Annual Meeting of the American Economic Association, May 2001, pp. 73–8.

rather than knowledge of the economy. This is reinforced by graduate economic education that stresses formal techniques over studying real-world problems.[1] A noted historian of economic thought summed up the state of the discipline thus: "Modern economics is 'sick.' Economics has increasingly become an intellectual game played for its own sake and not for its practical consequences."[2]

Though narrow models may help to frame policy questions, they do so at the cost of restricting the universe of possible policy objectives and alternatives. Neoclassical approaches are often used to defend the status quo, promoting a quiescent stance towards problems that in reality require innovative public-policy solutions. And the problems with such economic reasoning plague also the means, as well as the ends, of public policy. Economists have typically relied on simplified aggregate accounts of economic performance like gross domestic product and per capita income rather than quality-of-life measures. They have failed to explore the impediments to the development of human capabilities and inequalities that deny many people the means to lead the good life; indeed, given the model and approach employed, conventional economics made no claim as to just what "the good life" is. Instead, the conventional approach is limited to "positive" economics – the economics of what "is," not what ought to be. From this perspective economics claims to predict the consequences of different policies but attempts to leave normative concerns to the political process. Abba Learner puts this position succinctly "As a social critic, I may try to change some desires to others of which I approve more, but as an economist I must be concerned with the mechanisms for getting people what they want, no matter how these wants were acquired." Defending the sanctity of individual preferences, in his Nobel lecture Paul Samuelson argued for the "notion of giving people what *they* want." Yet taking preferences as given ignores the important role that economic arrangements play, fostering and facilitating (or discouraging) behaviors and disseminating beliefs. Also, if people act upon ethical and religious beliefs, then normative concerns play an important role in predictive economics.

Positive economics alone is not enough. Economics must be tempered by a discussion of ethical concerns; here modern economics can gain from the insights of Distributism. It is often forgotten that even economists such as Adam Smith and John Stuart Mill were not afraid to incorporate conceptions of the good life in their work. According to David Levy and Sandra

---

1. See "The Report of the Commission on Graduate Education in Economics," *Journal of Economic Literature* 29, September 1991, pp. 1035–87.

2. Mark Blaug "Disturbing Currents in Modern Economics," *Challenge* 41 (3), May/June 1998, pp. 11–34.

Peart, after about 1870 the ethical elements of Smith's and Mill's economics fell into disfavor.[1] Writing in his *Principles of Political Economy* (1878), W. Roscher notes,

> The isolation of the theory of Political Economy is peculiar to our own day. In more remote times, we find this study confounded with the other moral sciences, of which it was an integral part. When the genius of Adam Smith gave it a distinct character, he did not desire to separate it from those branches of knowledge without which it could only remain a bleached plant from the absence of the sunlight of ethics.[2]

Nobel laureate Amartya Sen argues that the separation between ethics and economics leads to an impoverished account of economic behavior: "the purely economic man is indeed close to being a social moron."[3]

New Economic Models

TODAY THE ECONOMIC problems confronting our world go well beyond the old debate between planning and free markets. The premonitions of the Distributists seem particularly prescient with the fall of the Soviet Union and the loss of faith in centrally planned economies. Although generally ignored by most historians of economic thought, the early Distributists exposed the weaknesses of centrally planned economies in stark terms.[4] Yet with the death of command economies, there has been a birth of many more kinds of economies, each with a unique cultural stamp. All have in common the reliance on markets, but the degree to which exchanges are shaped by cultural and extra-market concerns varies from country to country. The crop of Asian economies has produced the greatest variety in this harvest.

What is of interest from the Distributist perspective is that this economic tumult has given rise to economic models that defy easy classification. Just because former planned economies have moved away from central direction does not mean they have embraced unbridled capitalism – far from it. Coun-

---

1. Sandra J. Peart and David M. Levy *The "Vanity of the Philosopher": From Equality to Hierarchy in Post-Classical Economics* (Ann Arbor, Mich.: The University of Michigan Press, 2006).

2. Catholic economist Charles Devas was unhesitating in his willingness to categorize economics as a branch of moral philosophy: "If we are agreed on the true philosophical view of the nature and destiny of man and of his surroundings, we ought to have little difficulty in agreeing on the position of economics among the sciences. It is a part of moral philosophy or ethics, which, in the widest sense, is itself that part of philosophy which regards the moral order" (*Political Economy* [New York: Benzinger Bros., 1891], p. 538).—Ed.

3. Sen, *op. cit.*

4. Belloc's critique of socialism is particularly apt. See my introduction to *Economics for Helen, op. cit.*

tries that rushed to privatize faced disastrous consequences. These countries, which were advised by conventional economists who apparently believed that markets, like mushrooms, spring up overnight, faced many dislocating effects brought on by the transition to market relations.[1]

Conventional economic models and methods proved of limited help to the transitioning economies, just as they were limited in explaining the rise of new economic models around the world. For example, China's strong record of growth has coincided with the rise of township and village enterprises, while property rights have only been vaguely defined. Again, this is inconsistent with the tenants of conventional economics.

The case of Asia demonstrates how cultural factors influence economic performance. It has also shown how existing market theories and their narrow assumptions about the social conditions for their adequate functioning failed to adequately predict the Asian miracle.

These experiences underscore the need for more nuanced discussions of the kinds of non-economic factors that support economic performance. Distributism recognizes the importance of these factors, and has insisted upon a fuller and more complete consideration of the broader social, ethical, and psychological concerns of men and women in their economic activities.

Fairness

A CLASSICAL LIBERAL might be tempted to dismiss the issue of unfair work arrangements by suggesting workers are "free" to exit unfavorable exchanges. That is the flexibility and benefit of a free market, we are told. We are "free to choose," or so the story goes.[2] Others argue that since both workers and capitalists benefit from existing arrangements, those arrangements cannot possibly be unfair. Yet, as economic theory predicts and experience confirms, many different kinds of firms, when compared with the absence of any firms at all, can satisfy both owners *and* workers. Although capitalists and workers may in fact benefit from these arrangements, it still leaves the questions of fairness unanswered.

---

1. Joseph E. Stiglitz notes, "unlike these transition gurus who marched into Russia armed with textbook economics, Arrow recognized the limitations of these textbook models. He and I each stressed the importance of competition, of creating the institutional infrastructure for a market economy. Privatization was secondary" (*Globalization and Its Discontents* [New York and London: W.W. Norton], p. 182).

2. See Milton Friedman's book by the same name, *Free to Choose: A Personal Statement* (New York: Harcourt Brace Jovanovich, 1980), with Rose D. Friedman.

Fairness can be defined in terms of the distribution of rewards for work, the authority and command structures within the firm, the pace of work, and the nature and kind of work. A Distributist approach takes note of precisely these issues: how fairly the benefits of work are distributed, the degree of control that workers have over their work place, and the amount of individual freedom that their employment gives them to choose and pursue their own ends.

Are workers really "free to choose," as is claimed? What is the degree of control that workers have over their lives? Some see unhampered market exchange as providing this freedom. For Distributists, not only should people have access to markets, but also they should have the resources necessary to reap the benefits that markets afford.

One argument put forth against alternative work arrangements is that they would be unjust, insofar as they would violate the rights of those who own the resources that produce the goods. In a market system, it is argued, people get what they produce. Moving to a Distributist system where there is widespread ownership of the means of production would require redistribution and therefore entail a form of theft. This argument conflates property ownership with the actual production of output. In a world in which production requires multiple inputs, the notion that the owner of a resource has "produced" a particular amount of good or service begs the question of how one determines what portion of output is due to which particular input.[1]

One cannot rebut the charge that capitalism is unfair by demonstrating that the worker gains something from having a relationship with the capitalist firm and therefore is not worse off. That may be right, but the critical issue for the Distributist is not whether workers are better off than they would be if they were not working for capitalist firms. Neither is it whether they are getting marginally poorer or richer. Indeed, re-casting the debate as one of *some* benefit versus *no* benefit is to favor the status quo; the question is whether the benefits offered are shared in a reasonably proportionate way, and whether access to those benefits is provided for all who participate in the market. The substantial issue at stake is the moral one of the distribution of economic benefits and the freedom those arrangements engender. Distributists seek a better deal for the economic underdogs, Chesterton's "common man." And, most notably, they seek that better deal not just by modifying or tempering the interaction of workers, owners, and the markets with considerations of fairness and other ethical matters; they seek to fundamentally alter the relationship by making the workers *into* owners, thus eliminating many of the "bones of contention" that come up in modern economic life regarding the employer-worker relationship.

---

1. This theme is discussed in my introduction to *Economics for Helen, op. cit.*

One central question that emerges, then, from a consideration of the Distributist insight applied to current economic issues is not "should we use markets at all?" but "how are economic matters to be arranged?" Proponents of free-market capitalism find those questions all too easy to answer, believing they amount to the same question. The experience of the 20th century has shown that markets make possible exchange and specialization, without which economic prosperity is hard to achieve. Some would have Distributism attempting to thwart the forces of specialization and exchange, thus parodying Chester-Belloc economics as "three acres and a cow."

This is a manifestly unfair caricature, however. Conceding the usefulness of markets to any given extent does not equate to a credible critique or effective dismissal of the Distributist position. Distributism *is not a choice between markets and no markets.* Markets, whether local, national, or international, do not run of their own accord. They are simply tools brought to bear on circumstances that have numerous other attributes. Their performance depends on many "enabling conditions" or "rules of the game," such as the distribution of human and physical resources, the nature of business, the degree of community activity, types of economic arrangements in play, the extra-economic values of the participants, the reward mechanisms employed, etc.[1]

Here again the strengths of Distributism are revealed in their argument for community-level involvement to circumvent enforcement problems, for widespread property ownership, for giving people a stake in their community, and for giving them a voice in how that community enforces the rules of the game. These local solutions to problems take full advantage of concepts well-known to classical economists who recognized that individual agents and local communities know more about their own local economic arrangements than does some far away government official. This kind of solution helps to lubricate the wheels of social commerce.

Distributists realize that "the rules of the game" depend on cultural norms and political, economic, and social institutions. Distributists recognize that these factors do not impede the legitimate use of markets or make them somehow insignificant. Indeed, the former significantly affect the latter, and proper norms and institutions would serve to attenuate undesirable tendencies of the market.

---

1. As G. R. S. Taylor noted in his short but important sketch of the guilds (about which many Distributists wrote and which represent their ideal vision of cooperative employment, market exchange, and owner-worker relationship), "there is no reason to think that the guilds will immediately abolish [market] competition. It will be made a sane competition for the benefit of the community, instead of a very insane one, for the benefit of the profiteer. But it would be just as hasty to assume that all competition is a public evil as it would be for a man with sunstroke to dismiss the sun as a public nuisance" (*The Guild State* [Norfolk, Va.: IHS Press, 2006], p. 63).—Ed.

Issues over values are not the only concern of Distributism. Efficiency also comes in for scrutiny. It is not obvious that the contemporary capitalist firm is the most efficient or even the one most capable of providing technological advances. The efficiency of the capitalist firm may only be apparent, because its success is relative to existing arrangements. The capitalist firm may only be viable within existing arrangements, which would actively thwart one run on Distributist principles. Efficiency and survivability are not one and the same. Under a Distributist system there may well be gains that are unobtainable within an economy dominated by capitalist firms. Given space limitations, I briefly sketch just one argument in support.

According to Bowles and Gintis, capitalist firms use up resources monitoring their workers.[1] The Distributist firm can realize efficiency gains since the workers would own the output of the firm. Worker-owners would have an incentive to provide greater productivity. The Distributist firm would spend less on monitoring workers and therefore achieve greater output per unit of input. Moreover, these firms would be more inclined to use wage incentives to elicit work effort, rather than expending resources on monitoring techniques that would be comparatively less efficient. Distributist firms may be more innovative as well, since workers have an incentive to share improvements that they discover in the course of their work. Workers will have an incentive to invest in firm-specific "human capital." Given these advantages, why don't we see more worker-owned firms? Within existing economic arrangements, these firms tend to be capital-constrained and are often unable to find sufficient loans with which to run the business. It is evident, therefore, just how constraining the "rules of the game" can be, and the absence of these kinds of firms is hardly an endorsement of or a statement upon their inefficiency or undesirability.

Institutions, Inequality, and Market Expansion

EVEN WHILE ECONOMISTS defend markets, they must also see the legitimacy of those who criticize market relations. Those who argue for the expansion of market relations into social domains normally considered to be governed by non-market criteria, and who are committed to even freer markets without regard to the distributional issues involved, misdiagnose the main problems of modern capitalism. Distributist theory recognizes that these problems do not lie with the market per se, but with existing in-

---

1. Samuel Bowles and Herbert Gintis, *Recasting Egalitarianism* (London and New York: Verso, 1998).

stitutional arrangements. Distributism calls for serious reassessments of the institutions that characterize the contemporary world.

Before large-scale buying and selling could take place, certain norms, conventions, and institutions had to develop to sufficient levels of sophistication to facilitate exchange. These rules evolved with human society, and took millennia to take their present shape. What markets do so well is that they facilitate the exchange of the bundles of rights that characterize a commodity.[1] We rarely take notice of these bundles in our daily lives, yet their ramifications are enormous.[2] Markets are information-gathering devices, helping us to economize on costly information. Yet to achieve these benefits, the enabling conditions of markets such as the norms, institutions, conventions, legal structures, etc. all are necessary to undergird market exchange.

Distributist theory can benefit from a focused consideration of the enabling conditions of markets by calling on the recent advances in behavioral and experimental economics that allow a role for Distributist concerns. Such a consideration would help in its effort to thwart the push for unbridled capitalism. A commitment to the expansion of markets alone, without regard to the relevant enabling and limiting conditions, and to the numerous extra-market (and even intra-market) considerations that govern market exchanges, is an inadequate approach to economic prosperity. "Markets" in and of themselves are neither simple mathematical (and non-human) phenomena, nor is invocation of "the market" considered in this way a panacea for economic woe.

Distributism contributes also to a better and more accurate appreciation of these phenomena by its emphasis on democratic decision-making, by which I mean the notion that a broader base of individuals is allowed to participate in local economic processes. Milton Friedman used the language of democracy to describe and defend market exchanges: competition, he maintained, allows consumers to vote with their feet and with their dollars. Yet the democratic nature of this "participation through purchase" is questionable, at best.

If every dollar of household income had been cast as a vote in 2002, the average household in the richest fifth of the U.S. population would have had more than 14 times as many votes (143, 559) as the average household in the poorest fifth (9,931).[3]

---

1. For example, we may tend to think of a car as an object, but from an economic point of view any object is also a bundle of rights. If I own a car I have the right to sell that car to another person, but I do not have the right to drive that car into your living room.

2. See F. A. Hayek, "The Use of Knowledge in Society," *The American Economic Review* 35 (4), 1945, pp. 519–30.

3. Samuel Bowles, Richard Edwards, and Frank Roosevelt, *Understanding Capitalism: Competition, Command, and Change* 3rd edition (New York: Oxford University Press, 2005), p. 222.

As for "democratic" participation in the market, classical liberals have warned that political freedom may adversely affect economic freedom. Voters may pursue policies that restrain the economic tumult and insecurity brought on by a dynamic capitalist system. There is much evidence to suggest capitalist firms have acted upon this fear, and have themselves attempted to thwart democratic measures when they are inconvenient from the standpoint of "the bottom line." Some classical liberals indeed place economic freedom over and above political freedom, arguing that the former is necessary for maintaining the latter. For example, Friedrich Hayek preferred the order of a Pinochet to the democratically elected socialist Allende.[1] The business community echoes this point: George Soros has claimed that businesses prefer predictability and simplicity and therefore would rather deal with a single person or junta than a democratically elected governing body.

The prescient account of the political machine by Belloc and Chesterton holds that firms and the wealthy often express their own interests via support of elected representatives (and we can extend that to think tanks, special interest groups, and the media). The power of concentrated wealth finds expression in legal and tax systems that promote the interests of the managerial classes. This is precisely what Chesterton and Belloc feared when they wrote about "oligarchy." Since the property-rights structures of markets are themselves a product of the legal system and the government, when the laws that govern those rights change market outcomes will change.[2] Belloc's and Chesterton's oligarchs will seek to harness market forces for their benefit by changing rights to suit their interests.[3]

Princeton economist and *New York Times* columnist Paul Krugman echoes Chesterton and Belloc when he claims that "we have a rising oligarchy" and that the "growth in inequality may have as much to do with power relations as it does with market forces." For example, the average pay of the top 100 CEOs chosen by Forbes magazine in 1970 was 49 times that of the average worker. By 1998 that ratio had grown to 2,388 to 1! Krugman's concern is that "a rising economic tide has failed to lift most boats," and that "highly unequal societies also tend to be highly corrupt."[4]

In spite of the popular myths, in America a modern-day Horatio Alger story is not the norm. Upward mobility is greatly restricted. One study

---

1. Hayek's view was summarized in an interview he gave to the pro-government newspaper *El Mercurio* in 1981: "Personally I prefer a liberal dictator to democratic government lacking liberalism."

2. James M. Buchanan and Warren J. Samuels, "Two Views of Government: A Conversation," in David M. Levy and Sandra J. Peart, eds., *The Street Porter and the Philosopher* (Ann Arbor, Mich.: University of Michigan Press, 2007), pp. 139–61.

3. See Hilaire Belloc and Cecil Chesterton, *The Party System* (Norfolk, Va.: IHS Press, 2007 [1911]), for their expanded argument on this point.—Ed.

4. Paul Krugman, "Graduates Versus Oligarchs,"*New York Times*, February 27, 2006, p. A19.

found that children from the *bottom* tenth of the income distribution are about 15 times more likely than children from the *top* tenth to end up in the bottom 10 percent. Children of rich parents rarely move down the income distribution scale, contrary to another popular American myth that the wealthy "wayward kid" will receive his comeuppance for his sloth. Indeed, children from the richest tenth of the population end up as adults in the top 10 percent of the income distribution 20 times more frequently than do children from the poorest tenth of the population.[1]

In debates over alternative economic arrangements, it is sometimes claimed that the American economic system is the *best* because of the sheer size of U.S. output. The U.S. does have the largest per capita income of $31,872 in 1999 international dollars compared to Japan's $24,898. Yet, when it comes to quality-of-life measures such as life expectancy and infant mortality, the U.S. lags behind.[2] For example life expectancy at birth is 67.6 years in America, 71.8 years in Sweden and 73.6 years in Japan. The mortality rate of children per 1000 live births is 9 in the United States where Japan's is 5 and Sweden's only 4.

Democratic Firms

BELLOC AND CHESTERTON understood the notion of democratic ownership and the advantages of democratically owned firms, where "democracy" is here taken to consist of the broad participation and self-determination of the average employee in the firm or the economy. They knew that an environment conducive to the growth and expansion of the Distributist firm must be created and maintained. In *The Outline of Sanity* Chesterton advocates government measures to level the playing field. He is not advocating equality of outcomes, but equality of opportunity, which may mean treating different people and institutions differently depending upon circumstances. To level the playing field while ignoring the distribution of resources in the economy would be a mistake. The status quo distribution of resources cannot be sacrosanct if the playing field is to be truly equal.

Distributists have long realized that effective participatory democracy requires that people have access to resources so that they can participate in a meaningful way. Distributists see this democracy as tied intimately to self-development, autonomy, and self-control. They believe that this

---

1. Samuel Bowles and Herbert Gintis, "Intergenerational Inequality," *Journal of Economic Perspectives* 16 (3), Summer 2002, pp. 3–30.

2. Bowles, Edwards, and Roosevelt, *op. cit.*, p. 379.

kind of democracy serves a number of important functions: it makes decision-makers accountable, whether in the government or the marketplace; it enables people to have more control over their lives; and it makes them better.

This Distributist emphasis on democratic decision-making is not a claim that all decisions should be subject to the vote, but rather decisions with significant effects beyond the individual should be subject to a larger audience of participants – in effect, those who are affected should have a say in how. Actions that affect only the individual need not be subject to a democratic vote. When actions impose costs on others, collective decision-making should allow people to have a say in how they are affected. Their view also holds that decisions must have accountability, and this too is consistent with good economics. If people are not held accountable for their actions, then they have less incentive to take into account the costs they impose on others.

Work

THE ECONOMIST'S *homo economicus* derives utility from consuming goods and services, as well as from taking leisure, but he *avoids* work. Economists tend to treat work as a "bad," something of which people desire to consume less. The economist's awkward (though telling!) phrase for this is that a person "receives disutility" from work.

Distributism stresses that man is made in the image of the Creator. Man is a craftsman; he is a creator on a miniature scale. It focuses on the life-changing effects work has on the human person and wishes to take into account the multiple motivations that make people work. Distributists see work as something that can be spiritual or mystical. This is especially the case with work tied directly to creation itself, like artistic or intellectual pursuits or practical endeavors like rearing children, farming, or craftsmanship that involves working with raw materials. From this perspective people can enjoy work and find it fulfilling, and they are willing to work hard when they feel that they have some control over their lives, when they respect those in authority over them, and when their work is emotionally and intellectually rewarding. Yet when employers try to control workers and the pace of production, and reduce tasks to repetitive motions, the level of worker satisfaction falls. Although it is not possible to make all work tasks entirely pleasurable, it is possible to improve attitudes towards unpleasant work. Changing diapers is not a particularly enjoyable activity, but when it is your own child's diaper it takes on a different hue.

Distributists take issue with those who claim that by nature, people prefer leisure to work, or that they do not like taking orders from a boss, or even that the assembly-line nature of modern work is somehow necessary to achieve high productivity. Distributists do not believe that if workers are allowed a say in their conditions it leads to coddled workers who resist working for an advance of the firm's interests. This is the exception not the rule. Indeed such a worker can be created by the very strategies that capitalist firms have employed to elicit effort on the part of the worker. Distributism recognizes that an understanding of capitalism requires knowledge of who controls, benefits, and determines the pace of work. If workers bristle under management, it probably has more to do with how the workplace is organized than with the natural recalcitrance of the worker.

Distributist views on work are well described by Pope John Paul II:

> Through work, man *not only transforms nature*, adapting it to his own needs, but he also *achieves fulfillment* as a human being and indeed, in a sense, becomes "more a human being."[1]

Equity and Efficiency

DISTRIBUTISM IS OFTEN seen as an attempt to turn back the clock or escape from the modern world. There are surely these themes in Distributist literature that mount a critique of the hustle and bustle of modernity, the tearing of the social fabric, and the dislocations brought on by modern capitalism. Yet Distributism is broader than that. A longing for a time that is easier socially to navigate is a theme that other recent thinkers have come to embrace.[2] There is a growing recognition that people should not be mere flotsam and jetsam on the high seas of globalization but rather should have both a say in how their communities choose to allocate their scarce resources and the right to a share of economic gains. As John Maynard Keynes once remarked, "economists set themselves too easy a task if in tempestuous seas they can only tell us that when the storm is long past the ocean is flat again."[3] Keynes was responding to those who preferred to let markets adjust of their own accord, regardless of the enormous social costs that that may entail.

One school of thought argues that the economic system will work out the kinks over time, and that a necessary byproduct of our dynamic economic

---

1. Pope John Paul II, *Laborem Exercens*, §9 (translation and paragraph number from the Vatican edition, http://www.vatican.va).

2. John Gray, *False Dawn: The Delusions of Global Capitalism* (New York: New Press, 1998).

3. John Maynard Keynes, *A Tract on Monetary Reform* (London: Macmillan and Co., Ltd., 1923).

system is a skewed distribution of income. Hence the price, it is said, of a rapidly growing economy is income disparity. A vibrant capitalist economy with complex financial institutions must *necessarily* create winners and losers. To reduce this inequality would stifle the drive for innovation and risk taking. The best we can do is to create a minimum social safety net, remove market impediments, and let the effects of time and compounding work their magic.[1] In addition, it is feared that active measures to improve income equality through taxes and transfers may increase inefficiency and lead to slower economic growth. From this perspective income inequality could lead to greater work effort and innovation as management and labor struggle to improve their lot.

This conventional wisdom was expressed well in Arthur Okun's book *Equality and Efficiency: The Big Tradeoff.* This view, as he articulated it, became the hallmark of worldly wisdom and was trumpeted by both liberals and conservatives alike. Indeed Okun, a professed democratic liberal, claimed that "the conflict between equality and economic efficiency is inescapable," and that his message was a dose of reality.[2] Even liberals came to embrace the mantra, arguing that equality would be great if we could get it, but it was not worth the price.

Like so many other "inescapable conclusions" of economic policy, history has not been kind to this theory. Income inequality and productivity growth are inextricably and inversely linked. Countries such as Taiwan, South Korea, and Japan are among the most equal countries in the world, yet their growth in productivity has exceeded those of the most unequal countries, including the U.S. and the U.K. Even if only the wealthiest countries are examined, the tradeoff does not appear between equality and efficiency. Economists now realize that economic inequality may create inefficiencies and reduce the growth rate in productivity. Inequality can lead to labor unrest, an increase in conflicts between labor and management, and to wasteful expenditure of resources. When people feel they are treated unfairly they may avoid economic relationships that would have been mutually beneficial. Notwithstanding the moral or philosophical arguments, here we have hard economic evidence pointing in a Distributist direction.

That evidence further shows that people are willing to do things that are costly to themselves (e.g., foregoing a beneficial economic trade) to punish

---

1. Compounding here refers to the compounding effects of annual economic growth, i.e., a country whose total output grows at the rate of 1% per year will take 70 years for its total output to double. A country whose total output grows at the rate of 2% per year will double its output in only 35 years. The time it takes output to approximately double is easily calculated using the rule of 70: divide 70 by the annual growth rate.

2. Arthur M. Okun, *Equality and Efficiency, the Big Tradeoff* (Washington, D.C.: The Brookings Institution, 1975).

those they feel have treated them unfairly.[1] Thus, people walk away from the worker-employer relationship, increase their propensity to shirk on the job, avoid helping at the firm, preferring no slice of the economic pie to an unfair one. Worker-management relations can have such a strong effect on the quality of output that poor relations can be deadly. For example, there is evidence that the Firestone tire recall of 2000 is directly related to two of its production facilities that had particularly poor labor-management relations.[2]

Consistent with the insights of Distributist theory, inequality limits the entrepreneurial talents of those who lack capital to go into business for themselves. As a result, the main benefit that we are told comes from small-business ownership – the incentive to work hard for one's own – is lost. Oddly, critics of Distributism claim this attitude towards the small shop owner is backward looking, but it is obvious that promoting small businesses only enhances overall entrepreneurship by tapping into the creative powers of the poor but gifted business owner. Indeed, wealth inequalities ensure that many businesses are stillborn if these gifts remain untapped. It is indeed hard to imagine that such a positive perspective on entrepreneurship and initiative could be "backward."

Similar arguments apply to the role of democracy, or genuine popular participation in government, in economic growth. Just as it is claimed there exists a trade-off between efficiency and equality, some claim that political freedom and a democratic political process are also at odds with economic growth. Democratic governments lack the will to undertake unpopular economic reforms, it is said, since they require the marshalling of fickle public opinion that is often ignorant of economic realities. Further, democratic governments are subject to special-interest group and party politics. Hence, a dictator may well be better situated than a democratic government to achieve low government spending, low inflation, full employment and a high national saving rate.

Yet as with the efficiency-equality trade-off, this claim does not hold up to scrutiny. For example, Professor Jenny Minier of the University of Miami examined the growth rates of countries that experienced sharp changes in their level of democracy during the period 1965 to 1987. She found that increases in democracy tended to increase economic growth, and decreases in democracy tended to decrease economic growth.[3]

1. Chapter 3 of Bowles, *Microeconomics, op. cit.*, has an excellent overview of the experimental literature and provides helpful pointers to the relevant literature.

2. Alan B. Krueger and Alexandre Mas, "Strikes, Scabs, and Tread Separations: Labor Strife and the Production of Defective Bridgestone/Firestone Tires," *Journal of Political Economy* 112, April 2004, pp. 253–89.

3. Jenny A. Minier, "Democracy and Growth: Alternative Approaches," *Journal of Economic Growth* 3 (3) September 1998, pp. 241–266.

There are several reasons democracy may promote growth. Relative to dictatorships, democratic governments that command popular support may be more stable and less likely to start wars, and have better relations with the advanced industrial nations, most of which are democracies.[1]

Constitutional protection for both human and property-rights also increases the willingness of foreigners and residents to invest in a country. Freedoms of speech and expression are essential for full development of a nation's educational and scientific potential. Democratic governments also have a greater ability to respond to public demands to solve public-goods, collective-action, and coordination problems, all of which can lead to slower growth if left unresolved.

Conclusion

> 1. Economists do not know very much. 2. Other people, including the politicians who make economic policy, know even less than economists do . . . . These beliefs do not provide a platform from which to make strong pronouncements about economics or economic policy.[2]
>
> —Herbert Stein

I TAKE IT FROM Stein that we need to proceed with caution, but proceed we must. Today we have examples of successful experiments in work organized along Distributist lines, such as the cooperatives of Mondragon in the Basque region of Spain. We have the accumulated theoretical work that demonstrates the possibility of success from Distributist-directed firms. What remains is the desire to carve out some space in which Distributist principles can take hold. We need to think long and hard about policies that will help communities pursue their shared Distributist goals.

Looking back to the great Distributist and Catholic social thinkers for inspiration is not wishing for better days. Rather, it is the realization that with the tools of modern economic theory it is now possible to build upon the Distributist vision in a way that can boast of currency and familiarity with economic literature and research, no less than common sense. The recent developments within and without economics show promise, insofar as economists and social scientists are becoming aware both of the limitations

---

1. The Bush administration's recent behavior with respect to starting wars casts doubt on this claim. Democracies with a timid national press can be misled by an aggressive, single-minded administration. See D. L. O'Huallachain and J. Forrest Sharpe, eds., *Neo-CONNED! Again* (Vienna, Va.: Light in the Darkness Publications, 2005).

2. Herbert Stein, *Washington Bedtime Stories: The Politics of Money and Jobs* (New York, Free Press, 1986), p. xi.

of their discipline and of the benefits of new approaches. These recent developments in economic theory point to the same issues that interested Distributists. Thanks to this development, it is now possible to cast Distributist economics in terms that academic and professional economists can appreciate. And in the process we can conduct a fruitful conversation with the past that will hopefully reinvigorate today's economic debates.

~ III ~

SKETCHES PERSONAL
AND PRACTICAL

THE GREAT TASK OF THIS AND SUCCEEDING GENERATIONS IS TO LIMIT
AND PERHAPS FINALLY TO TRANSFORM INDUSTRIALISM, FOR ONLY WHEN
INDUSTRIALISM IS SUBORDINATED, MINIMIZED, AND CHANGED CAN HUMANITY
REGAIN ITS SENSE OF WHAT LIFE IS AND WHAT IS THE PURPOSE OF LIFE. HUMANITY
MUST LEARN EXPLICITLY, WHAT IT KNOWS IMPLICITLY BUT WILL ONLY IN ITS CYNICAL
OR DESPAIRING MOMENTS OPENLY ADMIT: THAT INDUSTRIALISM, AS WE NOW HAVE
EXPERIENCE OF IT, IS ANTI-HUMAN, ANTI-VITAL, IS INDEED THE WAY OF DEATH.

—Donald Davidson

"The few who have perceived these truths, the few who can contrast the modern man with that immediate ancestry of his age, but have forgotten, know that the remedy can only be found in a change of philosophy; that is, of religion. They know further that the material test of this change and at the same time the prime condition which would foster the change would be the reinstitution of private property and its extension to a determining number of the community. But those who see this are few. It is their duty to work upon the lines which their knowledge of the trouble suggests, but it is also their duty not to deceive themselves upon the conditions of their task. It is their duty to realize that this task has become exceedingly difficult of achievement, that the difficulty is increasing, and that therefore they must bear themselves as must all those who attempt a creative effort at reform: that is, as sufferers who will probably fail."

—HILAIRE BELLOC

～ 10 ～

The Economy of Salvation

How the Son of God Employs Fathers in the Work of Building the Kingdom of God

Father Lawrence Smith

> . . . be not solicitous for your life, what you shall eat, nor for the body, what you shall put on. Is not the life more than meat and the body more than raiment? . . . Seek ye therefore first the Kingdom of God and His justice: and all these things shall be added unto you.
>
> —St. Matthew vi:25, 33

MANY TODAY ARE UNCOMFORTABLE WITH THE blurring of lines between Rome and the rest of those claiming belief in Christ that has transpired since the Second Vatican Council. Indeed, Catholics are not Protestants. This is painfully obvious in the doctrinal areas of ecclesial governance, theology, and morality. But those concerned with the issue of whether or not Catholics and Protestants should share administrative structures, forms of worship, and proscriptions on certain behaviors seem to take no exception to the blurring of the lines – indeed the lines are so blurred as to constitute an actual identity of belief – between Catholics and Protestants over another issue, one of much longer standing and more deeply ingrained in Western man's collective psyche: namely, the way men make a living. No matter what people precisely understand by seeking the Bread of Life in Holy Communion, practically all moderns of any or no faith are agreed that the earning of our daily bread is and should be achieved by means of *capitalism*.

But the assumption that Catholics and Protestants do not and *need not* have different approaches to the pursuit of sustenance on earth is seriously flawed. First it must be recognized that there is no single voice that defines just what it means to be authentically Protestant. This leaves the door open for "Protestant" economic practices profoundly at variance with both Catholicism and other forms of Protestantism. The Amish sheep farmer and the Calvinist manufacturer have few shared principles guiding their respective decisions on pursuing a livelihood, exercising worship, and understanding the nature of sin. Curiously enough, however, the Amish farmer has at least a limited affinity with the detachment of St. Francis of Assisi, while at the same time the Calvinist industrialist seems to take little exception to the work ethic of St. Joseph.

At the root of the whatever is common to the Protestant understanding of the human person in all aspects of mortal experience is the notion of the individual's right to determine his own course. This is not merely a matter of Martin Luther parting ways with the Holy See, or the aforementioned Amish being "divorced" by the followers of Menno Simon, or John Wesley finding the retooled faith of Elizabeth I too confining, or the leaders of the Anglicans throughout the Third World vilifying Gene Robinson of New Hampshire. In addition to this shared Protestant penchant for seeking communion apart from one another, they share another, rather ironic pedigree. All Protestants look to the Catholic Church as their origin.

Amintore Fanfani, in his treatise *Catholicism, Protestantism, and Capitalism*,[1] spells out how Catholics tolerated, then pursued, and then mandated practices that became modern capitalism. In the same vein, it was from a unified Catholic culture and ethos that the Protestant multiplicity arose. This simultaneous set of departures by Catholics from Catholic ethics of economics, orthodoxy in doctrine, and adherence to ecclesial order did more than produce rival claimants to the name "Christian." Divergent understandings of faith and how it is played out in daily life also produced a dichotomy between Catholics and Protestants of what is permissible and *meritorious* in man's economic activities. It is not possible to make a final determination of which modern economic activities are acceptable to all Protestants, but it is easy to demonstrate how often modernity veers from definitive Catholic teaching on ethics, morals, and justice.

Men with common mores and a common worldview will meet with certain difficulty and probable failure in offering their fellows fair opportunities to produce food, shelter, and clothing. Men *without* a common set of truths at the basis of their vision as to how to pursue their livelihoods

---

1. Norfolk, Va.: IHS Press, 2003 (1934).

are *guaranteed* to suffer the exploitation of many men by others, *and the exploited will have no principle by which to correct their oppressors.* Appeals to sentimentality and emotionalism will be made on the one hand, and on the other there will be violent struggles by the deprived to take what they perceive was stolen by the privileged. Neither sentiment nor violence is a basis for a rational resolution to social injustice, and neither emotionalism nor strife can be the basis for an ongoing effort to preserve civilization.

Where no Protestant is able to speak for all Protestants about what constitutes fundamental departures from an "orthodox" *sine qua non*, the Vicar of Christ on earth, the Pope, holds an office whose responsibilities include teaching definitively what is authentic to the Gospel, what is required for salvation, and what will lead to damnation. It is the matter of a wholly other work to describe how this aspect of papal authority has been muted with regard to economic matters. What is of importance here is to acknowledge the power of Catholicism, through the papacy, to provide a consistent and coherent body of doctrines useful in man's daily life, *and* to outline several of the most egregious ways in which modern capitalism violates Catholic dogma, natural law, and the divine will. This capacity to articulate for all believers what is of the Faith and what is antithetical to it is an inherent and irreconcilable mark of difference between the Catholic Church and Protestant sects. The failure of Popes to exercise this capacity fully, coupled with Protestants' impotence to agree among themselves about matters of truth, has resulted in the extraordinary economic and social injustices rampant in the modern capitalist world.

Pride, lust, avarice, gluttony, envy, anger, and sloth are the seven deadly sins. They feed off of and lead towards each other. Capitalism encourages men to cultivate these sins in many ways. Protestants have no agreed upon set of principles to counter capitalism's claims of the legitimacy of these vices at work in man's economic life. Catholicism has defined over the centuries many principles that clearly condemn fundamental activities within capitalism that nonetheless have become commonplace in the average man's daily experience. Billions are invested, trillions exchanged, and incalculable losses incurred based on an exclusively this-worldly understanding of man's ultimate purpose.

Is that the last word on what should occupy the space between the womb and the tomb? Heavens no! God has *much* more to say to man than Madison Avenue. Our Lord gets His word out through His Vicar, through His clergy, and through His sons who head the families where He is made to be at home.

Feed My Sheep!: How the Holy Father and the Bishops Can Help Jesus Save the World

> [L]et them not cease to impress upon men of all ranks the principles of Christian living as found in the Gospel; by all means in their power let them strive for the well-being of people; and especially let them aim both to preserve in themselves and to arouse in others, in the highest equally as well as in the lowest, the mistress and queen of the virtues, Charity. Certainly, the well-being which is so longed for is chiefly to be expected from an abundant outpouring of charity; of Christian charity, We mean, which is in epitome the law of the Gospel, and which, always ready to sacrifice itself for the benefit of others, is man's surest antidote against the insolence of the world and immoderate love of self, the divine office and features of this virtue being described by the Apostle Paul in these words: "Charity is patient, is kind . . . seeketh not her own . . . beareth with all things . . . endureth all things" (1 Corinthians xiii:4–7).
>
> —*Rerum Novarum*, §83

JESUS CHRIST CAME not to be served, but to serve. His Mystical Body, the Catholic Church, continues His work. It is not the place of the Church to change economics; it is the place of the Church to announce the Good News of salvation. Those who hear the Good News will live lives according to its mandates. It is not for the world to dictate how the Gospel is tolerated in men's lives, but for the Gospel to mold a world in keeping with obligations that lead to eternal life. His Holiness the Pope and the Bishops in union with Him have the charge from God Himself to offer food to His Flock in such a way as to free them to do the work of building up the Kingdom of Heaven. God's law, the natural law, and the laws of the Church are not intended to restrict the citizens subject to Christ the King, but to provide for them a context in which to exercise the freedom of the sons of God.

Towards that end, the hierarchy of the Church should refrain from offering yet another encyclical letter on social justice or a pastoral letter on human rights or, Heaven forbid, a blue-ribbon committee to study the problem with secular and religious leaders. Instead, the Church and the world need to hear the Good News, the Gospel of Jesus Christ – and that Church leaders are taking it seriously. This is to say that as *spiritual* leaders they set the tone for the conversation. It is not an estimation of the present state of things that requires exposition, but a constant iteration of eternal things. Our work in this passing world must ever be directed by a desire to live in the world that will never end.

Jesus Christ, the same yesterday, today, and forever, is the patrimony of the Church. His Birth in Bethlehem forms the basis for our understanding of what a life pleasing to God looks like. Jesus was born a poor child, in poor circumstances, to a poor family. He lived His life among poor people and proclaimed the good news that the poor are *blessed!* Jesus died a criminal's death literally lacking the shirt on His back.

In that death, Jesus empties Himself of all human dignity, of creaturely life, of the honor due Him as God. He is left with absolutely nothing. The very torments of hell become His sole possession. During His teaching ministry He stressed that it is *only* through the Cross that God's will is accomplished, that life is preserved, and that the sinner shows himself a true disciple.

Jesus then takes up His life again on Easter Sunday. He enters into His Father's glory on Ascension Thursday. One day – soon, let us pray – He will return in that glory to judge the living and the dead. Those who would go on living are commanded to do as the Lord of Life has done: to lay down this life; to reject the allurements of the world, the flesh, and the devil; and to trust in the Providence of God to provide *all* that is needed: food, shelter, clothing, and life itself.

The Pope is the successor to St. Peter and the Bishops are the successors to the other Apostles. As the original Twelve went forth to the ends of the earth and proclaimed the Kingship of Christ Crucified and Risen, each succeeding generation of the Magisterium is charged with the labor of spreading the Gospel. Jesus did not wield a kingship shaped of worldly things. The Princes of the Church, although stewards of material goods, have as their primary authority the power of binding and loosing on earth and in Heaven. Their sons and daughters in the clergy and laity stand in profound want of the voice of Christ calling mankind to sanctity in every aspect of earthly life. As such, the preaching task, far more than administration, is at the heart of the role of shepherd given to the Pope and the Bishops in communion with him.

Christendom was not a wonderful economic system put in place supporting nice people who ended up becoming holy. The Social Reign of Christ the King was pursued in the daily life of countless martyrs, confessors, and virgins, who through their tireless witness to Christ and Him Crucified gave birth to a society predicated on perfecting man through the grace of God mediated through the Sacraments of the Church. Our Bishops should remember this as efforts are made to confront a world grown godless once more. The world will not be met and defeated on its terms, but by bringing to bear the power of grace, the gift of the Sacraments, and the wealth of divine charity shared among the children of God. The best service that the hierarchy could offer the Church is not to dictate *what* we are to do, but to articulate *why* the Church exists on earth: *Jesus Christ is Lord of all! He has given us an example of holy poverty. He has promised a reward to those who sacrifice all with Him. And He commands all to love as He loves, unto death, to new life, for ever and ever. Amen!*

Do This in Memory of Me! The Role of the Parish Priest in Christ's Work in the World

> It is clear, however, that moral and religious perfection ought to be regarded as their principal goal, and their social organization as such ought above all to be directed completely by this goal . . . . Therefore, having taken their principles from God, let those associations provide ample opportunity for religious instruction so that individual members may understand their duties to God, that they may well know what to believe, what to hope for, and what to do for eternal salvation, and that with special care they may be fortified against erroneous opinions and various forms of corruption. Let the worker be exhorted to the worship of God and the pursuit of piety, especially to religious observance of Sundays and Holy Days. Let him learn to reverence and love the Church, the common Mother of all, and likewise to observe her precepts and to frequent her Sacraments, which are the divine means for purifying the soul from the stains of sin and for attaining sanctity.
>
> —*Rerum Novarum*, §77

IT IS NECESSARY for the faithful to hear two words from their priests in the pulpit to understand how to conform their economic lives to their Faith: *Go home!* Where will we find the means to transform the world from the den of Mammon to the House of God? *Go home!* How can we make a difference in our large economy to bring greater justice to bear on our economics? *Go home!* Who is responsible for ensuring that the Gospel is at the heart of decisions that affect our material well being? *Go home!*

Perhaps the most devastating aspect of the ills wrought by a worldly economics is the accelerating destruction of the family. Parishes throughout the world are contributing to this phenomenon. Whether it is the extraordinary expense of the physical plants, or the immense size of staffs doing work of dubious worth, or a chaos of activities that demand the presence of parishioners at meetings, fundraisers, and, every now and then, Mass, the parish has become a true burden to the average family. Add to all of this the dizzying array of events attached to the few remaining and barely Catholic schools, and it becomes evident that the family spends more time at work, at school, and at socializing than with one another.

An irony in this age of lay "empowerment" is that Church activities have become tied up with a physical location. The parish hall, rectory and school have replaced the front porch, back yard, and kitchen as the places most Catholics engage one another. Since parishes are so rarely neighborhood realities in the twenty-first century, the *only* time that parishioners see one another is on Sunday. Thus, coffee-and-doughnuts hour becomes the primary context for the majority of the laity to learn to love their fellows sufficiently to sell all and give to the poor, to lay down their lives for their friends, and to take up their crosses each day and follow Jesus.

Father Needs to Tell Everybody to *Go Home!*

THE PARISH SHOULD not be a surrogate living room. Glorifying God should be the emphasis when the parish priest is exhorting his parishioners to greater efforts at sanctity, not appeals for capital campaigns, or selling candy for school computers, or raffles to beef up the endowment. *Father should not encourage consumerism and materialism in the name of advancing the work of God.* The parish priest sets the tone that the children of God in their parish family live in a house devoted to *prayer.* Anyone can show hospitality in his own home. The unique role of the Church is to bring the people together to receive from God what He has to offer – Christ Crucified – and to offer in return humble thanks, joyful praise, and reverent awe.

When everybody does *Go home!* the fruits of God's gifts can be shared. It is in the home that the lessons learned in the Church are applied. We are here, not to buy more things or to have "better" things or to earn more to have more things. The tone set by the parish priest goes a long way toward reminding parishioners that, as Christ's Kingdom is not of this world, His flock is laboring for a reign not of this world. But if the parish is caught up in frenetic activity, material acquisition, and misplaced priorities that neglect the spiritual altogether, then when it comes to personal decisions on purchases, employment, and investment, it is not to be expected that suddenly a flock whose shepherds have never guided them in a sense of holy poverty will suddenly insist that their houses, cars, home-entertainment systems, Disneyland vacations, and usurious credit cards will reflect a desire to imitate Jesus.

Insofar as the parishioners are at the church, they will be in need of their priests being at the altar, in the confessional, and on their knees. It is absurd to think that the lay faithful at work in the world will on the whole be more spiritually centered and fervent than their priests. Like fathers, like sons. Parish priests who set an example of worldly anxiety, committee-driven decision making, and material avarice will have a parish full of worried, tired, and unsatisfied – and unsatisfiable – basket cases. The priest who leads in prayer, who demonstrates a desire for sanctity, who rejoices in holy poverty, sets a standard for his people that, if they strive to meet it, will result in a peace that this world cannot give.

Father Pastor is not an administrator. He is not a businessman. He is not an employer. Father is ordained *in persona Christi* to offer the Holy Sacrifice of the Mass, to forgive sins, and to mediate grace to a sinful world. The priest who makes prayer, penance, and service in love of God above all things and neighbor above himself will go far towards helping his people escape the trap set by the world. As Dorothy Day said in a fundraising letter sent from her base in New York in 1967, "The less one takes from Caesar, the less one must render to Caesar!" The parish priest can offer a tremendous gift to his parishioners by modeling for them and exhorting them to a life given to laying up treasures in Heaven, where neither rust, moth, nor thief – nor inflation – can diminish them.

"As Christ Also Loved the Church and Delivered Himself Up for It": Holy Fathers at Home

> Rights of this kind which reside in individuals are seen to have much greater validity when viewed as fitted into and connected with the obligations of human beings in family life . . . . No law of man can abolish the natural and primeval right of marriage, or in any way set aside the chief purpose of matrimony established in the beginning by the authority of God: 'Increase and multiply' (Genesis 1:28). Behold, therefore, the family, or rather the society of the household, a very small society indeed, but a true one, and older than any polity! For that reason it must have certain rights and duties of its own entirely independent of the State . . . . As already noted, the family, like the State, is by the same token a society in the strictest sense of the term, and it is governed by its own proper authority, namely, by that of the father . . . . To desire, therefore, that the civil power should enter arbitrarily into the privacy of homes is a great and pernicious error . . . . Paternal authority is such that it can neither be abolished or absorbed by the State, because it has the same origin in common with that of man's own life . . . . Inasmuch as Socialists, therefore, disregard care by parents and in its place introduce care by the State, they act *against natural justice* and dissolve the structure of the home.
>
> —*Rerum Novarum*, §§18–21

IT IS IN the home that the freedom of the sons of God is exercised by the laity. No one can keep a father from exercising paternal service to his little flock, the family, in perfect conformity with the teachings of the Church, the message of the Gospel, and the example of Our Lord. Husband-fathers hold a priestly role in the home. They are nourished by sound teachings, strengthened by Sacramental grace, and encouraged by their priests' examples to guide their families in emulating the Holy Family. Dad is responsible for insisting that the family's home is a house of prayer. That Jesus is the primary member of the family. That the honor due to mother and father flows from placing God the Father at the head of the family and obedience to Him in all things as the fundamental rule of the house. The Fourth Commandment is dependent on adherence to the First.

Fathers are given to families for leadership. Of utmost importance is their leadership in striving for Heaven. Dad should lead the family daily Rosary, gathering the family to go to frequent Confession, preparing the family at home in prayer on Sunday and Holy Days before heading to church for Mass, insisting on having time each day to nurture his own spiritual life in private prayer, as well as making time for family retreats, pilgrimages, and pursuing the corporal and spiritual works of mercy. Dad should speak frequently to his children about the vocation to which God is calling them, and he should cleave faithfully to his wife as they together fulfill their vocation as parents and spouses.

Embracing such spiritual disciplines will bear fruit in filial piety, love of God, and confidence in His promise of salvation. A family led in this way will not want television polluting their home. They will hold popular music, material acquisitiveness, immodesty, profane language, and irreverence in utter disdain. Christmas will be preceded by a holy Advent bent on the penitential preparation for receiving God's Son into their midst, not a feeding frenzy at the trough of Mammon to fuel a bloated economy. Such a family will be bound together so strongly that the children growing up will not have an uncontrollable urge to leave home, but will instead understand that their family is always their home, and the next generation will be lovingly received into the bosom of a group of people who know themselves and who they are as a family, and who have a well-founded hope for achieving their ultimate goal of living together forever in Heaven.

Before the revolution is mounted to sweep away the excesses of capitalism and make the world safe for whatever a revolution of that kind would deem worthwhile, it must be considered what kind of men are making things change. Good men will make changes for the better, bad men for the worse, and men without a sense of good and bad who insist that no one should impose such sentiments on others will be the most evil. Too much time is lost, too much breath is wasted, and too much energy dissipated waiting for the "system" to change. Beyond the fact that no "system" has a will to change and is entirely at the behest of its human creators and users, is the fact that only a fool would leave something as important as his immortal soul – and his family's immortal souls – in the hands of bureaucrats, politicians, and "market forces."

True power lies in each man governing his own affairs in keeping with the universal call to holiness. The Browns have no control over whether or not the Joneses will cooperate in building the Kingdom of Heaven, but both the Browns and the Joneses have absolute control over what happens in their respective homes. The key to transforming the world is to transform the individual soul and then the family. It is the father within the family who must decide the direction of such a transformation. There is no coincidence that the destruction of the family began not with forcing women into the workplace or putting children in compulsory public schools or taxing income and non-productive real estate, but *in removing the father from the family farm or the family trade.* Much of the cure to what ails us is dependent on returning the father to his proper place at the head of the family and *in the home.*

Pride is at work among those who ignore the essential work of making families holy under the headship of the father. The mindset that sees such efforts as inconsequential encourages the very problems attacking the family. Strong families are not a by-product of good economics or social theory. Mankind must strengthen the family or all economics will be a matter of slavery and the community that of inmates in prisons. It is not a waste of time or a distraction to begin the task of correcting the imbalances in macroeconomics by focusing on the domestic economy.

The macro-economy exists to support the home economy, and the home economy exists to support the needs of the body in service to spiritual perfection. Families are not made for work, but work is meant to nurture the family. Prayer is not intended to sustain man in his daily life of toil, but his daily life of toil makes sense only as a means to sustain the effort to attain eternal life. We do not work all day and grudgingly give a little time to prayer at infrequent intervals. We pray each day and throughout the day, taking time periodically to do the work that makes prayer possible. People incapable of ordering their lives towards the eternal will find themselves laboring for that which is ephemeral, dehumanizing, and, ultimately, deadly.

So, the father in a family must be keenly aware of his responsibility to guide his little flock to good pastures. Where he interacts on a community level, it will be with the desire and understanding that public efforts are intended for the preservation and enrichment of his family and all families. The common good is not merely a matter of what is good for all, but what is good for each. A collection of people inattentive to being good at home will not accomplish any good together. Conversely, a society of strong families has a firm foundation on which to increase justice, peace, and, in proper proportion, prosperity.

Conclusion: A (Very) Few Practical Considerations

> Through past events we can, without temerity, foresee the future. Age presses hard upon age, but there are wondrous similarities in history, governed as it is by the Providence of God, who guides and directs the continuity and the chain of events in accordance with that purpose which He set before Himself in creating the human race . . . . And since religion alone, as We said in the beginning, can remove the evil, root and branch, let all reflect upon this: First and foremost, Christian morals must be re-established, without which even the weapons of prudence, which are considered especially effective, will be of no avail to secure well-being.
>
> —*Rerum Novarum*, §§80, 82

HERE ARE A few suggestions for the Catholic who desires to serve God more than Mammon: Believe what Jesus teaches through His Church, pray fervently and constantly, and spend more time at home than anywhere else. Most people will think this too vague and general. It is an indication of our collective paucity of imagination and the decline of the *sensus Catholicus* that such simplicity is thought to be too little to be effective. The lack of a simple life, of simple desires, of simple work is what has gotten us into the current morass. We have forgotten that searching the depths of the wisdom of God is denied to the learned and clever, but revealed to the merest children, of whom is made the Kingdom of Heaven. In its typical penchant for contrariness, modernity also balks at explanations that require thought, study, and discipline.

To be more specific, then, a suggestion for the hierarchy to take to heart: declare a Holy Year to celebrate the primary truths of Catholic Faith. Begin in Advent with an emphasis on *Emmanuel,* God with us, particularly in His Real Presence in the Blessed Sacrament of the Altar. Encourage the faithful to bring the reality of Our Lord's loving abiding with us to the end of time from the Church to the home out into the world. Celebrate the Christmas Mystery around the Sacred Mysteries of the Mass and throughout the entirety of the Christmas Season right up to the Feast of the Presentation.

Continue the Holy Year observance with an emphasis on Our Lord's Sacrifice at Calvary. Shift the focus in the Mass from Our Lord being with us, to His salvific action in our midst. Approach Lent having received the awe-inspiring gift of Christ in the Incarnation with the intent of returning that gift through sacrifice, penance, and mortification. Allow the Lenten disciplines to be an expression of the willingness to love as Jesus loves, to obey the Father as Jesus obeys Him, and to offer all in sacrifice along with the perfect holocaust of Good Friday.

From Easter until after Pentecost is a time to emphasize in the Mass how the Cross accomplishes the forgiveness of sins, and how the gifts of the Holy Ghost bear fruit in the hearts, minds, souls, and bodies of those who conform entirely to Jesus. It is during this period of the year that the faithful give witness to the world that indeed the Lord Jesus saves and that real hope is present that fallen man can rise above his miserable state in the world and dare to claim unity with God Himself! The glory of God in Christ is present in the Mass where the work of salvation goes on unceasingly and bears fruit in the Body of Christ bringing His offer of eternal life to the whole world.

Once the hierarchy has declared this Holy Year, the parish priest has an outline for the work ahead of him in the local community. In addition to observing the universal Church's celebration of the Holy Year, the parish priest can use it to make permanent changes in the spiritual lives of his flock. One simple yet profoundly significant gesture would be to change the parish's fiscal year to reflect the liturgical year. This would allow all of the parish's material labors to refer back to their spiritual bases and more readily reflect the truer goals of parish activities.

Thus, the period of Advent and Christmas would become a time to focus the parish on examining how they go about their work, examining themselves for adherence to lives that are receptive of Christ in all things. As the calendar year comes to an end, and the liturgical year begins, the world becomes quieter, darker, and more introspective. This is a great context for whatever might be necessary by way of preparing the parish for appeals to support the material needs of the parish and broader community. Christmas, then, becomes a time to rejoice in what God has given, rather than in offering more of the same of what the world calls wealth. The parish should never descend into being self-serving, but should always strive to be of service in assisting one another to be holy, providing for the poor, *and making converts to the Faith to join the parish in its service.* The new year should be the time the parish renews its resolve to be holy as God is holy, to be perfect as the Father is perfect, and to be compassionate as the Lord is compassionate.

That resolve becomes the basis for the Lenten sacrifices that follow shortly after the Christmas Season. Sacrificial giving, both in terms of the corporal and spiritual works of mercy, prayer, and material goods, can form part of the parish's collective taking up of the Cross with Jesus. If it is necessary to ask for money beyond what is offered in the weekly collection (and this need should be examined for its underlying cause, for such need should be rare), then Lent lends the proper focus for why, how much, and how to use what is given. However, far more than parish needs, the priest should encourage and guide his people toward finding needs outside of their immediate community, to broaden the scope of the true mission of the Church to preach the Gospel, offer the Sacraments, *and save souls.*

In the time of Easter and after Pentecost this work of seeking souls to bring to Christ's salvation becomes the heart of the life of the parish. Having recognized the immensity of the gift of Christ at Christmas and rallying the parish to offer themselves with Him at Lent, the parish then can burst forth from their "upper room" and live out what they believe and what they have promised. This will bear fruit in the homes of the parish, in the Sacramental life of the community, and in their willingness to give witness to the desire of the Church to bring Christ to the whole world. These efforts flow much more soundly from the liturgical calendar than from a fiscal calendar or a school calendar, and the parish thus gives a far stronger message about their priorities built on God and His Providence rather than the arbitrary dictates of man.

Lastly, and mostly, this will to receive Christ, to unite His Body more firmly to Him as the Head, *and never to rest until every soul on earth is a member of His Body,* finds its greatest effects in the homes of the faithful. Individual souls, not parishes or dioceses or episcopal conferences, are given salvation. Those individuals are born to, raised in, and learn from families in the home.

Most learning should be in the home. Mothers and fathers are children's first and primary teachers. Collective education in the modern world is nothing short of catastrophic. Those who insist that somehow other people's children benefit from being subjected to the indifference and neglect that the average parent inflicts on his children, the hostility to good sense and morals characteristic of school bureaucracies, and the outright godlessness of most curricula, probably claim never to have inhaled, to read only the articles and not look at the pictures, and to always obey the speed limit. In a world where second-hand cigarette smoke is attacked with a vengeance not seen since the Salem witch hunts, it is obscene to suggest that any parent should allow his child's body, mind, and soul to be exposed in schools to widespread filth, teachers' warped philosophies, and government malignancy in setting school policy.

There is nothing more beneficial for fathers to do than establish the home as the locus for *all* family activities. If at all possible, he should work for the family's sustenance from the home. The mother should be the primary caretaker of the home. And the children should receive instruction, play, and learn to pray in the home. The family should do nothing elsewhere that it does not do in the home.

Fathers and mothers should use their skill, imagination, and prayer to impart to their children the wonders of life, the responsibilities of being in a family, and the joys of serving and loving God with one's whole heart, mind, soul, and strength. Children should understand from a very early age that to live differently from the Catholic ideal is abnormal, self-destructive, and against common sense as well as deleterious to a saintly life. The child raised in a Catholic home should understand that God comes first, that the Church is a generous Mother, that the family is a tremendous gift always to be treasured, and that the things of this world are subservient to the needs of supporting the family, becoming holy, and obeying God. Modern man needs to teach his children the life lesson that modern life has gone horribly awry. The Catholic family needs to revive the tradition of proclaiming Jesus Christ as Sovereign King – so that generations to come will not find that to be an extraordinary assertion, but the truest and happiest statement of fact.

Perseverance

No matter how the night oppresses, I
will always make my way back home to Dawn;
regardless how the dark might make me cry
in pain, through pain to Day I press anon.
Undaunted by the wounds of mounting years
and heedless of my ever waning youth,
no ancient terror nor my childish fears
shall stop my search for Heaven's deathless Truth.
Although assail'd by sins' temptations fierce
when naught seems hidden but the help of grace,
the veil that veils the nations I shall pierce
until at last I see God's holy Face.
Take this to be the declaration for
my part 'gainst hell in right'ous, ruthless war.

Do not think I have come to bring peace on earth; I have not come to bring peace, but a sword! —St. Matthew x:34

Why, even the hairs of your head are all numbered, therefore, fear not! —St. Luke xii:7

~ 11 ~

"For the Life of This Pig"
or, An Essay on the Benevolence of the Butcher

William Edmund Fahey, Ph.D.

T**HE OLD MAN KNEW HOW TO KILL THE PIG. W**E DE-sired to know. With our thoughts of health, and our longing for tradition, we desired to participate in a nearly forgotten ritual, but our desire was that born of *books*, and of a certain suspicion that the promises of this world were but vain smoke.

I. Setting Out

> My heart is longing for them day by day
> Where I spent life's golden hours
> In the veil of Shenadoah
> Mid the green fields of Virginia far away.
>
> —Traditional Virginia Ballad

T**HAT WINTER MORNING** I had crossed the Shenandoah before dawn at Morgan's Ford. I had with me my two eldest daughters and a stranger, who had heard of our community and wanted to see something of it for himself. The waters of the river flowed north out of the great valley of Virginia. Up and down the uneven banks, ice held to the shores and a dull grey light revealed snow between the black trunks dusting a season or more of fallen leaves. We crossed as a western wind churned up the waters. I was reminded of the sea hard by where my father's people lived in Maine, the land which gave joy to my youth.

We traveled through an ancient wood of oaks, through a place once known as Milldale. The place had long since lost the water mills which gave the settlement its name, and even their location is forgotten, though it is remembered that there were two. And though there is not a living soul, the name of the place recalls the former vitality and independence of a people for whom the grinding of grain was neither an inconvenience to be sourced elsewhere nor a convenience to be neglected, but a natural part of feeding one's self and of being neighborly. That was long ago. Now there is only the name on a map.

Along the road one finds strange contrasts: brambly woodland choked by long neglect, bordering upon nearly a thousand acres under cultivation as a rich man's tax shelter – all monoculture crops and sustained only by heavy equipment and petro-fertilization. On a small parcel, horses stamp against the damp chill, while fifty yards away the rusted hulk of a car is vanishing slowly into the vegetation. Here and there a new house faces off against a tired old one; vinyl siding vying with blistering clapboard. There is not a human soul to be seen. All about nature lies in potency – where it is not paralyzed by tidy chemical management or lawless thickets. A valley, still rich, yearns for the men who knew how to cultivate her; but the original homesteaders crossed the wide waters long ago and died further west.

Near Milldale is Fair Knowe, the house of my friend and our destination. The name is a variant of Sir Walter Scott's Fairy Knowe, which the unnamed traveler sets out to discover in *Old Mortality*: "I wish to know the way to Fairy Knowe." A fairy knowe, or in Gaelic, *dun sithean*, is the sort of mound which allows the little people to move between our world and their own. In a way, we all wish to know the path to such places. As strangers in our own world, we are comforted by the thought that perhaps what strikes our eyes may only be the surface of things. Perhaps what is more distant, but more familiar, lies just beyond, but now connected. That a grove might be the habitation of some ethereal race bestows upon our transient way of understanding our lives a sense for the permanence of what was and may be. The gravel road to Fair Knowe takes you along a straight course until the trees gather round you, their dark arches flecked with hoarfrost. Then the land rises and falls. The hedgerow gives way to walnut and tulip poplar, the bare Judas tree, white ash and black cherry, choirs of beech; and as the road lowers into a hollow, the keen may see the slender dogwood drawing the eye into the deep woods before the road rises among once golden shagbark and pignut hickories. That is how one arrives. All the trees watched us silently as we approached that morning.

A landscape that has recorded the long interaction of man and nature does not forget its partners, and my friend, a professor of philosophy, has been working steadily to keep that partnership alive. His twenty-some acres sit atop the ridges that slope down to the Shenandoah. His is flanked by the land of his brother-in-law and his father, some three hundred acres that nurture flocks of cattle and sheep, bee hives, several large orchards, chicken coops, gardens and acre upon acre of forest, which they and others hunt every autumn. The land is well-tended and beautiful, supporting several ventures in husbandry and farming, and, more importantly, allowing three families and their many friends to cooperate in the work of creation, extending it, enriching it and themselves, and in so doing imitating the Creator in His own activity.

My friend's home is simply designed, spacious, and bright. I have seen it in every season and am pleased to have helped floor the kitchen with cherry cut from the land. The sun was just below the tree line when we pulled around the circling drive. Behind the house was a merry gathering. A few former and current students ringed an open fire. Their talk was of absent friends, of the day's sharp, purifying cold, and, of course, of the slaughter. Most clutched mugs, of coffee or tea, of things that keep one warm. Ukrainian sweet breads had been baked by the woman of the house. Among the little curve of oaks, we did not mind the wind. Hickory wood crackled into our imagination the idea of warmth. The air smelt faintly of tobacco and the long moldering of leaves; and the old man's eyes were fixed on the fire as he began to recall the steps for us.

II. Preparations

> Hear, my son, your father's instruction, and reject not your mother's teaching.
>
> —Proverbs i:8

THE PROPER BEGINNING to any affair is always in relationship to its end, but only a man with tried experience knows how to properly pursue it. Therein lies the difficulty of tradition. Had the old man not been there, we would have been nearly cut off from actions that, in spite of our ignorance and inexperience, ultimately seemed engraved on our hearts like some sempeternal law. Yet what mortal art lies so deep without care? The seeds of all good affections, such as love and courage, may be in our hearts, but poetry and soldiering require training. It is a matter of calling forth, with discipline and dedication, the habits of art and virtue that, while to some extent lying within us, need the nurturing of an older, wiser, and more experienced hand to develop.

The slaughtering of animals is surely contemporary with the birth of tool craft. Indeed, it may be father to the craft. Nevertheless, this most ancient art is yet an art. Civilized order is not maintained without effort, instruction, and fidelity. For the mind to understand something truly, there is required the keenness of imagination and the senses acting to acquire knowledge, but there is greater need for an overarching and directing experience, and a willingness to repeat the activity until it is done so rightly that one forgets exactly how it is done. As in the mind, so in thriving cultures, the past must preside over the court of experience. For us, the old man was the Past articulate.

Everything set down here finds its cause in the old man, for they did not slaughter hogs when I was a boy in Hudson, Ohio. My friend, our host, had lived his early life in one of Maryland's first planned communities. As the old will remember, butchering sessions normally fall between early December and February. The exact date varies slightly, sometimes by region, but behind the region is typically religion. Catholics tend to slaughter pigs near the Feast of Saint Nicholas. An early December slaughter gives one just enough time to hang hams in one's chimney and have the meat smoked by Christmas. Such chimneys are rare today, now that function and beauty have been divorced. In Virginia, the original harvest feast of St. Martin marked the earliest point of slaughter. The old man, however, remained true to the traditions of his own valley: slaughters always fell within two days of Thanksgiving. There was good planning in this, since the autumn feast provides abundant "leftovers" for the men, and a country man can rarely stand a full day of inactivity. The timing is tempered to the season by long experience. For by December, much of the surplus crops and waste have been eaten. The hogs are over two hundred pounds. Their flesh is crucial fare during the winter. The cool air protects the savor of the pig. In warm climates, slaughter and consumption were side by side, for culinary reasons as well as for health.

The old man remembered that his family would often slaughter a dozen or more pigs in a single day. Good work for six men and a boy. Was it as boisterous as this day's gathering, I wondered aloud. "Oh, yes. There was always more than a little fun in it. Even the Baptists took a little Bourbon. The women worked as well, bringing coffee and lending a hand wherever it was needed; everyone knew what was to be done. Everyone was involved. Partially, because you had to be, but mostly because you wouldn't have had it another way."

The old man had brought the ropes and tackle, scrapers, galvanized buckets, and scalding vat. My friend and two young men had filled the vat with spring water and started a fire beneath, long before dawn, just as instructed. I knew both young men well. Both were strapping men, just the sort you wanted. One was finishing his degree and soon would return to Kansas to take up farming on his father's land. The other hailed from Pittsburgh and viewed this as part of his apprenticeship before buying a parcel for himself and his young wife. Neither had slaughtered a pig before. There were several young ladies there as well; there were reasons beyond simple fellowship for being present. They were there to see what cast of man slaughtered a pig, for it was judged that such a man might make a boon companion for life. The discerning ways of women are mysterious and wise.

My good neighbor, also a professor, hailed me. I introduced the stranger and he was welcomed. To a person everyone there was somehow associated with the little liberal arts college where I once taught, apart from one friend, a wine merchant, who came because poor scholars and old farmers enjoy life considerably more than the rich men to whom he sold wine. It must be made clear that not a single one of us knew first hand what would happen. Every motion depended on the old man's words.

The old man went over the basic steps of the slaughter again, for repetition is the mother of every discipline. I was surprised at the simple elegance of it all – the ordering of each part which seemed to unfold before us naturally and well-paced like the cadence of the old man's speech. For when he spoke, I imagined it like the phrases and homespun rhythm that once were heard as butternut soldiers marched north with Lee on a summer's day. But now it was winter and my thoughts turned back to practical matters, for the rustling of the leaves and a little snort heralded the presence of the pig.

The pig was a Tamworth – descended of the English boar, hardy and made for the open life, now rare. My friend had raised twelve. The one that rustled about in the crisp leaves was the smallest of his family. His brethren had already gone the way of all pork. The Tamworth is an attractive pig. Indeed, were there still country inns, one would fully expect – stepping into a Beatrix Potter tale – to find a Tamworth standing beside a roaring fire, tankard in hand, drawing heavily from his clay pipe. Such a fanciful vision obscures the fact that the Tamworth is for the sustenance of the body, more than the imagination. Fattened on acorns, the flesh is as succulent as one could desire. Horace once said that he wished to be a pig from the herd of Epicurus. Considering this Tamworth's life, I can now understand the remark. The pig had lived to his maturity with his brethren in the shade of oaks, while eating happily from the land and enjoying splendid air and plenty of roaming ground. Having lived within yards of one family, sharing the same round of sun and rain, and hearing nothing but the sound of the woods and the laughter of children, he was about to move from the life of a pig to the stuff of man.

III. The Blessing

> Benedic, Domine, creaturam istam, ut sit remedium salutare
> generi humano: et praesta per invocationem sancti nominis tui; ut,
> quicumque ex ea sumsperint, corporis sanitatem et animae tutelam
> percipiant. Per Christum Dominum nostrum.
>
> —Benedictio ad omnia quae volueris[1]

A T THAT MOMENT the merry-eyed priest approached. He was a Virginian, but not of the Valley; and though recently appointed to the parish, already in love with it. As he trod across the frost and leaves, I knew what my friend and host was thinking. He had not arranged this moment properly; that is to say, the old man had not requested a priest, and as Father approached in the pastor's biretta, with breviary in hand, my friend was concerned that the depths of the old man's blood would be stirred and that he would look with a Covenanter's eye upon the priest and his blessing as something outside the natural course of things and not in keeping with tradition. For a long moment there was only the sound of crushed leaves and the hushed sweep of a cassock. My friend broached the issue manfully. "I thought it right to have Father bless the pig and our work." More than a few dry throats swallowed before the old man spoke. "You did right there, John (for that was my friend's name). My father always, always blessed the pig, or had it done. It is a pig, but it is a life. There's no sense in doing something without gratitude. That's just plain ignorant."

Then came the blessing. The old man withdrew a space. Among old men I have often noticed this sort of reserve at a blessing, as if they wish to make more room for the young, compelled both by shame and hope, content to act as a solemn witness, harrowed by hard experience and sustained by dogged belief, wondering if the rising generation will fare bet-

---

1. In English, this "Blessing for any use (or any kind of creature, esp. food) whatsoever" reads: "Bless, O Lord, this creature so that it may be wholesome nourishment for mankind; and grant that those who eat of it may, through the invocation of Thy Holy Name, receive bodily health and spiritual protection. Through Christ Our Lord." Upon being approached for a translation, the author initially balked, suggesting that "those interested in the restoration of traditions would do well to learn to read or at least pray in Latin, and a good start could be made by consulting Abbot Cabrol's *The Roman Missal*, especially its various blessings." Happily, he relented in the end. This particular blessing can be found in the same work.—Ed.

ter. A basin was filled, exorcised, and blessed. Then the priest aspersed the Tamworth and all who were there, while the children rushed forward to be sure to receive a good lashing of the waters. Old Roman Cato records that the pig was one of the three animals set aside for the rites of purification. There too, the pig was aspersed and then offered as an oblation for the sake of the community. Of all the animals, only the pig, the lamb, and the ox were deemed right for cleansing a family and its land. Among that company, the pig took pride of place. Many find the Catholic rituals of blessing and purification – if ever they see or hear them – as simply too close to the pagan, too arcane for sensible Christianity, as if an avalanche of doubt would bury their souls in discovering the rude and hoary foundations of our religion. Yet I count it a consolation to know that our ancient Roman fathers never abandoned their prayers and duties, but found them more fully fulfilled with the Advent of the Christ Child.

IV. Killing

> What will I do gin my hoggie die?
> My joy, my pride, my hoggie!
> My only beast, I had na mae,
> And wow! but I was vogie!
>
> —Traditional Scottish peasant song

FAINTLY, MODERN MEN still know some of the ancient affection that a farmer might hold for his animals. The love a city dweller has for his Siamese is overly sentimental and a result of the displacement of children, but felt truly enough. Rarely, though, do his feelings have that depth which can only come for something that lives side by side with you, that has required considerable time and sacrifice to raise, that shares the regular cycle of the day, that lives under the power of the elements, and that brings some material blessing to the entire family. The story of the Good Shepherd is increasingly inaccessible to people who can afford with ease to give their Tabby medical treatment unaffordable to most mortal men. *My host was not such a man.* He had purchased a dozen pigs with some reservation and only after consulting with several friends and pooling funds together. The apparently thoughtless act of feeding hogs was a risky affair financially. As he would later learn, an entire litter of pigs can be lost in one bitter storm, and a sow can crush her brood trying to keep them warm during a freezing autumn downpour. "It is a pig, but it is a life," as the old man said, and it is just when a man has dug a trench to bury an entire litter of newly born pigs that he experiences the real fragility of existence.

To look at the bloated creatures raised in vast pig factories today, one would have trouble comprehending any attachment or understanding between creature and master. In my favorite bookstore, housed in a three-hundred year old barn, I once turned a corner to meet a small black pig, who seemed to have the run of the place and, indeed, sat in a wicker basket opposite the proprietor in the warmth of a cast iron stove, the proprietor reading books, the pig wondering at the proprietor. Sir Walter Scott had a small pig as companion. Certain breeds, like the Tamworth, are handsome and, if not intelligent looking, they are expressive and creaturely: they are a life. My friend had kept back the runt for a few weeks when all the others had been slaughtered. The runt would be fed a while longer and provide meat for his family. That runt was not meant to be a pet, although it did trot happily behind him and children for a time, but lasting companionship was not what that pig was for.

Whether a man who has killed a hundred pigs pauses long or not before the slaughter, I cannot say, but even the old man seemed to have pulled back for a moment into a respectful quiet. Then he broke the silence, telling us that this moment was one of the clearest and fondest from childhood: when he would be out with his family just at dawn, and dozens of shots went out down the valley signaling the official commencement of the slaughter. On this morning there would be only one shot maintaining that folkway. My friend had prepared a board with a small amount of feed to be lowered into the pen. The pig was to come over and be shot and thus removed from his pen clean. One shoots the pig downward through the triangle made by his ears and snout well above the eyes. "Now, when you shoot him, make sure it's a good clean shot. Straight through the head now. He's to go down in one blow." (At that word the old man made to clap, but stopped short so as not to disturb the Tamworth.) "You don't want him running around in pain. That'll be a disaster for all." My friend nodded. "Then, you'll want that fence down, and to go in and stick him quick."

"Stick him?"

"Just like in hunting. Stick him. You want that heart to pour his blood out. That makes for good pudding and he'll go faster."

Clearly my friend had not anticipated this part.

"And these two fellows will want to come down on top of him and help the blood out. The sooner he's bled, the sooner he's gone."

At this the finality and the instrumentality of action joined sharply in my friend's mind. We were no longer slaughtering *a* pig, but *this* pig, *his* pig. The indefinite had shifted to the definite, and the definite to the possessive. Nor was the pig to be slaughtered in the passive voice any more. Now we moved to the active voice. He would shoot his Tamworth, the runt which he had spent autumn evenings watching. Now he would end its life.

The board was lowered in silence and the grain spilled. Several of the children had now disappeared and I suspect a few adults wished they were still children. The Tamworth stepped out and began to eat. My friend knelt in front of the pig with his revolver. The excited swaying of the pig's head and the interposing lines of the fence seemed to prevent a straight shot. There were times when the shot seemed possible for a second, and then the moment passed. Suddenly, my friend stood up with the revolver slack at his side and it hit me hard how difficult such a thing must be the first time, or perhaps anytime. He let out a slow breath and said, "Lord, we thank you for the life of this pig." The old man nodded. The pig simply stopped and lowered his head. The shot was clean and before the crack left my ear, two men were on the Tamworth and his dark blood ran out into the earth.

Old Roman Varro calls the butcher the "conciliator" between man and the animals, bringing together man and what in nature is *for* man. It struck me again how life on the land attuned man for the ancient faith. How could one walk away from this scene and not understand the role and responsibility of offering a sacrifice? How could one not see the strange shared suffering between man and his beast? And what would it mean for a culture to lack men who understood these things? How could bloodless sacrifice be understood without real bloodshed?

V. The Scalding and Scraping

> And innumerable swine, with flashing white teeth and fat thick upon them were singed and stretched out on the flames of Hephaistos.
>
> —Homer, *Iliad*, Book 23

ONCE THE PIG is down and bled, two separate paths can be followed, depending upon one's tradition. The hair of the pig, so useful for shaving, must be removed, and this can be done by burning or scraping.

The tradition surrounding the Hampshire pig is to burn layers of straw over the pig. The hog must be dry for the hairs to come out properly. The flames tighten the skin and give the meat a unique flavor. The burning is a protracted affair and requires an earlier start and a continuous bonfire—a pleasing task and even more delightful sight before dawn. Our pig, however, was a Tamworth.

The pig was carried with a little groaning and a little staggering to its steamy bath. After a few minutes' dip, it was brought out and eight hands began rapidly scraping. There was little trouble at all. Like the shaving of a mature face, the skin yields up the bristles quickly and with mild effort, and the continuous flow of action, the swirling of the arms, the regular laver of vaporous waters, all gave this stage a soothing, quiet quality. No one spoke a word. There was only the hiss of the water and the scraping of knives.

VI. Hanging

> Evans: I pray you, have your remembrance, child: 'accusative, hung, hang, hog.'
> Quickly: 'Hang-hog' is Latin for bacon, I warrant you.
>
> —Shakespeare, *The Merry Wives of Windsor*

ASK A FARMER why it is a "gambrel" that a pig is hung upon, and he will not say more than that is the *word*, that is what his father and his father's brothers called the thing. The gambrel in some regions goes by the name "single tree," when a horse harness is added, or – with frankness – the "spreader." It is now that the beast must be uplifted and freed from the earth so that his meat may be taken without the taint of lower things. The gambrel is often, as it was that winter day, two sturdy poles with iron hooks, which pierce the hind tendons, and behind these a third pole for support.

Oh, if ever the naturalness of slaughter can be seen, it is now, as the massive pig is raised, his body securely fixed to the spreader. No matter the weight, the particular tendons of each pig will always have developed to support his mass above the earth; that is at least for swine who roam and root freely as had ours. Nature does nothing in vain.

And so, the Tamworth swung, and in so doing revealed the secret of the gambrel. For if the old man could have made the journey through time, hearing what his forefathers had called in Virginia and England "the gambrel," he would have heard the echo of strong Norman voices saying "gamberel," and before these the Roman "gamba" (hoofed leg); further still and eastward the conversation would run back to the Greek "kambê" (that which swings). But what would be gained in the scholars' game of chasing echoes when the old man, more than these, possessed the word from his own father, its meaning known because experienced through long use? Through the speaking of words tuned by long memory to the actions of his body the old man stood outside of time, and where he stood remained the West. In our attempt to recover a tradition, we still labored under the burden of our own age. When the old man spoke, that burden became lighter and freed us to pursue, with a unity beyond mere imagination, the task for which we came.

VII. Gutting

> The inwards are next taken out, and if the wife be not a slattern, here, in the mere offal, in the mere garbage, there is food, and delicate food, too, for a large family for a week; and hog's puddings for the children, and some for the neighbours' children, who come to play with them; for these things are by no means to be overlooked . . . .
>
> —William Cobbett, *Cottage Economy*

IN SOLEMN SILENCE swung the pig. Even with such a creature there is a respect that must be shown towards the body. Even in such a moment as this – perhaps especially in moments such as this. The old man directed practically and precisely how to work the knife: down and with care, for the skin must be cut while simultaneously tying that lowest of organs to prevent a loss of dignity to pig and man alike. The slightest knick of the intestine will produce a sulfurous smell, and worse. The gut twined, the belly skin must be parted downward to the jaw. The breast bone must be split with determination. The object in mind is to divide the body in half. Which of the two requires greater dexterity – cutting the skin near the intestine or cracking the breast bone – is hard to say. Both were done with an intense though somewhat hesitant force by my friend; he was a hunter, but a pig is not a deer and this was a new rite of passage. The old man kept nodding and quietly saying "that's right," and so under his guidance my friend knit this novelty to his experience and finished neatly before he knew.

Now a large washtub must be at hand. We had many near by, for the old man had ordered our tools as well as our actions. It is with great ease and relief that the organs will tumble earthward, as if reluctant to be parted with earth, as if they still shared too much with the soil. To one having never seen a gutting, it is always remarkable how clean the thing is; nothing at all like a filthy charnel house. As with a hunted animal, the pig's innards are separated absolutely from the good meat by a membrane, and nature seems to have placed the muscles of the diaphragm in such a way as to distinguish – and keep safe – the nobler organs of the heart and lungs from their lesser companions. The organs were then divided: the stomach, the kidney, the liver, the mysterious "sweet breads," and the mirth-making bladder. Cleaned, even the intestine should take its place among the salubrious meats. The spleen, the old man told us, was to be cast away. It was done, and tradition thus observed.

When we examined the heart, it struck me how natural each action of the slaughter was for a man who married the guidance of tradition with his own experience; it became so deep and internal as to be unlearned and purely enacted. As for ourselves, we by and large were only acting out the old man's vision; his actions were guided by the hard-earned grace of practice, habits formed by long memories so deep that it would be truer to say that the man who had acquired them was *of the memory*, than that the memory was his own. My friend, who had pierced the heart, was in a middle state between inexperience and old practice. By coupling his understanding of hunting with the old man's directives, my friend struck once and swiftly with near effortless thought – thought that met no resistance in action. And in sticking that pig, the heart was halved so perfectly that one would have concluded that pigs, like men, lived with divided hearts.

VIII. The Cutting

> Then they cut up the pig, and Eumaios began by putting raw pieces from each joint on to some of the fat; these he sprinkled with meal of barley, and placed them upon the embers; they cut the remaining meat, spit it, and roasted it to satisfaction; when they had taken them off the spits they piled them on trenchers. The swineherd, a man most fair, then stood and gave each his due portion – seven in total. One of these he set apart for Hermes the son of Maia, as well as his nymphs, praying to them as he worked; the others he distributed to each man. He gave Odysseus some slices cut lengthways down the loin of the white-toothed pig: a mark of special honor, and Odysseus was much pleased. "I pray, Eumaios," he said, "that our father Zeus will be as well disposed towards you as I am, for the good grace that you are showing to a wanderer like myself."
>
> —Homer, *Odyssey*, Book 14

THE HARD COLD of the day allowed events to continue at a pleasant pace. In warmer weather one must balance the need to let the flesh cool with the singular fact that pork is not suited to delays. So there was time to look at the fire for a few moments and drink coffee. While we were a little weary, the first flush of the slaughter having passed and the release of tension having led to a state of anticipatory satisfaction, the old man had become most animated, as he stepped back into every slaughter of his youth and lost the distinctiveness of our faces. He chanted out story after story, mentioning the names of men and women who should have been as intimate to us as they were to him. With a little repetition they did begin to become something more than shades.

For the old man, the slaughter of hogs had always been a pursuit that brought together the generations. As a boy, long before he could speak much at all, he had gathered kindling for his equally quiet great grandmother, who, seated beside the fire, rendered the lard and doled out fresh crackling, salt-dipped, to grateful little hands. His mother and father were always in sight, as with most activities on the homestead. And though there were the occasional tart comments, and though this work was hard, there remained the abiding joy of good work done with and for his family. The affair was under the direction of his father and grandfather; and no distinction was made between education and home-making. The old man's own sons had walked away from such customs, walked to the lively beat of progress, and unwittingly jeopardized the fragile continuity required for handing on knowledge. The boys had taken office jobs. The old man did not quite understand what they did or did not know how to speak about it, and so we returned to our work. It was at this point that the sawing began.

The backbone of the hanging pig had to be removed. When it was done it was a wonderful thing to see. What we did with it I cannot recall, but I remember it as bright with blood and suggestive of roasting. But now I have got ahead of things, for as I have said, I too was learning.

The head was removed. This act was done in silence. The head is, after all, the seat of (some sort of) intelligence in any beast (even a bureaucrat). To many people, the head of a pig is frightening, perhaps conjuring up fears of mortality. The most ancient of storytellers among the Greeks speak of the terrible quest for a man-devouring boar. The sad lays of the Celts agree. Perhaps the severed head of the pig disturbs some primordial ghost within who reminds us that not every hunter returns to the feast. That warning gives poignancy to a feast, for there can be no earthly feast without the thought of those absent. A feast recalls with intention the transitory nature of things, but it does so to defy it. By definition a feast commemorates the dying and the renewing of our affairs. Thus, absence itself becomes essential to the hopefulness and joy of a feast. As for me, my mind was enlivened with one of the merriest carols of old Christendom:

> The boar's head in hand bring I,
> Bedeck'd with bays and rosemary.
> I pray you, my masters, merry be
> *Quot estis in convivio.*
>
> *Caput apri defero*
> *Reddens laudes Domino!*
>
> The boar's head, as I understand,
> Is the rarest dish in all this land,
> Which thus bedeck'd with a gay garland
> Let us *servire cantico.*
>
> *Caput apri defero*
> *Reddens laudes Domino!*
>
> Our steward hath provided this
> In honor of the King of Bliss;
> Which, on this day to be served is
> *In Reginensi atrio.*
>
> *Caput apri defero*
> *Reddens laudes Domino!*[1]

Why the head of a boar, or of his humbler brother pig, is the "rarest dish in all this land" is simple enough to understand: it contains the most succulent meat. It is with good reason that illustrations of ancient feasts place the boar's head before the king. The jowl and neck and meat around the face are delicious. The ears will transform a pottage of beans into a savory meal, and all the other scraps are sought as ingredients for the choicest of pies. The great skull should be boiled until all the flesh falls away from the bones. These scraps, when cooled and blended with cloves and pepper, salt and sweet marjoram – which Lucretius says boars fear when alive – are excellent served cold with horseradish, or pan-fried like a sausage.

After the head and back bones have been removed, there are four primal cuts, each one yielding – even in a modest pig – at least a dozen pounds of meat. Under the direct tutelage of nature, man long ago established these cuts. The old man knew them; the wine merchant as well, although the names dif-

---

1. A traditional English Christmas carol, first published in 1521 and referred to as the "Boar's Head Carol." The refrain is rendered in English as: "The boar's head I bring / Giving praises to the Lord." The Latin from the last lines of each of the three verses is, in English, respectively: "As you all feast so heartily"; "Let us serve with a song"; and, "In the Queen's hall." According to tradition, the song arises from an event in the 14th century. A scholar of Queen's College, Oxford, was on his way to midnight Mass, carrying with him a book of Aristotle. He was suddenly attacked by a wild boar, and he promptly defended himself by ramming the book down the boar's throat. The song was written in thanksgiving for the subsequent Christmas feasting.—Ed.

fered, as names do in a living culture. Consult whom and what and where you may, the cuts have become universal and only an entrepreneur could unmake them. Though the carving of these portions be done by two or even one man alone, it is done with a community in mind. Even a suckling pig, such as the first of several pigs Eumaios offered Odysseus, has been made for two or three men together. As the pieces are cut and set aside for seasoning, few, even of those poor souls who have only paid for meat dismembered and divided in equally weighed units for simple profit and solitary consumption, few indeed could miss the fact that nature has structured the pig for joint consumption. But this should be obvious. The wise man has observed that even an onion is made for two men to consume, for no single man will eat an entire onion.

What are the primal cuts? I myself did not know. They are the shoulder, the back (or loin) the belly, and the ham. Each of these cuts subdivides further into a series of portions, meals that will satisfy a family or several hardy men.

First comes the shoulder, which divides into the Boston shoulder, or, properly, the Pork Shoulder Blade Boston Roast; the lengthy name reflects the slow roast that this cut should enjoy while covered in apple gravy or encrusted in coriander and garlic. Then comes the fore leg, also known as a picnic shoulder, meant for braising, or to be shredded and cooked in bubbling lard in a kettle of beaten copper. One should not forget the trotters, which in Portugal are made into chorizo and stewed with thyme, white wine, and mussels.

The mid-section consists of the coveted loin, with its tender center cut, and then the ordinary ribs or back ribs (as well as the country ribs, which are actually fatty chops), the chops proper and the hip end, or sirloin as it is more politely dubbed. Man's ingenuity knows no limits as to how these should be consumed: rolled in flour and pepper; daubed with vinegar, molasses, and sugar; brined in oranges and soy; bathed in Riesling and apricots; massaged with olive oil, paprika, and sage; always treated with salt and garlic; frequently grilled, sometimes roasted or fried, rarely disappointing to those gathered at table.

Properly speaking, the belly is also of the mid-section, but as the life-sustaining bacon comes from it and as it yields an additional dozen or more pounds of worthy meats, it is treated separately. Here one finds the true spare ribs, down low near the belly fat, rich in flavor. Belly fat is little known. It is the unsmoked portion of the hog's belly, which is so seductively tender that it could be easily mistaken for clotted cream. Here, as I have said, is the bacon. Of ribs, nothing will be said since the traditions vary with violence on how they are to be prepared. Of bacon, I shall say only: even Long John Silver and his rogues knew how to fry their own bacon to accompany their biscuits, for truly man does not live by bread alone. "I'll stay here a bit," said Billy Bones upon entering the Admiral Benbow. "I'm a plain man; rum and bacon and eggs is what I want, and that head up there for to watch ships off." While men could be found who contented themselves with rum and bacon and eggs, and a view of the sea, Christendom lived well and strong. Until bacon is elevated again, we should expect little but continued decline.

Then there is the ham: salted or smoked with apple wood, glazed and roasted or fried as steaks, shaved and sliced, the ham is still well known and can even be seen swinging on hooks in the most conventional of supermarkets. Ham is the single hind quarters, usually kept intact and either cured wet or dry. Wet curing, or brining, yields the famed Wiltshire hams; dry cured are known throughout the West – *prosciutto crudo*, Westphalian, Ardennes, and, of course, Virginia country ham.

Finally, there is the long process of "rendering" the parts of fat which are trimmed away from the beast and melted so that nothing may go to waste: the lard and crackling, that flavorful skin which will not melt. All offer a savor and satisfaction to the palate, and almost all are studiously neglected by the modern consumer. Lard is maligned terribly in our day. Largely this is due to our fear of the natural end of the body – that little happy girth which marks the transition from youth to maturity. Yet one can scarcely find a more delightful snack than lard which has been mixed with rosemary and a little salt spread over fresh bread. Such marginal dishes were once the staff of a good life. Of the slow melting, and cooling, and skimming of the lard, or the delicate, lace-like tissue that held the organs together and is so prized by bakers and pastry cooks, I cannot speak, for at this point it was necessary for the stranger to depart. There was still plenty of daylight, still considerable work to be done, and a considerable meal to eat, but the dictates of flight times and e-tickets, of heightened security and short-term parking, all the many "conveniences" of modern travel demanded that I take the stranger back to the city. Never mind that he longed to stay.

IX. A Modest Reflection

> It is not from the benevolence of the butcher, the brewer, or the baker, that we expect our dinner, but from their regard to their own interest. We address ourselves, not to their humanity but to their self-love, and never talk to them of our own necessities but of their advantages.
>
> —Adam Smith, *The Wealth of Nations*

IT HAS BEEN some time since I have seen either the old man or the stranger. Of the old man, I have heard he continues to counsel my friend in various fading arts. The stranger's last words to me were of how much he desired to live in a community like ours. I hope that happens. It is not entirely a matter of choice. The world of choice and self-advantage does not understand the world of tradition. For to enter the world of tradition requires a kind of invitation. Choice on the personal level is only exercised as an affirmation or rejection of the sudden awareness that one is part of something, something not entirely of one's own choosing. The disciplines and arts of any community rely obviously on the efforts of single persons at sustaining discipline. Nevertheless, a single person cannot create an art, a tradition, or a community. It is precisely the benevolence of those already within a tradition that allows us to enter and be initiated. The coherence necessary to sustain a community and its arts reposes chiefly on benevolence – benevolence that initiates good will towards a fellow, and continues in the trust that he will sustain the conventions "handed on," even long after he has left one's company. Human action moves along grooves of benevolence; we follow customs and manners and standards developed and affirmed long before our birth.

We may reject such conventions, but in so doing, we reject the invitation of previous generations. We reject our humanity, a quality derived from our attention to our fellow man and the limits we place on our own self-love. When we shift our gaze away from the traditional end of human action – a shared life of goodness – we seek a solitary life, an individual life, but hardly a humane life. It may well be a life carefully protected by rights. It may well be, by material indicators, a prosperous life, but it will be a life enervated by the demands of creating a new and personalized (or, as they say, "authentic") existence, and it will be haunted by the nagging suspicion of incompleteness, even in the face of absolute freedom from material want. For vanished now are even those days when the woman of the house could at least debate and appreciate the merits of a prepared piece of the meat of which I was privileged to have myself witnessed the preparation. Indeed it was not long ago when those who cooked – though they neither raised nor slaughtered – knew the worth of a particular cut. And it was with that knowledge, and a trucking disposition, she could appeal to the butcher's noble self-interest, a self-interest attuned not so much to profit as to a genuine interest in the art and pride in the craft. Now a mute exchange occurs. Not even the interest of the other is given consideration, only that of the self. The consumer and the clerk alike, never allowing their faces to meet, obey the flickering judgment of a scanner. Eyes they have but cannot see; ears they have but cannot hear. The only thing they share in that moment is the pursuit of solitary interest and the common touch of dead and sterile money.

Of late, my friend has informed me that the old man is dying. No doubt he has long been dying. Apart from a few simple actions, his role in the slaughter was that of intelligence directing muscular movement and the marshalling of youthful enthusiasm. His outward frailty was evident to all. But only those who had spent time with him could perceive that such frailty was but the worn sheath of courage: the courage to stand fast by his traditions in the wake of changing fashions and the broad abandonment of his way of living. To many city people, this man would be just another broken-down redneck. Yet his vitality was evident to those who had eyes. The worker of the industrial city, sustained by chemicals and machinery, may live a longer life than the old man will, but in the end, one will have to ask, did he *live* during his decades? Shut up in offices and cubicles, standing in homogenous and superficial "coffeehouses," he no doubt has ideas of his own, recurring dreams and flickering desires, but do these ever move from imagined states into incarnated reality? Does he ever see the fruit of his labors in this world, or is it only measured in the pale, virtual shades of the computer screen and in the quarterly reports about his money that others manage and that others, principally, enjoy?

In the country air and on his own land, the old man has chosen daily from among a variety of traditional means how to pursue his happiness and live in virtuous modesty. A tradition handed on to him by his own father marked a range of activities and taught him how to unify his actions to the season and the work at hand. What of the city worker? Promised a life without limits, he pursues a career – seven times no less; for where there are no limits there are no rules or relationships to mind seriously. There is no continuity in work, except for the biweekly check, which is swallowed by mortgage, insurance, taxes, and keeping abreast of fashion.

The old man will die in fidelity to his fathers, and though his sons may have been prodigal, he never leveraged away their inheritance; it remains still and goes by the name of home. My friend informs me that the old man speaks little; he has little need. His wife and he have transcended spoken words long since. With the proverbial old dog at his side, he looks over his honest parcel of land and is sustained by its memories, just as he was sustained for so many years by his responsible cultivation of it.

The modern worker's death will come shrouded in cold irony as he moves into his "autumn" years – as if the cycle of his life, at least, reflects a natural order. He has moved from house to house, longing for communion among strangers, haunted by novel anonymity. His final estate is a place called Heritage House, or Spring Rise, or the Breakers. There he lives like a transient in a room that someone else had died in and someone else will need to die in, waiting his turn, free from obligations to family, land, or vocation. There he will die broken, stewing in his own filth like the industrial hogs he spent his life eating. None of his wives come to him; he is crowded by the shades of his aborted love: he is not touched by fidelity. He is not moved by the absence of those once present, but rather turns in constant anxiety before the presence of all that is absent. He will not play a part in any remembered story, except the statistics of the nursing station and the state social worker's report. He is forgotten by all but God.

The old man, who stood in a specific place and for a specific tradition and sought to share his abundance, will be remembered. Love never departed from his work or from his resolve to keep intact old ways. Love makes work endure. Even his sons' forfeiting of their inheritance will not bar his remembrance, for by his participation and transmission of a craft, his sweat and knowledge and particular grace are absorbed and maintained, so long as the continuity of such folkways is maintained.

"In a sense, the Southern Agrarians led the last significant American campaign in behalf of property and the humane concerns so well expressed in the ancient right to property. One can even argue that the Agrarians were the last original group of critics in America, with anything close to a national audience, who took property and property rights seriously. An alternative way of expressing this point is that they fought the last significant, rearguard, and losing battle against either socialist or corporate forms of collectivism – against large accumulations of capital, narrowly centralized and bureaucratic management, and wage dependent, non-owning workers."

—PAUL KEITH CONKIN

～ 12 ～

Economics Begins at Home

Tobias J. Lanz, Ph.D.

THE DESTRUCTION OF THE HOUSEHOLD ECONOMY IS one of the most significant consequences of the modern revolutions of the last two centuries.[1] However, it is a subject that has received little attention. Professional economists find it trivial when compared to the workings of business corporations or national economies. The average American, including most Catholics, sees it as a positive development that has meant greater mobility, money, and freedom from menial labor. Yet, this seemingly benign death of the household economy is correlated with some serious social ills – from rampant crime and violence to widespread divorce, reproductive dysfunction, and mental illness. Most noticeably, the decline of the household is closely connected to the decline of the community and religious life.

The main cause of the decline of the household economy can be traced to the industrial revolution and the subsequent rise of the modern state and business corporation. The industrial revolution separated economic production from the traditional family and communal setting, and the state and business corporation were able to control and direct these new economic processes to their benefit.[2] While society did receive, in exchange, some material benefits from many of these new organizational and technical changes, the price paid was a high one: most of the traditional socio-economic func-

---

1. See, e.g., Allan C. Carlson, *From Cottage to Workstation* (San Francisco: Ignatius Press, 1993).

2. James Burnham aptly termed this phenomenon the "Managerial Revolution," for both the modern state and corporation are institutions that are run by a managerial class comprised of technicians, analysts and administrators. And it is these bureaucrats who displaced an older elite that were still in some way connected to the family and community. See James Burnham, *The Managerial Revolution: What is Happening in the World* (New York: John Day, 1941).

tions of the household were lost to the state and the corporation. The state took over "primary-care" functions such as education, health, and care of children and the elderly, while the corporation took over those of economic production for provision of food, clothing, shelter, entertainment, and even, to some extent, biological reproduction. As a result, the modern household has become almost completely dependent upon these institutions for its survival. Moreover, this dependency has meant that the reliance people once had on themselves, their family members, their communities, and their churches have declined proportionately.

In effect, the state and the business corporation have monopolized economic (as well as political and cultural) power in America and in the entire industrialized world. It is a revolution that is also now international, as witnessed in the process of so-called "globalization." This monopolization of power is the essence of both socialism and capitalism, which are, at least in theory, the two so-called "competing" ideologies of the modern age. Both ideologies exaggerate and hence distort one aspect of socio-economic and political life at the expense of all others. Socialism is fixated on the exclusive power of the state, whereas capitalism is fixated on that of the market. As socialism and capitalism have struggled against one another for preeminence, they have turned societies into ideological battlegrounds in which the traditional socio-economic order centered on family, community, and Church has been the ultimate casualty.

This is why the Catholic Church has always been critical of both socialism and capitalism, because both try to monopolize power at the expense of the intermediary social institutions that form the basis of the traditional social order. The Church has never condemned the role of the market to the extent that it provides goods and private property, nor has it condemned the role of government to regulate, tax, or provide social benefits. According to Church teaching, the proper roles of the state and market are to support and facilitate family, community, and religious life rather than compete against and destroy them. The former must subordinate themselves to latter – at least in terms of their ends or purposes – if they are to be rightly ordered. And in a healthy body politic, the market itself must be subordinate to the state, for the enforcement of prudent and proper limits, where such subordination is called for. Such an approach is the only way in which these institutions can be assured of working to provide for, rather than militating against, a fuller realization of human potential and the spiritual gifts given by God, as well as an equitable and stable economy.

If Catholics, and Christians generally, are serious about changing the current social and economic conditions in America and other nations that have fallen into the narrow and destructive "left vs. right" paradigm of socialism and capitalism, they must begin by placing the family and community once again at the center of economic life. It is only when the household again becomes a viable actor in social and economic life that a Catholic cultural renewal will even become possible. After all, the home is the center of all civilized existence, and it is where economics begins.

Subsidiarity and the Natural Economy

THE SHIFT OF the most basic economic functions (especially food production, cooking, household chores, entertainment) away from the household to the marketplace accounts for much of the economic growth of the last several decades. It is what is euphemistically called the "service economy." But its essence is consumer*ism*, ultimately a product of the divorce of the consumption of economic goods from their production: the modern household has been almost universally transformed into a center of consumption by workers who are no longer themselves producers, but mere employees in a "service industry." The traditional connection, so much insisted upon by Fr. McNabb and others,[1] between the production of goods and their consumption *by those who produced them*, or at least by members of the neighborhood or community where the goods are produced, has given place to the "dormitory" model of the American household. It is today nothing more than a place where one retires at the end of the day to eat industrially processed food, watch TV, and sleep. Production, meanwhile, of the goods consumed in the "dorm" takes place hundreds if not thousands of miles away.

The early (nineteenth-century) criticisms of socialism and capitalism by the Church focused, among other things, on the exploitative and alienating aspects of work under centralized economic systems. However, more recent papal encyclicals have focused on the socially and spiritually destructive aspects of consumerism as almost a psychological and ideological problem of its own. As Pope John Paul exclaimed in 1991 in *Centesimus Annus* (*CA*):

> In advanced economics the demand is no longer for quantity, but for quality. Hence the issue of consumerism arises. The new material, physical, and instinctive needs should remain subordinate to humanity's interior and spiritual needs. Appealing to instinct only may create lifestyles and consumer attitudes that are damaging to spiritual and physical health. The education

---

1. See the essays by Anthony Cooney and Dr. Chojnowski in this volume for more on the Distributist (normative) "law" that seeks to re-unite the areas of production and consumption.

and cultural formation of consumers and producers and of the mass media are urgently needed, as well as the intervention of public authority (§36).

The only thing that can really counter the consumer culture would be a "producer culture."[1] Naturally, the first step towards creating a producer culture would be to cut consumption. The modern economy is constantly trying to create new demand for goods and services, many of which are unnecessary and wasteful, if not downright sinful. Consumption creates dependency upon the sources of goods that we "can't live without," and relegates ever more power to the state and business corporations which thrive from the profits and taxes generated by these massive consumer industries. Consumerism also directly contradicts the most basic Christian principle of poverty. While not all Catholics are called to a life of radical poverty, all are called to a life of simplicity. The simple life is only possible when the "consumer impulse" is thwarted.

The second and most critical step in returning to a producer culture is when people actually produce more of what they consume, and this can only occur at the level of the household and community. To modern ears this sounds like a romantic and unworkable program. Yet the idea of a producer culture is at the heart of the natural economy advocated by Catholic social teaching. The principle that underlies this economy is *subsidiarity*, whose importance Pope Pius XI explains in this way in his 1931 *Quadragesimo Anno*:

> [T]hat most weighty principle, which cannot be set aside or changed, remains fixed and unshaken in social philosophy: just as it is gravely wrong to take from individuals what they can accomplish by their own initiative and industry and give it to the community, so also it is an injustice and at the same time a grave evil and disturbance of right order to assign to a greater and higher association what lesser and subordinate organizations can do. For every social activity ought of its very nature to furnish help to the members of the body social, and never destroy and absorb them (§79).[2]

Thus, if an economic function can be performed at the level of the household, it should be. And it is only if it cannot be done there, that higher levels of institutional complexity (i.e., the state or business corporation) should be called upon to perform the task. It comes as no surprise that the modern world has totally abandoned the principle of subsidiarity. In fact, it has it exactly backwards, for modern economies prod man to constantly adopt the most complex means to achieve simple tasks. In the end the household and community lose all of their socio-economic functions and become de-

---

1. This is a term first coined by the contemporary agrarian writer Wendell Berry, who has made this argument in many of his books on agrarian life and farming in America.

2.From the Vatican edition, published at http://www.vatican.va.

pendent on massive and impersonal bureaucracies to fulfill even the basic needs.

Historically, the social body where subsidiarity was most fully practiced was the family farm. It was here that people relied on simple forms of energy, technology, and technique – namely the human being and his labor – to provide for basic needs. The family farm was also the center of human reproduction. And it is where the active ingredients of religious faith – the feelings of trust, obedience, discipline, and fidelity – were cultivated. The family nurtured and sustained these bonds of love, which was the "glue" that held society together. Thus, the family farm was the cultural foundation of society, because it is the only social body where both spiritual and material reproduction co-existed.

So when the Southern Agrarians, the English Distributists and other radical Christians defended the family farm and rural life, they were not simply spewing forth nostalgic pap – they were defending the only economic culture that could truly counter the spiritual and material destructiveness of modernity. Theirs was a rational argument based on thousands of years of empirical evidence that the family farm is the foundation of a healthy and properly religious society. They were also echoing the received wisdom of the Catholic Church's most respected thinkers. As Pope Pius XII said in 1941, "Of all the goods that can be the object of private property, none is more conformable to nature, according to the teaching of *Rerum Novarum*, than the land, the holding on which the family lives, and from the products of which it draws all or part of its subsistence"; and "only that stability which is rooted in one's own holding makes of the family the vital and most perfect and fecund cell of society . . . . "[1] Five years later he would only strengthen his judgment: "[T]he tiller of the soil still represents the natural order of things willed by God."[2] Here we was simply expounding upon the judgment of Catholic tradition, which saw "the ideal of all great statesmen from Solon to Leo XIII" as "flourishing populations of small farmers or peasants."[3]

Because self-reliant agrarian communities did not have to depend on the corporation and the state, they were able to keep corporate and state power in check. And it is for this reason that the family farm remains the most important socio-economic entity for traditional Christians, just as the business corporation is the icon of liberals and the state that of socialists. Chris-

---

1. *La Solennità della Pentecoste*, from *Principles for Peace* (Washington, D.C.: National Catholic Welfare Conference, 1943), p. 727.

2. Speech delivered to the delegates at the Convention of the National Confederation of Farm Owner-Operators, Rome, November 15, 1946.

3. Charles S. Devas, *The Catholic Encyclopedia* (New York: Robert Appleton Company, 1907–12; online edition K. Knight, 2003), s.v., "Agrarianism."

tians know all too well that once the family farm disintegrates, a culture's ability to reproduce itself spiritually, morally, and psychologically, as well as physically, diminishes, and a civilization begins to die.

Today the family farm is virtually extinct. Some of this is due to an indifferent if not hostile government, which created polices that failed to promote the family farm aggressively. But perhaps more damaging was the seduction of the consumer lifestyle, in which one's interaction with economic goods is principally to consume them, and not to produce them. While the Church must continue to defend the family farm and the virtues of rural life, as a beacon and ideal, as well as a viable alternative, the greatest economic and cultural struggle lies in suburban America, for it is at the center of the consumer culture, and it is here that Catholics must find ways both to cut consumption and become economically more self-reliant.

Steps Towards Restoring a Natural Economy

I F CATHOLICS AND other Christians want to restore economic sanity and moral stability to society, they must begin by reapplying subsidiarity to *every* sphere of life. In a world dominated by big business and big government, this might appear to be impossible. But it is not. Leviathan thrives on the illusion of its own inevitable triumph. It may dominate the public square, but it should never win in the home. And this is where economic (as well as political and cultural) resistance is possible. Serious Catholics and others of good will can effectively undermine the economic principles of modernity – namely the unbridled desire for power – just as modernity has violated the Christian principle of subsidiarity. The easiest way to reduce the power of the state and business corporation is to reduce reliance on them and strengthen the family, the community, and the Church. This is the essence of subsidiarity and the basis of a more fully lived Christian social life.

The first application of subsidiarity applies to work. Those interested in beginning the slow but steady transformation should, if possible, seek to work where they live. Those who cannot work at home should at least try to live as close to work (as well as school and Church) as possible. Home or local employment *must* be the desired option for both Catholics and all others desiring a more sane and healthy life because of its many social and cultural benefits. First, families can spend more time together and in their communities. Second, a thriving business can be a multi-generational affair that can cement family relations and keep family members close to home. Third, small businesses bring life to a neighborhood. Most neighborhoods today have become ghost towns. Women, children, and the elderly were once common community fixtures. They were, in fact, the foundation of all communal life. Now they are all off at work, at day care, or deposited in facilities for the aged. The only human life forms left in the neighborhood are delivery people and "pest" exterminators – a weak foundation indeed upon which to sustain a living community.

Integrating home and work can lead not only to more fulfilling family and community life, it can also create towns and cities that are more environmentally and socially sustainable than the high consumption, mass-sprawl metropolises that now scar the American landscape. Those who work at or close to home can also reduce their reliance on the automobile, which is not only an expensive machine to maintain, but has many hidden (and not so hidden) social and ecological costs. It is the leading cause of two of the urban world's most pervasive problems: smog and traffic (not to mention stress). More importantly, the reliance on the automobile is probably the single major cause for the explosion of state and corporate power in the last one hundred years. As E. Michael Jones has written, the automobile is highly conducive to manipulation by big business and the government. As such, it has become the basis of some of the most powerful forms of social control and social engineering ever witnessed in America and the industrial world in general. The result has been the explosive growth of suburbia and the high-mobility, high-consumption lifestyle that has dealt such a serious blow to the traditional social order.[1]

One of the paradoxes of suburbia, in particular, is that all of these homeowners possess land (even if it is only mortgaged), yet few use it for any economic purpose. For those who have land, the first application of subsidiarity is to grow food. This applies to *all* landowners. Even a tiny quarter acre suburban plot, with good sun and soil, can produce enough fruit and vegetables to support a family of four for an entire year! Most Americans are not aware of this. They would rather work the day away in an energy-consuming office and then purchase their input-intensive agri-goods at the local supermarket. Home food production makes particular economic sense for middle and lower income families with a little land, where the mother does not desire full-time work or work outside the home. Here the cost of full employment (including the expense of an additional car, eating out, day care, a new wardrobe, etc.) is usually not worth it. Growing and cooking one's own food at home is not only attractive, it is a viable economic solution to the worker-consumer treadmill. Once again we see the wisdom of the attempt to re-integrate production and consumption.

1. E. Michael Jones, *Slaughter of the Cities: Urban Renewal as Ethnic Cleansing* (South Bend, Ind.: St. Augustine Press, 2002).

Growing food is not simply a quaint hobby; it is, rather, a serious economic endeavor. There is a growing area of agriculture that is focused explicitly on producing food on small plots, especially in urban areas. This discipline is known as permanent agriculture or "permaculture." [1] Its advocates have demonstrated that small plots are not only highly productive, but that they can yield two to three times the amount of produce per unit of land as the average farm. Moreover, permaculture production techniques are based on low-input methods coupled with superior garden designs to achieve maximum results. These principles are slowly being put into practice throughout Europe and Asia, where land is scarce, but not so much in America, where land is still cheap and abundant. There is great potential here that has yet to be realized.

Aside from its clear ecological and economic benefits, gardening should be a specific priority for Catholics and all Christians. After all, the garden is one of the most important spiritual symbols in Christianity. In our worldly struggle Christians always yearn for the beauty, bounty, and innocence of a lost Eden. Although one can never undo the mark of original sin, we can nonetheless make our own homes into places that radiate with life and beauty and stand as a spiritual counterweight to an increasingly materialistic and ugly urban world. All Catholics should make it a priority to restore even the smallest piece of land to its intended function, which is the creation of life.

Another important Christian symbol that is related to the garden and food is the table. It represents the idea of the shared meal and most importantly the Last Supper. Sadly, just as the garden has been abandoned in modern society, so has the table. Today it is not uncommon for families either to eat out or not to eat together at all! Taking raw materials and turning them into the sustenance of life is the most humanly binding and spiritually enriching form of economic production. In all cultures, except the modern consumer culture, eating, like biological reproduction, is a hallowed activity because it sustains life. And like that reproduction, eating should be done in the privacy of the home and enshrined in a distinctive set of mores and manners that serve to underscore its vital importance to life itself. Because cooking and eating together are so integral to material and spiritual well-being, it is essential that these activities be faithfully upheld in Catholic – and all seriously religious – homes.

Eating at home has many practical advantages, in addition to its social and spiritual importance. It is cheaper, healthier, and less wasteful than eating out. Restaurants, like the agribusinesses that supply them, are horren-

1. Bill Mollison and David Holgren are two of the pioneers in permaculture design and have written several books on the topic. To date, no writer has fused permaculture with Catholic social teaching, although it would be a suitable match.

dous food and energy wasters. This is especially the case with large national chains that buy in bulk, serve in bulk, and waste in bulk. When eating out, seek out smaller local establishments. By buying local, one is also supporting the community. Moreover, because of their smaller size, these restaurants also tend to be less wasteful. They are also more likely to carry fresh products, especially natural and locally grown goods. But, all in all, restaurants should be reserved for special occasions. They are expensive consumer havens – designed for convenience and sensate pleasure. Subsidiarity says eat in, not out.

Growing and preparing food can be taken a step further by promoting these economic activities at the community level. The trading and selling of foodstuffs is another economic activity that was once performed almost exclusively at the community level. Today it is virtually monopolized by large grocery chains. Thus, when purchasing food and other goods, subsidiarity says that local markets (for example farmers' markets) should be patronized. For the more ambitious, local markets as well as trade and barter networks can actually be established to coordinate the buying and selling of a number of home-grown and home-made products. Again, these types of activities are particularly well suited to families who work or raise children at home.

Perhaps the most important application of subsidiarity is to technology. The proliferation of technology has greatly facilitated the sweeping socioeconomic, political, and spiritual changes of the modern era. Naturally the modern view of technology is positive. Technology is good and more is better. Sadly, most Catholics have also adopted this naïve position. They see technology simply as a tool that can enhance human abilities and improve the human condition. But technology is more than a tool. A tool is dependent on living energy forms, namely human or animal energy, i.e., a shovel or plow. In contrast, technology requires non-living energy forms such as electricity or fossil fuels. To bring these massive stores of energy to "life" requires the inevitable involvement of equally massive social institutions – namely the state and the business corporation.

Technology has permeated every facet of modern life. In fact, it is synonymous with modern life. By its very nature, a great deal of modern technology militates against the principle of subsidiarity. Generally speaking, technology makes life easy and comfortable, but it often requires large and complex institutions for its very existence. More significantly, technology breeds dependence and feeds the industrial spiral of endless consumption, production, regulation, and taxation. Using less technology helps keep this spiral under control. Thus, the Catholic response to technology is not so much the puritanical one advocated by the Amish, where all forms are banished, but a reasonable and prudent one that asks first whether a technology is necessary and, second, whether it brings one closer to God, family, and community. If technology creates dependency or isolates one from the traditional social order, then it must be used selectively or even jettisoned.

Along with the automobile, the most insidious example of this destructive type of technology is the television set. It is not only a means of social control by both the state and corporation; it is a direct path to sloth and stupidity. It has also become the principle cultural organ of industrial society. As such, it has replaced the role of the Church in defining and disseminating cultural values. The struggle to rid oneself of the influence of television is essential to restoring sanity in the household and rekindling human relationships, conversation, hobbies, prayer, and many other forgotten human activities. Other technologies should also be treated with a similar skeptical eye. Technology is the modern pagan fetish; much of it is unnecessary, and most of it can be easily relegated to a secondary role in one's life.

Another critical application of subsidiarity is to education. In the modern world, the state and corporation have effectively monopolized the production and dissemination of knowledge. Children have become, as a consequence, their compliant consumers. One of the most important ways to challenge this monopoly and undermine the secular worldview of modern education is to remove children from public schools. Educating children at private academies, at religious schools, or at home are all ways to exercise educational subsidiarity. The home-school movement, in particular, is growing, and it is one area in the "culture war" where Catholics and other Christians are actually winning.

Home schooling networks are flourishing, allowing many families to share information and create a social environment that is free from the poisonous influences of consumerist and materialist secularism. More importantly, since many "home schoolers" are Catholics, the movement is one of the most viable ways to sustain the Catholic culture. It may prove to be a real cultural revolution if all "home schoolers" can win the legal victories necessary to repeal property taxes for those families that chose not to support the corrupt and immoral public school system. If this ever happens, an authentic Christian counter culture can take shape – one that is ideologically and financially free from government and corporate control.

One area of modern economic life that is now completely under the control of government and the business corporations is investment and especially insurance. To invest means literally to furnish or clothe (from the Latin *vestio* meaning to clothe). From a social standpoint it also means to grant power or authority. Thus, from an economic standpoint, the question is to whom should Catholics give the authority to provide their economic means. Today, investment is defined almost exclusively in monetary terms, especially investment in government and corporate stocks and bonds. From the standpoint of subsidiary, the definition of investment must first be broadened to include all aspects of social life. Second, when it *is* applied to economics, it must begin at home. Thus, the first and most significant investment must be a home and property from which economic security and sustenance can be derived, in keeping with our vision of the unity, as far as possible, of the locations of production and consumption. Even when the home is not or cannot be used explicitly for economic purposes, Catholics and all sincere Christians must resist treating the home as a commodity to be bought and sold.

The home should grow naturally with the growth of a family. Thus, rather than "trading up," which is the norm in America, seekers after economic sanity should try to build up, adding onto smaller structures to create ones that can fulfill the growing needs of the family. In older American and European neighborhoods this has always been the case. As such, both homes and neighborhoods mature gracefully and reflect a range of social and economic differences – i.e., large and small homes, as well as apartments for those unmarried, all coexist in a single neighborhood. The modern suburb and the "trading-up" mentality have changed all this. Rather than staying put and building a larger home, people move from a subdivision comprised exclusively of small homes to one comprised exclusively of large homes. The modern subdivision reflects the essence of the consumer society: a world that is standardized, sterile, and despiritualized. A concerted and collective effort to invest in one home over the long term can transform even the drabbest suburb into a living neighborhood, especially if child-rearing and businesses can coexist there as well.

The principle of subsidiarity also applies to investing in government and corporate stocks and bonds. Catholics, in particular, should invest in those entities that support rather than compete against the natural economy, and only where investment itself is at least to an extent an extension of natural economic activity, and not simply another form of perpetuating the divorce between essential economic activity and ownership and consumption, or, what's worse, pure speculation.[1] Investment should also have a moral purpose. The American government and most corporations support a "moral" agenda that runs counter to Catholic teaching, especially on issues such as abortion, homosexuality, divorce, feminism, and the just-war doctrine. Entities that support these policies should *never* receive Catholic money. Thus,

---

1. As Richard Weaver put it, "the abstract property of stocks and bonds, the legal ownership of enterprises never seen, actually destroy the connection between man and his substance . . . . Property in this sense becomes a fiction useful for exploitation and makes impossible the sanctification of work" (*Ideas Have Consequences* [Chicago: The University of Chicago Press, 1984 (1948)], pp. 132–3).

it is incumbent upon Catholic investors to educate themselves fully, not only about the monetary risks associated with these investments, but more importantly, the moral risks. Fortunately, there are companies and mutual funds that are specifically tailored to Catholic social and moral concerns, and these are the entities that must be sought out.

The question of insurance is even thornier, especially that of health insurance. Serious illness, injury, or long-term care can lead to bankruptcy. And for these scenarios, insurance has a proper place. But Catholics must also begin to rethink the entire logic of health insurance. Unlike most types of insurance, health plans cover more than just catastrophe; they frequently cover routine medical procedures (this is the case with dental insurance in particular). The application of subsidiarity would approach health and illness differently. Rather than cover every aspect of health care, Catholics should accept some risk and responsibility by paying for routine and minor medical procedures.[1] This approach is radical, even counterintuitive to the modern ethos, which eschews risk at every turn.

A prudent approach to health care would first ask what is the risk, and, second, who should bear the cost of that risk. The family should pay basic health costs. A higher social level (extended family and friends) would be called upon in cases with a higher financial and emotional cost. This would be followed by the community and parish. Finally the greatest burdens would be shared by the diocese or national Church. If subsidiarity were ever instituted in such a manner, the Catholic Church could provide a social network that could seriously reduce the reliance upon government or corporate health providers. Given, however, the insufficient understanding and application of subsidiarity among Catholic communities on this and other serious socio-economic questions, all health decisions have been left in the hands of professional bureaucrats. As a result, the health debate is defined in exclusively secular terms. This is why people now have greater faith in "the system" than in God and their religious communities.

Concluding Thoughts

THE FOREGOING EXAMPLES are some of the most important applications of the principle of subsidiarity, but there are many ways

---

1. The importance of accepting suffering as part of our Christian faith is never even considered in the national health debate in America or elsewhere. Yet, facing this possibility with courage and commitment would also reduce the fear of not having adequate or any insurance.

and degrees to which subsidiarity can be applied. It will be the collective impact of thousands (and hopefully, some day, of millions), of consumers-turned-producers that can radically change the present political-economic situation in America and other industrial nations. The goal of such a movement must be modest. It will not create sweeping social-economic changes, nor will it create a new communal Christian golden age (a point liberal cynics never fail to mention about any anti-modern movement). But if enough households can establish a level of economic self-reliance, and establish stronger communities and supportive social networks, a modicum of religious and political autonomy may be achieved. Anywhere this can be done on a merely local, small-neighborhood level, involving even just tens of families, it should be; and to the extent that it is done, it will be a victory.

It must be stressed that the application of subsidiarity is far from being an idealistic endeavor. On the contrary: it is a realistic attempt to return prudence and sanity to economic life. What the idea of subsidiarity really represents is a different economic strategy from that which currently reigns over modern industrial societies. It is one that seeks to *optimize* wealth, rather than *maximize* it. Optimization implies limits and boundaries to human behavior, which, in a manner of speaking, is the definition of morality. This cultivates habits and patterns informed by grace that are consistent with the teachings of the Catholic Church. In contrast, maximization is only interested in the constant amassing of material and the unbridled pursuit of power, which results in the breaking and constant changing of boundaries. It destroys all sense of limit and proportion, rejects morality, and contradicts and undermines the fundamental teachings of the Church.

The rebuilding of household and communal economies is also a political act, because it seeks to change the power relations in society from one that is concentrated among large institutions to one that is diffused among many intermediary social institutions, of which the family is the most important. At the level of national politics, such ideas may never gain currency. But Catholics and all those of good will are nonetheless called to be involved in the political process to help bring about the changes that can support the growth and development of a natural economy, such as pressing for more favorable tax rates and zoning policies. In keeping with the principle of subsidiarity, it is establishing control over *local* politics that is most critical. Catholics and all Christians must begin to choose their battles carefully, and win the small victories on the political margin where their strengths are greatest. Enough small victories can eventually add up to more significant political changes in the long run.

Those who sincerely pursue the natural economic path – articulated by the Catholic Church for centuries – will certainly need to sacrifice monetary wealth and social status. But they will gain something more valuable. First: a degree of economic independence and a freedom from material desire; second: the genuine health and emotional satisfaction that comes from a life dedicated to physical labor, simplicity, and thrift; and finally: the recapturing of time, and with it, leisure. Indeed, as the Catholic philosopher Joseph Pieper so poignantly wrote back in 1948,[1] leisure is the basis of love, friendship, and spiritual well-being. As such, it is the essence of a living culture. These are the very things that can never be found in the modern consumer culture, which is, as Pope John Paul II aptly termed it, the culture of death.

---

1. Joseph Pieper, *Leisure, the Basis of Culture* (London: Faber and Faber, 1952).

Suggestions for Further Reading

WHILE THE SPECIFIC ORGANIZATIONS, JOURNALS, men, and movements that advocated widespread owner-ship of productive property in the 1930s have for the most part passed out of existence, there remain, happily, numer-ous initiatives and organizations dedicated to the preservation of the aims and ideals that our authors herein vindicate. One of the original Ameri-can groups, the National Catholic Rural Life Conference, is still extant and committed to "a spiritual tradition that brings together the Church, care of community, and care of creation." A robust organic and "green" movement, though predominantly "leftist" and liberal today owing to the passing of Catholics from the field in this area of endeavor, remains in existence and is supported by well known writers such as John Seymour (who died in 2004) and Wendell Berry and journals from all and no sides of the political spec-trum, such as *Chronicles, Resurgence, Mother Earth News, The American Con-servative,* and *Countryside.* There are, additionally, the Catholic/Christian Homesteading Movement, the American Chesterton Society, the Agrarian Foundation, the Christian Homesteaders Association, the E. F. Schumacher Society, the Howard Center, Chelsea Green and similar publishers, the Land Institute of Kansas, and others still who today preserve, if in many cases unconsciously, the aims and methods of the original Distributist-Agrarian movement. The Southern Agrarians of Nashville still enjoy a wide following among paleo-conservatives and neo-confederates, as reflected in numerous journals and monographs, even though the contemporary interpretation of their original movement as "conservative" is perhaps more strained than self-evident.

The following list of books and websites, the various contents of which it would be impossible for us to endorse in their entirety, but whose broad

subject matter may be of use and of interest for the prospective student of
the "traditionalist" social-economic critique or the budding small farmer, is
offered by way of reference and resource. Many of the books listed are not
currently in print, but can still be found in secondhand bookshop or via an
Internet search at, e.g., *www.booksold.com*. Major papal encyclicals are available
via a number of websites (e.g., *www.newadvent.com* or *www.papalencyclicals.net*),
but other resources containing the lesser-known papal documents
may need to be consulted for the other pronouncements.

—The Publishers

Catholic Social Movement

Henry Somerville, *The Catholic Social Movement*
(forthcoming from IHS Press)

Paul Misner, *Social Catholicism in Europe*

Martin Conway, *Catholic Politics in Europe*
---*Political Catholicism*

Giorgiana Putnam McEntee, *The Catholic Social Movement in Great
Britain*

Parker Moon, *The Labor Problem and the Social Catholic Movement in
France*

Harold Robbins, *The Last of the Realists: A Distributist Biography of G. K.
Chesterton* (forthcoming from IHS Press)

Fr. Edward Cahill, *The Framework of a Christian State*

Catholic Social Teaching

Luigi Civardi, *How Christ Changed the World
Christianity and Social Justice*

Charles Devas, *The Key to the World's Progress*

Fr. Denis Fahey, *The Mystical Body of Christ and the Reorganization of
Society*

Emile Guerry, *The Social Doctrine of the Catholic Church*

Joseph Husslein, S.J., *Christian Social Manifesto*

Amintore Fanfani, *Catechism of Catholic Social Doctrine*

Carol Robinson, *My Life with Thomas Aquinas*

Harold Robbins, *The Sun of Justice* (forthcoming from IHS Press)

Ed Willock, *Ye Gods*

Papal Pronouncements

Leo XIII, *Rerum Novarum* (1891)
---*Laetitiae Sanctae* (1892)

Pius XI, *Ubi Arcano Dei* (1922)
---*Quadragesimo Anno* (1931)

Pius XII, *Sertum Latitiae* (1939)
---*La Solennità della Pentecoste* (1941)
---*Oggi al compiersi* (1944)
---*Address to Italian Farmers* (1946)

Distributism

Fr. Vincent McNabb, O.P., *The Church and the Land*
---*Nazareth or Social Chaos*
---*Old Principles and the New Order*

Hilaire Belloc, *The Servile State*
---*Economics for Helen*
---*An Essay on the Restoration of Property*

G. K. Chesterton, *The Outline of Sanity*
---*Utopia of Usurers*
---*The Well and the Shallows*

Various, *Distributist Perspectives*, Volume I
---*Distributist Perspectives*, Volume II (forthcoming from
 IHS Press)

Race Mathews, *Jobs of Our Own: Building A Stake-Holder Society*

Allan Carlson, *Third Ways*

Corporatism

Matthew Elbow, *French Corporative Theory*

Ralph Bowen, *German Theories of the Corporative State*

Johannes Messner, *Dollfuss: An Austrian Patriot*

Joaquin Azpiazu, *Corporatism*

The Guild System

A. J. Penty, *The Gauntlet* (a first anthology)
---*Means and Ends*
---*The Restoration of the Guild System*
---*Guilds and the Social Crisis*
---*Guilds, Trade, and Agriculture*
---*Post-Industrialism*

---*Tradition and Modernism in Politics*
---*Communism and the Alternative*
---*Protection and the Social Problem*
---*Towards a Christian Sociology*
---*Old Worlds for New*

G. R. S. Taylor, *The Guild State*

Peter C. Grosvenor, *The Medieval Future of Arthur Joseph Penty* (forthcoming from IHS Press)

Solidarism

Rupert Ederer, trans. and ed., the works of Heinrich Pesch, S.J.

Heinrich Pesch, S.J., *Ethics and the National Economy*

Richard Mulcahy, S.J., *The Economics of Heinrich Pesch*

Ruralism and Back-to-the-Land Movements

H. J. Massingham, *The Wisdom of the Fields*
---*The Tree of Life*

William Cobbett, *Cottage Economy*

John Seymour, *Getting It Together*
---*The Small Holder*
---*The Complete Book of Self-Sufficiency*

Philip Conford, *The Origins of the Organic Movement*

M. G. Kains, *Five Acres and Independence*

G. C. Heseltine, *The Change*

Luigi Ligutti and John Rawe, S.J., *Rural Roads to Security*

Various, *The Rural Solution*

Various, *Flee to the Fields*

Rev. George H. Speltz, *The Importance of Rural Life According to the Philosophy of St. Thomas Aquinas*

Raymond Philip Witte and the National Catholic Rural Life Conference, *Twenty-Five Years of Crusading: a History of the National Catholic Rural Life Conference*

Troy Jesse Cauley, *Agrarianism*

Paul Keith Conkin, *Tomorrow a New World: the New Deal Community Program*

Jack Temple Kirby, *Rural Worlds Lost: the American South, 1920–1960*

Sympathetic and Other Related Works in Economic and Social Thought and History

Jorian Jenks, *From the Ground Up*

Walter John Marx, *Mechanization and Culture* (forthcoming from IHS Press)

Henry Slesser, *The Middles Ages in the West*

Herbert Agar, *Land of the Free*

Twelve Southerners, *I'll Take My Stand*

Various, *Who Owns America?*

Emily S. Bingham and Thomas A. Underwood, eds. *The Southern Agrarians and the New Deal: Essays After* I'll Take My Stand

William C. Havard and Walter Sullivan, eds., *A Band of Prophets: the Vanderbilt Agrarians After Fifty Years*

Fifteen southerners, *Why the South Will Survive*

Donald Davidson, *The Attack on Leviathan: Regionalism and Nationalism in the United States*
---*Southern Writers in the Modern World*

Richard M. Weaver, *Ideas Have Consequences*
---*The Southern Essays of Richard M. Weaver*
---*Visions of Order: the Cultural Crisis of Our Time*
---*The Ethics of Rhetoric*

Paul Keith Conkin, *The Southern Agrarians*

Eugene D. Genovese, *The Southern Tradition: the Achievement and Limitations of an American Conservatism*

Virginia Jean Rock, *The Making and Meaning of* I'll Take My Stand: *A Study in Utopian Conservatism, 1925–1939*

Thomas Daniel Young, *Waking Their Neighbors Up: the Nashville Agrarians Rediscovered*

Paul V. Murphy, *The Rebuke of History: the Southern Agrarians and American Conservative Thought*

John Médaille, *The Vocation of Business: Social Justice in the Marketplace*

Gary Taylor, *Orage and the New Age*
---*Socialism and Christianity*
---*G. D. H. Cole and the National Guilds*

John A. Ryan, *Distributive Justice*
---*The Living Wage*

Matteo Liberatore, S.J., *Political Economy*

Charles Devas, *Political Economy*

Christopher Hollis, *Christianity and Economics*
---*The American Heresy*
---*The Two Nations*

Joseph Clayton, *Economics for Chrtistians*

Amintore Fanfani, *Catholicism, Protestantism, and Capitalism*

George O'Brien, *The Economic Effects of the Reformation*
---*Medieval Economic Teaching* (forthcoming from IHS Press)

Oswald von Nell-Breuning, S.J., *The Reorganization of the Social Economy*

Herbert Shove, *The Fairy Ring of Commerce*

Joseph Husslein, S.J., *World Problem: Capital, Labor, and the Church*
---*Work, Wealth, and Wages*
---*Industrial Democracy*

Allen Carlson, *The New Agrarian Mind*
---*From Cottage to Workstation*

Wilhelm Röpke, *Humane Economy*

T. J. Jackson Lears, *No Place of Grace: Antimodernism and the Transformation of American Culture, 1880–1920*

Human-scale economy and living

Sally Fallon, *Nourishing Traditions*

John Lane, *Timeless Simplicity*

E. F. Schumacher, *Small is Beautiful*
---*A Guide for the Perplexed*

The End of Techno-materialist "Civilization"

Howard Kuntsler, *The Long Emergency*

Jean Gimpel, *The End of the Future: The Waning of the High-Tech World*

Kirkpatrick Sale, *Rebels Against the Future*

Krishan Kumar, *Progress and Prophecy*

Eric Schlosser, *Fast Food Nation*

Websites

CarFree.com

TheMeatrix.com

NewUrbanism.org

Distributism.org (or *.com*)

Chesterton.org

The Chesterbelloc Mandate
(distributist.blogspot.com)

The Distributist Review
(distributism.blogspot.com)

The New Distributist League
(distributistleague.blogspot.com)

About the Contributors

DR. TOBIAS J. LANZ has degrees in Wildlife Science and Agricultural Economics from Texas A&M University and a Ph.D. in International Politics from the University of South Carolina where he currently teaches. He has written numerous articles and reviews on economics, rural development, and Catholic social teaching and has done fieldwork on the relationship between conservation and rural development in West Africa and India. He lives in Columbia, SC with his wife and two children.

KIRKPATRICK SALE is the author of twelve books, including *The Conquest of Paradise: Christopher Columbus and the Columbian Legacy*; *Human Scale*; *Rebels Against the Future: The Luddites and Their War on the Industrial Revolution*; and *After Eden: The Evolution of Human Domination*. He is a contributing editor to *The Nation* and director of the Middlebury Institute for the study of separatism, secession, and self-determination.

JOHN SHARPE is a 1993 distinguished graduate of the United States Naval Academy at Annapolis, Maryland, where he received a Bachelor of Science degree with honors in English, and emphases in political thought and history. He served for seven years as a Navy Submarine Officer and has experience in America's major military headquarters such as the U.S. Atlantic Fleet, Norfolk, Va.; U.S. Joint Forces Command, Norfolk, Va.; and the Pentagon. In 2001 he co-founded IHS Press, and has re-issued, edited, and annotated works of Hilaire Belloc, G. K. Chesterton, Arthur Penty, Fr. Vincent McNabb, Amintore Fanfani, and Heinrich Pesch. He has contributed to *The Angelus, The Remnant, Catholic Family News*, and the *Encyclopedia of Catholic Social Thought, Social Science, and Social Policy*. He was also invited in 2005 to join the Academy of Letters at the Catholic Institute of Arts and Letters.

A IDAN MACKEY was born in Manchester, England in 1922 and became a Chesterton devotee at the age of 14 when his brother challenged him to "read something useful." His passion led him to found the Distributist Association along with H. D. C. Pepler in 1947 and launch a small monthly journal, *The Distributist*, which saw publication from 1953 to 1960. He has written several books on Distributism, including *Hilaire Belloc and His Critics* (1991) and *G. K. Chesterton: A Prophet for the 21st Century* (2007). He was instrumental in establishing the G. K. Chesterton Centre at Plater College, Oxford.

A NTHONY COONEY was born in Liverpool and graduated from the Open University. He was editor of the *Liverpool Newsletter* (1973–1993) and is author of several books, including *The Leonine Corpus as a Third Way*, *Bread in the Wilderness*, *Sources of Poverty*, and *St. George: Kinght of Lydda*. He lives in Liverpool, England with his wife Margaret. He has two daughters and two grandchildren.

G ARY POTTER is a native of California. After attending public schools, a professional theater academy, and college, he spent two years sailing in the Merchant Marine and another four living in France, where he discovered the Faith. Following time working in advertising in New York, he began his career in Catholic journalism in 1966 as a founding editor of the legendary *Triumph* magazine. Besides *Triumph* and two publications of which he later was editor, *Truth & Justice* and *CCPA News & Views* (the publication of Catholics for Christian Political Action), articles by him have appeared in *National Review, Human Events*, the *New York Times*, the *Washington Post*, the *National Catholic Register, Faith & Reason, The Wanderer, The Remnant* and numerous other places.

D ALE AHLQUIST is the President of the American Chesterton Society and creator and host of the EWTN television series, "G. K. Chesterton: The Apostle of Common Sense." He is the author of *Common Sense 101: Lessons from G. K. Chesterton*, the publisher of *Gilbert! Magazine*, editor of *The Annotated Lepanto*, and associate editor of the *Collected Works of G. K. Chesterton*. He has written and lectured on Chesterton so much that he has not bothered getting a real job. He lives near Minneapolis with his wife and six children.

D R. CHRISTOPHER BLUM was educated at the University of Virginia and the University of Notre Dame. He was formerly Chairman of the History Department at Christendom College. He is currently Professor of Humanities at Thomas More College of the Liberal Arts. He teaches and writes about French Catholic thought from Bossuet to Bonald and European religious art and architecture. He is editor of *Critics of the Enlightenment: Readings in the French Counter-Revolutionary Tradition* (2004). He is married with two children.

D R. PETER CHOJNOWSKI has degrees in political science and philosophy from Christendom College, Virginia, and a Ph.D. in Philosophy from Fordham University, New York. He specializes in the philosophy of St. Thomas Aquinas and Catholic Social Thought and has written over 100 articles and reviews on Catholic topics. He currently teaches at Gonzaga University and Immaculate Conception Academy. He lives with his wife and six children on a three-acre farm in Washington State.

T HOMAS STORCK was educated at Kenyon College and St. John's College, Santa Fe. He is the author of numerous articles, essays and books on Catholic social teaching and culture, and his most recent book was *Christendom and the West* (2000). He is a member of the editorial board of *The Chesterton Review*. A convert to Catholicism (1978), he is married to the former Inez Marie Fitzgerald. They have four children and four grandchildren.

D R. RUPERT EDERER was born in Germany in 1923 and immigrated to America in 1926. He was educated at St. Bonaventure University and St. Louis University. He taught at various colleges and retired from the State University of New York College at Buffalo. Dr. Ederer has written some 200 articles and written or translated 20 books, including Heinrich Pesch's *Liberalism, Socialism and Christian Social Order* and *Lehrbuch der Nationalökonomie*. He is the recognized living authority on Heinrich Pesch.

D R. EDWARD MCPHAIL was educated at Washington University and the University of Virginia. He received his doctorate at the University of Massachusetts. He is currently chairman of the Economics Department at Dickinson College. His research specialties include international trade theory, eugenics and economics, socialism and its critics, and the political economy of G. K. Chesterton and Hilaire Belloc.

F R. LAWRENCE SMITH is a native of Davenport, Iowa. He has an undergraduate degree in music from DePaul University and a Masters of Divinity from Kenrick Seminary, St Louis. He has been involved in parochial ministry since the early 1990's. He has taught students from kindergarten to postgraduate levels and has been retreat director for parishes in four states. His writings have appeared in *Gilbert! Magazine*, *The Catholic Yearbook*, *Lyrical Iowa*, *The Press-Citizen* (Iowa City), and *The Clinton Herald*.

D R. WILLIAM EDMUND FAHEY was educated in Classics and History at Xavier University and the University of St. Andrews. He holds his doctorate from The Catholic University of America. He was the founder and chairman of the Department of Classical and Early Christian Studies at Christendom College. Dr. Fahey is currently Professor of Humanities and Provost at Thomas More College of the Liberal Arts. His interest in Distributism is nourished by the regular consumption of Catholic social encyclicals, cask-conditioned ale, and bacon, all in vast quantities. He has returned to the lands of the Pennacooks and Abnekis (to some, New England), where his family has dwelt since the eighteenth century. Near an obscure tributary of the Merrimack river, he is restoring two acres with his wife and four children.

Index

About IHS Press

IHS Press believes that the key to the restoration of Catholic Society is the recovery and the implementation of the wisdom our Fathers in the Faith possessed so fully less than a century ago. At a time when numerous ideologies were competing for supremacy, these men articulated, with precision and vigor, and *without* apology or compromise, the only genuine alternative to the then- (and still-) prevailing currents of thought: value-free and yet bureaucratic "progressivism" on the one hand, and the rehashed, *laissez-faire* free-for-all of "conservatism" on the other. That alternative is the Social Teaching of the Catholic Church.

Catholic Social Teaching offers the solutions to the political, economic, and social problems that plague modern society; problems that stem from the false principles of the Reformation, Renaissance, and Revolution, and which are exacerbated by the industrialization and the secularization of society that has continued for several centuries. Defending, explaining, and applying this Teaching was the business of the great Social Catholics of last century. Unfortunately, much of their work is today both unknown and unavailable.

Thus, IHS Press was founded in September of 2001A.D. as the only publisher dedicated exclusively to the Social Teaching of the Church, helping Catholics of the third millennium pick up where those of last century left off. IHS Press is committed to recovering, and *helping others to rediscover*, the valuable works of the Catholic economists, historians, and social critics. To that end, IHS Press is in the business of issuing critical editions of works on society, politics, and economics by writers, thinkers, and men of action such as Hilaire Belloc, Gilbert Chesterton, Arthur Penty, Fr. Vincent McNabb, Fr. Denis Fahey, Jean Ousset, Amintore Fanfani, George O'Brien, and others, making the wisdom they contain available to the current generation.

It is the aim of IHS Press to issue these vitally important works in high-quality volumes and at reasonable prices, to enable the widest possible audience to acquire, enjoy, and benefit from them. Such an undertaking cannot be maintained without the support of generous benefactors. With that in mind, IHS Press was constituted as a not-for-profit corporation which is exempt from federal tax according to Section 501(c)(3) of the United States Internal Revenue Code. Donations to IHS Press are, therefore, tax deductible, and are especially welcome to support its continued operation, and to help it with the publication of new titles and the more widespread dissemination of those already in print.

For more information, contact us at:

mail: 222 W. 21st St., Suite F-122~Norfolk, VA 23517 USA
toll-free telephone or fax: 877-IHS-PRES (877.447.7737)
e-mail: order@ihspress.com • *internet:* www.ihspress.com

IHS Press is a tax-exempt 501(c)(3) corporation; EIN: 54-2057581.
Applicable documentation is available upon request.

More titles available direct from IHS Press.

The Outline of Sanity, by G. K. Chesterton
184pp, 6"x9", ISBN 0-9714894-0-8, Item No. GKC001 **$14.95**

The Free Press, by Hilaire Belloc
96pp, 5½"x8½", ISBN 0-9714894-1-6, Item No. HB001 **$8.95**

Action: A Manual for the Reconstruction of Christendom, by Jean Ousset
272pp, 6"x9", ISBN 0-9714894-2-4, Item No. JO001 **$16.95**

An Essay on the Restoration of Property, by Hilaire Belloc
104pp, 5½"x8½", ISBN 0-9714894-4-0, Item No. HB002 **$8.95**

Utopia of Usurers, by G. K. Chesterton
136pp, 5½"x8½", ISBN 0-9714894-3-2, Item No. GKC002 **$11.95**

Irish Impressions, by G. K. Chesterton
152pp, 5½"x8½", ISBN 0-9714894-5-9, Item No. GKC003 **$12.95**

The Church and the Land, by Fr. Vincent McNabb
192pp, 6"x9", ISBN 0-9714894-6-7, Item No. VM001 **$14.95**

Capitalism, Protestantism and Catholicism, by Amintore Fanfani
192pp, 6"x9", ISBN 0-9714894-7-5, Item No. AF001 **$14.95**

Twelve Types, by G. K. Chesterton
96pp, 5½"x8½", ISBN 0-9714894-8-3, Item No. GKC004 **$8.95**

The Gauntlet: A Challenge to the Myth of Progress, A first anthology of the writings of Arthur J. Penty
96pp, 5½"x8½", ISBN 0-9714894-9-1, Item No. AP001 **$8.95**

Flee to the Fields, the papers of the Catholic Land Movement
160pp, 5½"x8½", ISBN 0-9718286-0-1, Item No. FF001 **$12.95**

An Essay on the Economic Effects of the Reformation, by George O'Brien
160pp, 5½"x8½", ISBN 0-9718286-2-8, Item No. GO001 **$12.95**

Charles I, by Hilaire Belloc
288pp, 6"x9", ISBN 0-9718286-3-6, Item No. HB003 **$16.95**

Charles II: the Last Rally, by Hilaire Belloc
224pp, 6"x9", ISBN 0-9718286-4-4, Item No. HB004 **$15.95**

A Miscellany of Men, by G. K. Chesterton
184pp, 5½"x8½", ISBN 0-9718286-1-X, Item No. GKC005 **$13.95**

Distributist Perspectives, Vol. I, by the chief Distibutists
96pp, 5½"x8½", ISBN 0-9718286-7-9, Item No. DP001 **$8.95**

Dollfuss: An Austrian Patriot, by Fr. Johannes Messner
160pp, 5½"x8½", ISBN 0-9718286-6-0, Item No. JM001 **$12.95**

Economics for Helen, by Hilaire Belloc
160pp, 5½"x8½", ISBN 1-932528-03-2, Item No. HB006 **$12.95**

Richelieu, by Hilaire Belloc
272pp, 6"x9", ISBN 0-9718286-8-7, Item No. HB005 **$16.95**

The Guild State, by G. R. S. Taylor
128pp, 5½"x8½", ISBN 1-932528-00-8, Item No. GT001 **$11.95**

The Party System, by Hilaire Belloc and Cecil Chesterton
160pp, 5½"x8½", ISBN 1-932528-11-3, Item No. HB007 **$12.95**

The Church at the Turning Points of History, by Godrfey Kurth
160pp, 5½"x8½", ISBN 1-932528-09-1, Item No. GK001 **$12.95**

The Death of Christian Culture, by John Senior
192pp, 5½"x8½", with dust jacket, ISBN 1-932528-15-6, Item No. JS001 **$21.95**

The Restoration of Christian Culture, by John Senior
144pp, 5½"x8½", with dust jacket, ISBN 1-932528-16-4, Item No. JS002 **$21.95**

Order direct today: by phone, fax, mail, e-mail, online.
s/h: $4.00 per book; $1.50 ea. add'l. book. Check, m.o., credit.

See the other side of this page for contact information.

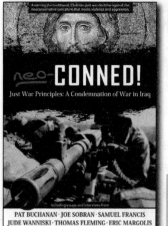